THE MODERN WRITER AND HIS WORLD

THE GOLDEN WEB IN THE WORK

THE
MODERN WRITER
AND HIS WORLD

BY

G. S. FRASER

CRITERION BOOKS
New York

PRINTED IN GREAT BRITAIN

BY WILLIAM CLOWES AND SONS LTD, LONDON AND BECCLES

CONTENTS

CONTENTS

PREFACE

The bulk of this book was written, or rather dictated to my wife and polished as I copied her notes on my typewriter, at Lake Chusenji in Japan in the summer of 1950. My object was to provide Japanese students of English literature, who had been cut off from contact with us during the war, with a fairly clear guide-book to modern tendencies. In Japan, where it has gone into two editions in English, and also been translated into Japanese, the book, I think, has been found reasonably useful. In England, however, I heard that some of my friends who had looked at it – and who had always, for instance, found modern poetry puzzling – also thought it useful; and I knew that, both when I was an undergraduate exploring modern English literature for the first time, and later preparing lectures for soldiers or for Adult Education classes, I myself should have been grateful for such a book. But I am not blind to the faults which, in these days of close criticism, must be found in such a sweeping and cursory survey. In covering such a wide field, one exposes very clearly gaps in one's reading, inadequacies in one's thinking, and deficiencies in one's sensibility. It is with these in mind that I have added to my chapters on modernism in general, on the drama, on fiction, and on poetry, a new chapter on criticism which has taken me, if not more pains, at least more time than all the rest of the book. I hope it will send readers who are looking here for a general picture of the lie of the land to more competent writers on many particular themes. The pattern I have had in mind, in producing this book, is that, for instance, of Dr Joad's excellent guides to philosophy and ethics, or some of Mr G.D.H.Cole's popular books on economic theory; such works no doubt bore specialists, by seeming to labour the obvious, and by avoiding the really tricky questions, but they do start the plain man off on the right road. It is the plain man and his needs that I have chiefly thought of here; in the long run, and even in the comparatively short run, the provision of an adequate popular education is the most urgent social task that lies ahead of us. I hope, however, that this purpose has not betrayed me into a tone of condescension, and I am fairly sure that, though it may sometimes have induced a fell loquacity, it has not betrayed me into over-simplification; I am, after all, like most of my readers, in most things a plain man myself.

I am indebted to the following authors and publishers for permission to quote from works in copyright: Messrs Allen and Unwin (J. M. Synge's preface to *The Playboy of the Western World*); Messrs Jonathan Cape and the Society of Authors as the literary representatives of the estate of the late A. E. Housman (A. E. Housman's *Collected Poems*); Mr Edmund Blunden (Edmund Blunden's *Collected Poems 1914–1930*); Mrs Harold Munro (Harold Munro's *Collected Poems*); Messrs Chatto and Windus (William Empson's *Poems* and *Collected Poems* and *The Poems of Wilfred Owen*); Messrs J. M. Dent (*Collected Poems of Dylan Thomas*); Messrs Duckworth (Hilaire Belloc's *Sonnets and Verses*); Editions Poetry London (Kathleen Raine's *Stone and Flower*, Keith Douglas' *Collected Poems*, Ronald Bottrall's *Selected Poems*, David Gascoyne's *Poems*); Messrs Faber and Faber (T. S. Eliot's *Collected Poems* and *The Cocktail Party*, Roy Campbell's *Collected Poems* and *Adamastor*, W. H. Auden's *Collected Shorter Poems* and *The Orators*; William Empson's *The Gathering Storm*; W. S. Graham's *The White Threshold*, Louis MacNeice's *Collected Poems*, Edwin Muir's *Collected Poems*, Stephen Spender's *Poems*, translations of passages by Eluard, Soupault, Picasso and Chirico from *Surrealism*, edited by Sir Herbert Read, and also to the Committee for Ezra Pound (Ezra Pound's *Personae* and *The Pisan Cantos*); Mrs Helen Thomas (the *Poems* of Edward Thomas); Messrs Hamish Hamilton (Kathleen Raine's *The Pythoness and Other Poems*); Messrs William Heinemann and Mrs Frieda Lawrence (D. H. Lawrence's *Collected Short Stories* and *Classical American Literature*); The Hogarth Press (C. Day Lewis's *Collected Poems 1929–1936*, Edwin Muir's *The Story and the Fable*); Messrs Macmillan, Messrs Methuen and Mrs George Bambridge (Kipling's *Collected Poems*); Messrs. Macmillan and Mrs Yeats (W. B. Yeat's *Collected Poems*); Messrs Macmillan and The Trustees of the Hardy Estate (Hardy's *Collected Poems*, *Poems* by T. Sturge Moore [and to Mrs Sturge Moore], and Dame Edith Sitwell's *Green Song*); Messrs John Murray (John Betjeman's *Selected Poems*); Messrs Methuen (*Collected Poems* of G. K. Chesterton, John Heath Stubbs' *A Charm against the Toothache*); The Oxford University Press (*The Poetical Works of Robert Bridges*, *The Poems of Gerard Manley Hopkins*, and Christopher Fry's *A Phoenix Too Frequent*); The Pound Press (Peter Russell's *Quintilius* and a prose passage from an article in the magazine *Nine* by Iain Fletcher); Messrs Routledge (Derek Stanford's *Music For Statues*); Messrs Sidgewick and Jackson (*The Poetical Works of Rupert Brooke*); Messrs Cassells (Robert Graves's *Collected Poems 1914–1947*) and Mr. Robert Graves.

G. S. FRASER

CHAPTER ONE

THE BACKGROUND OF IDEAS

Section 1: What Do We Mean by 'Modernity' in Literature?

This whole book is an extensive but summary (in a sense, necessarily summary *because* extensive) consideration of the set of tendencies which we call the 'modern movement' in English literature. In a book of this sort, it is impossible, of course, and it would also be undesirable, to exclude one's personal judgments, but I am at least attempting to be as objective as possible; where I find that my personal appreciation of a writer differs very widely from that of critics I respect, I am, without concealing my own opinion, making allowances for the possibility that I am lazy, or have blind spots. This book expresses my own judgments, but they are all judgments I think still open to discussion and reversal. My task, in fact, is less the final task of criticism than the preliminary task of getting a literary scene into perspective. I have attempted as it were to dig out and put tidily upon the page that rough working scheme of the development of English literature in the last fifty years which, I suppose, every practising critic has somewhere at the back of his head. I have taken the novel, the drama, and poetry as the three main kinds of literature demanding consideration and I have added a more tentative essay on the general trends of literary criticism. For each subdivision of my period, I have made no attempt at all at an exhaustive coverage, but I have directed my attention to these writers only who seemed to me vividly to express the mood of the time. Many writers whom I admire, or who would be worth considering in another context, I have omitted because they lacked the crude illustrative value I was looking for.

Illustrative of what? Roughly, I have, as I say, been directing my attention chiefly to those writers who seem to throw most light on the vast, complicated, subtle pattern of changes that has been transforming English society in the last fifty years. I ask myself if a writer mirrors some critical or questioning moment in the nation's history. There are excellent writers, on the other hand, whose significance lies in their personalities rather than in their relation to the spirit of the age; one can think, for instance, of Max Beerbohm, of Norman Douglas, or, at another level and from another point of view, Harold Monro. About such writers I have less to say. On the other hand, there are writers of less even excellence whose significance is that they mirror rather some *uncritical* or *unquestioning* moment in the nation's history. Their work reflects hopes or enthusiasms which the mere passing of time shows to be unfounded. H. G. Wells and Rudyard Kipling, in spite of the completely opposite and mutually hostile relation of their social philosophies, are writers of this type. Neither Kipling's militant Imperialism, nor Wells's optimistic Liberalism, has stood the test of time. But they were both men of genius. And for my own purpose the errors of great writers are as relevant as their insights. For my subject, very broadly, is the relation of the writer to his age.

I would like to make some reserves here. I do not think that literature can be 'explained' by setting it against the historical background that it springs from, any more than I think that historical background can ultimately be 'explained' itself, by reducing the operative agents involved in it to some definite set of factors. I think literature and life are both ultimately mysterious. I do think, however, that the attempt to relate the literature of a period to the more general life of a period can increase our understanding of both; we feel more at home, we find our way about better. As to *why* we should study the literature and the life even of the fairly recent past, there are a good many answers to that. One of them is that if we do, we shall feel more at home and find our way about better in the present. The more important answer is that the literature and the life of the past are interesting for their own sakes and that the disinterested curiosity we are capable of feeling about something that does not immediately practically concern us is part of our human dignity and part, also, of what refines the individual sensibility and enriches the individual life.

This then is a study of modern literature in relation to modern life – and the setting is England, but I think the study has more than a merely local relevance. What we call specifically 'modern' or 'modernist' literature has certain common characteristics in all countries; and so of course has the development of modern history in all countries. The problems which Englishmen have faced, and to which English writers have given literary expression, in the last fifty years or so are not merely local ones.

They have a general topical and contemporary interest. In this first chapter, I want to consider the question of what some of these common characteristics of 'modernity' are. For when we describe a work of literature as 'modern,' we do not merely mean that it has been published (according to the stretch of our historical perspective) in the last year or two, or since the beginning of the century, or perhaps since the Renaissance, or perhaps since the decline of the Roman Empire and the earliest poems and chronicles written in a vernacular European tongue. (For 'modern times' might be thought to begin, from some points of view, with the Christian era itself.) No, when we describe a work as 'modern,' we are ascribing certain intrinsic qualities to it, though we may be vague in our minds about what these qualities are. Thus the question of date need not rise at all. We may find Catullus or Petronius 'modern,' in a way in which we do not find Virgil 'modern'; or Villon in a way in which we do not find Ronsard, or Donne in a way in which we do not find Spenser, or Clough in a way in which we do not find Tennyson. That is to say, all through the literature of the past, there are certain works, which, in the attitudes they express and the problems they deal with, have a peculiar affinity with the spirit of our own time. It is well worth our while then (for it will increase our understanding of the world we live in) to try to isolate some of these characteristics which, wherever we come across them, give us the feeling of 'modernity.'

Section 2: The Historical Sense in Modern Literature

Paradoxically enough, one of the main marks of 'modernism' in literature is often a lively interest in the past for its own sake. We can push the beginnings of 'modern' literature indefinitely back and back, and it is as a mere matter of convenience that in this book I have started off, in my consideration of the novel, poetry, and the drama with the 1890s. On a book of a larger scale, the English romantic movement around 1800 might have seemed a more logical starting-point. One of the most important aspects of that movement was, of course, a new sense of reverence for the past. In the Augustan age, both Englishmen and Frenchmen tended to assume that, after centuries of comparative barbarism, they had at last achieved a civilisation comparable to that of Greece and Rome, and that this civilisation could be preserved, without essential alteration, for an indefinite number of years. What was the impulse that, as the eighteenth century wore on, made Horace Walpole ornament his house in a mock-Gothic manner, made Chatterton forge poems in a mock-Middle-English, caused Bishop Percy not only to collect old ballads but to add to them and alter them in what he thought was the same style, made Mrs Radcliffe set her gloomy romances in the castles of mediaeval Italy, and turned *connoisseurs* of buildings and scenery everywhere away from formal gardens and Palladian mansions towards the contemplation of ruins (they would even have ruins specially built, to set up in their parks, and would sometimes hire hermits to live in them) and the 'wild,' and the 'romantic' (the original meaning of the word is, resembling scenes or episodes in the old fantastic romances of chivalry), and the 'picturesque'? No movement so rich, complex, and various can be explained in any simple or straightforward fashion. It may be that there was in many minds a subconscious realisation that the static civilisation of the eighteenth century could not, in fact, be preserved indefinitely, that man was rather controlled by historical forces, than controlled them. If man lost, in this way, the dignity of being the master of events, at least he could enlarge himself in another sense by uniting himself with the long perspectives of history; and the new passionate interest in nature of poets like Wordsworth sprang perhaps from a similar impulse of enlargement, a wish to belong to something more invigorating and life-inspiring than some mere stiff, conventional urban social circle. The inspiring ideas of Augustan classicism had been reason and decorum. Mystery had been cast out. With the French Revolution it became clear enough, even if there had not been Edmund Burke to emphasise it with his matchless eloquence, that Tradition was a safer watchword for the ruling classes than Reason. The existence of a stable community like that of Great Britain was in essence a mystery, to be approached with reverence, not with a prying criticism or a carping superiority. There was a strange shaping wisdom in history, there was something awesome about established institutions. Our ancestors whom we had been thinking of, till the other day, as uncouth 'gothick' creatures, whose errors our new refinement had exploded, had built better than they knew. The man who tried to live by pure abstract reason was a strutting, dangerous, destructive *doctrinaire*. Man in relation to the past, like man in relation to the natural world about him, was a mystery; that was his dignity.

This new romantic interest in history was, of course, to be one of the most important factors shaping the development of English culture in the nineteenth century. One might almost say that, in many important respects, the Victorian age had no conscious style of its own and was thus for ever covering its nakedness in fancy costumes out of the past.

Thus, as the fine tradition of eighteenth-century classical architecture decayed, not only churches but railway stations and hotels were built, under the inspiration of Pugin and Ruskin, on the model of Gothic cathedrals. It was not only, often, a matter of imitation in an inappropriate context but of imitation with unworthy materials; thus an enterprising business man in the north of England invented a way of prefabricating the structural and ornamental elements of small Gothic churches out of cast iron. And certainly an air of comedy hangs about a great deal of Victorian mediaevalism; one thinks of Disraeli's 'Young England' group going to an enormous expense to reproduce all the settings and circumstances of a mediaeval tournament and being thwarted, as those who plan open-air festivities so often are in England, by a thrashing downpour of rain.

In a wider sense, one may feel that something that could be called not merely an interest in, but almost an obsession with, the past prevented many Victorian poets doing justice to their own age. Tennyson turns to classical legend and the Arthurian romances, Browning to Renaissance Italy, Rossetti and Morris, in tone as well as in theme, to the mediaeval world. Even Matthew Arnold, a poet more uneasily aware of contemporary issues than any of these, allows his mind to dally with a vision of Oxford in the seventeenth century, at a time when 'wits ran clear beside the sparkling Thames.' A writer, again, like Walter Pater, who is fundamentally, as Mr T. S. Eliot has said, a moralist rather than a critic, nevertheless, sets his moralisings against a richly evoked background of late Roman or High Renaissance life – he does not relate them directly (what might, in any case, have been tactless and dangerous) to the life around him.

This Victorian feeling for history, then, is a complicated thing. Sometimes it is not wholly a true feeling; it is less true, for instance, in Tennyson (whose Arthurian knights are too obviously sober Victorian gentlemen in disguise) than in the Browning, say, of *The Ring and the Book*. Yet it might be said that Browning's chief curiosity about and interest in his characters is always a psychological one, that the local colour and the historical setting are, for him, a secondary matter. In Rossetti and Morris on the other hand a highly individualised vision of the past embodies certain values of which they feel the lack, more bitterly and consciously than Tennyson or Browning, in the contemporary scene. Their feeling for the past is beginning to be almost a religious feeling, and when they look around at the actual world about them, the world that the Industrial Revolution has produced, they have a sense of

13

desecration. Yeats inherited from the Pre-Raphaelites this nobly re-actionary attitude, and it is of them that he is thinking when he writes,

> We were the last romantics – chose for theme
> Traditional sanctity and loveliness;
> Whatever's written in what poets name
> The book of the people; whatever most can bless
> The mind of man or elevate a rhyme;
> But all is changed, that high horse riderless,
> Though mounted in that saddle Homer rode
> Were the swan drifts upon a darkening flood.

For Yeats, as for Morris before him, the sense of the past has come to include an acceptance of the validity, at their own proper level, of myths and legends as well as of actual historical facts. He also sees, as Morris saw, that myths and legends spring from 'the book of the people' – that is, from traditional folk culture – and that when folk culture is destroyed, as it so largely has been by the industrial revolution, the poet is in danger of being cut off from his sources. Homer *rode* Pegasus. But the tide of change has now flooded the scene and the swan of poetry drifts weakly and without purpose, no longer controlling man's dreams, but controlled by his fate.

That sense of drift and of the darkening flood is evoked, too, but almost briskly and cheerfully, and certainly with none of Yeats's sense of foreboding, by Walter Pater in the opening pages of his *Plato and Platonism*. There he asks himself, and is perhaps the first Victorian thinker to ask himself, what is the deeper meaning of this 'historical' attitude, which he recognises to be the dominant attitude of the age. Its deeper meaning, for Pater, is that it implies an acceptance of the relativity of all values.* Can we ask, or answer the question, he demands, whether Plato's philosophical theories are 'true' or not? No, he says, we cannot ask or answer that question. We can merely try to understand Plato the man, try to understand his background, and relate the two to each other as far as we can. It was natural that such a man, at such a time, should evolve such theories, but the theories in abstraction from the man and the time are meaningless to us. Thus the historical attitude implies, in Pater's interpretation, at once a distinctly concrete approach and a permanent suspension of judgment; it also implies an acceptance of the fact that *our own* theories about life will seem meaning-

---

* Mr Graham Hough has written very brilliantly on the relation of Pater to Yeats, and in the next two or three pages I am largely summarising his ideas as I remember them.

less to future scholars except in relation to our personalities and to the age which we lived in. How far Yeats would have followed Pater in all this, it would be hard to say. He had more of a dogmatic temperament and more of a hunger for the absolute: at the same time, he does say somewhere, like Pater (but quoting Vico, if I remember, as his authority) that he is less interested in the ideas of Socrates than in Socrates the man.

Vico, a seventeenth-century Italian scholar, who was forgotten for many years after his death, but who has now become extremely fashionable once more, was the first philosopher of history. God, he said, made nature, but man made history, and therefore history was the more proper human study. He fascinated writers like Yeats and Joyce, because of his insistence that the earliest and most primitive force in human society was the concrete, intuitive poetic imagination (such imagination, for instance, as is embodied in the wonderful primitive cave-drawings of animals at Lascaux and at several other places in Europe), and that society develops, sorts itself out, specialises its functions, with the growing abstraction of language from its original, poetic concrete force; law and reason and debate are late developments. With nothing but a knowledge of philology, and a feeling for literature, to guide him Vico was nevertheless much nearer the truth in his guesses about early society than the Whig legalists who imagined primitive individuals arriving at a contract to live together under the rule of law.

He fascinated Yeats and Joyce, also, because, like Nietzsche, he believed in an eternal recurrence. It was in the nature of human society when it had reached a certain stage of civilisation to collapse into primitivism again, and then the whole scheme of human development which Vico had sketched out would start off once more. Spengler, in our time, in a crude, wordy, and popular book, has put forth a similar theory, and Yeats was to develop a recurrence-theory himself, with occult and magical trimmings, in *A Vision*. In Joyce's last very obscure and difficult work, *Finnegan's Wake*, the opening page begins in the middle of a sentence and the beginning of the sentence is the last thing in the book; so that theoretically one could turn back to the beginning from the end, and go on for ever, which, according to Joyce, is what history does.

The reasons why great poets and philosophers have accepted this theory of eternal recurrence are obviously not principally rational ones; it enables them to escape from that complete acceptance of relativity which had failed to worry Pater. It offers a kind of earthly immortality.

It is a strange illustration of the contrast between the European and the Oriental temperaments that this eternal recurrence is just the great wheel of existence from which all world-denying religions like Hinduism and Buddhism seek for the self's ultimate escape. It should be noted that Marxism, another influential historicist philosophy in our time, has more than a little in common as a pattern of ideas with the theories of Vico and Spengler (since it is never explained by Marxists why a classless society, supposing one achieved, will not sort itself out into classes again, as primitive classless societies have done in the past): it has in common too that *amor fati*, or joyful embracing of one's destiny, which is the way in which Vico and Nietzsche and Spengler and their disciples solve (or rather evade, in an emotionally satisfactory way) the old puzzles about determinism and free will. (It is not really a solution, but an embodied self-contradiction; for if my destiny is predetermined, so is the fashion in which I will embrace it; and if the latter is not wholly predetermined, then neither is the former.)

We have seen then how a mere curiosity about the past could develop in the course of a century into an elaborate and all-inclusive philosophy of history. But other attitudes to history than those of Yeats and Joyce were, of course, possible. There was, for instance, the old Victorian belief in the inevitability, given the mounting up of human assets, and every generation's addition to them, and the growing spirit of rationality among civilised peoples, of material and moral progress. This is reflected in the works of a writer like H. G. Wells. Wells, at the end of the nineteenth century, has the same curiosity about the future as Walter Scott, at the beginning, has about the past. He has not, of course, the same materials for satisfying his curiosity. Nevertheless, he is able to make good guesses about the growth of mechanical invention, and rather bad guesses about the development of human nature; and, however far off the mark he is, he can always tell a good story and keep our interest alive. There is a similar spirit in Bernard Shaw, except that Shaw, with a more religious and a less scientific turn of mind than Wells, postulates a 'life-force' – a sort of immanent deity, a divine spirit working and moving in human history – that will ensure the progress of the race, however many blunders and errors individuals may make. Shaw's rather ruthless optimism has a singularly hollow air to-day, and one might be inclined to think that if there is indeed a god shut up in history he is to-day chafing and trying to break free from his narrow bounds. And with his optimism of immanence one might contrast an attitude that could be called the pessimism of transcendence; a distinctively Christian attitude, unlike the others so far discussed.

This pessimism of transcendence is well expressed in the famous *Speculations* of T. E. Hulme. For Hulme, man is a limited, sinful creature, bitterly aware of perfection, but aware, also, of how much he falls short, and must fall short, of perfection. By strict discipline he can achieve a limited decency, but it is folly for him to dream of a world in any however distant future of 'men like gods.' This attitude was taken over, refined and elaborated by Mr T. S. Eliot, in a more ortho-doxly Christian fashion. For him the meaning of history is not to be found *in* history, but outside it, in man's relation to God, and God's relation to man. In history itself, no final order is ever achieved, and it is in this, not in any absolute sense, that Mr Eliot's attitude could be called pessimistic; for if the time is always in need of redemption, it is always, also, redeemable. We are not to make sense of time and history by inventing imaginary patterns of eternal recurrence, nor, on the other hand, by boarding, like Wells and Shaw, a fast train with no known destination. We are rather to make sense of time in our own lives by relating it to eternity, by self-examination, by prayer, by the purification of our souls. In the larger sense, just as man depends on God and time on eternity, so for society at large culture depends on religion. In a civilisation *without* faith, such as our own, everything tends to disintegrate and everybody tends to drift. That is one of the meanings of the most famous poem of Mr Eliot's early period, *The Waste Land*, a poem about society, where his later poems, like *Ash Wednesday* and *Four Quartets*, are rather religious examinations of his own individual experience.

The awareness of living in a period of peculiar crisis is not, of course, confined to writers with an elaborate, esoteric philosophy of history, like Yeats and Joyce, or with a definite and orthodox religious belief, like Mr Eliot. In the 1930s many young English poets, like Mr W. H. Auden, Mr Stephen Spender, Mr Cecil Day Lewis, and Mr Louis MacNeice saw the crisis as acute but temporary, the result of a transi-tion in society between a capitalistic and a socialistic method of organis-ing production, and sought for a resolution of the crisis in political terms. Many, though not all, of these poets in the 1930s were veering towards Marxism, though, like Queen Gertrude with her rue, they wore their Marxism 'with a difference.' The war, and recent political developments in the world, have tended to shatter these too rosy hopes, and in their recent poetry – Mr Auden, for instance, who is now living in the United States, has become an orthodox Anglican – these poets have tended to revert to more traditional attitudes.

The title of one of Mr Auden's latest poems, *The Age of Anxiety*, suggests one of the moods of the post-war world – a mood of what is often called *angst*, a word borrowed from the Danish religious thinker of the early nineteenth century, Sören Kierkegaard. Kierkegaard is the father of what is called to-day 'existentialist' philosophy; this is not a philosophy which has had much technical influence on English literature, but some of its attitudes – particularly the awareness of a general latent anxiety, not as the product of some particular pressure of events, but as intrinsic to the human condition itself – are shared by many English writers.

Kierkegaard was especially aware of the burden and mystery of one's individual existence to oneself – a burden which he thought ambitious, speculative philosophers like Hegel tended to ignore. Philosophers talk about the movement of ideas, or the development of tendencies, but our world is not a world of ideas and tendencies, it is a world of men, each of whom is an ultimate mystery both in and to himself. The most important thing in life for Kierkegaard was the relation of the individual soul to a transcendent God, who was in a position to judge that soul; it was from the extreme loneliness, and perhaps from the over-scrupulousness, of his own religious life that his emphasis on dread, awe, and anxiety (he has little, I am afraid, to say about joy) springs. In a sense he represents a genuine religious attitude, but a crippled one.

The most successful purely artistic development of Kierkegaard's ideas is to be found probably in the strange novels and tales of Kafka. Few modern writers are more lucid than Kafka; his two most famous novels, *The Trial* and *The Castle*, invite comparison, for direct narrative simplicity, both with Bunyan and Swift. Such simplicity can be, as it is in Swift's case, deceptive; and the profound deeper ambiguity of Kafka's 'message,' or the fundamentally elusive structure of his 'allegory,' has exposed him to more various interpretations than any other modern writer. *The Trial* is about a man who finds himself condemned and in the end punished – and he accepts his punishment abjectly – for some crime which he is not aware of having committed. *The Castle* is about a man who strives to get in touch with a local source of authority, which he has been told to get in touch with, and after all sorts of humiliating misadventures does not in the end really succeed in doing so. Thus in a sense the novels are 'about' the nature of sin, or guilt, and the nature of a kind of authority that might redeem or absolve us from them. But they cannot be read as straight religious allegories either in the Christian or in Kafka's own specifically Jewish tradition. We can take Kafka, of course, as meaning that we are guilty by inheritance, by our fallen nature, of original sin, whatever actual sins we may or may not have committed; and that though we reach out to God seeking forgiveness for our sins (or forgiveness for being the fallen creatures we are) we can never be sure of having reached God, and not merely some idol or substitute, or some institution, like a Church, which claims to speak for God but, in making that claim, may be betraying us. But the effect of these narratives – like the effect, perhaps, on some readers of *The Book of Job* – is to arouse a profound sympathy with the bewildered victim or the suffering seeker and to raise two fundamental questions: is there really a final authority at all, and, if there is, is it a just one? Thus some critics have taken these two novels not as religious allegories at all but as reflections of the helplessness of the individual in an elaborate decaying bureaucracy like that of the Austrian Empire; the citizen is always wrong, and he can never reach the department that could put things right, and perhaps there is no such department. Hostile critics of Kafka have even found in his work the climate of opinion that could lead to Fascism. He makes his wide appeal to contemporary readers not, perhaps, because they are eager to give their own answer to his riddles, but because he conveys with unparalleled purity and intensity the generalised anxiety of our time; it is all too easy for almost any contemporary reader to identify his own fears and worries with those of Kafka's heroes. Whether, to a more confident age, he would appear as he does to ours a writer of central significance may be doubted. He belongs, though in time he a little preceded it, very much to our special world of organised propaganda, control of the individual by government offices, permanent crisis of one sort or another, and crowded mental hospitals. He diagnosed a disease with frightening brilliance, but it is doubtful whether, either in his work or in his rather lonely and unhappy life, overshadowed by his father, he suggested a remedy.

Some of Kierkegaard's later successors, like the French philosopher and novelist and playwright, Jean-Paul Sartre, are not men of religious belief but atheists; but they find that the dread and awe and anxiety with which they regard the prospect of their own ultimate annihilation makes them as anxious as Kierkegaard was to insist on the unique significance of every individual human life. Moreover, they insist, if there is no God, it is man who makes man (that is to say, it is individual choices that define our ideals of what human nature should be). Therefore, in every choice I make, I must be overburdened with a weight of terrible responsibility, for I am choosing not only for myself but, ideally at least, for all other men. For the existentialists, then, we are not merely living through a period of crisis, but human existence itself is, in its very nature, a permanent crisis. There is a flavour in this philosophy like that of Jansenism. It can lead both to over-scrupulousness and intolerance. But it is, at least, very interestingly symptomatic of the troubled times we are living through.

Existentialism, whether in its theist or atheist versions, transcends, like Mr Eliot's Christian piety, a *merely* historical attitude to experience and it seems possible that the period when what we can call, in a wide sense, historicism was a main mark of modern literature may be coming to an end. In a period of recurrent calamities like our own, the mere passing of time gradually comes to have less significance than it may have in more settled or more expansive epochs. The conditions of human life, sad and limiting as they are, assume a certain air of permanence; and individuals accept what periods of peace and happiness and constructive activity they are granted less as a right than as a grace. They count their blessings, and are grateful.

Thus a certain reaction against the somewhat monotonous introspection and gloom of the existentialist position can be seen, for instance, in the group of interesting young writers who are connected with the English periodicals *Nine* and *Colonnade*. It would be wrong to say that these writers, Peter Russell, Iain Fletcher, Donald Carne-Ross, and others, have a common philosophy of life, but they have a common attitude of respect towards the great traditions of art and literature, the great historical achievements, of Europe. They feel that, just because we are in a bad way just now, we ought not to write off our whole historical culture, nevertheless, as a bad debt; that the great poems and prose works of the past can still give us spiritual refreshment, and that we owe a debt to our ancestors which we ought to repay.

Some of them have been very much influenced by the American poet, Ezra Pound, whose most ambitious work, *The Cantos*, an outwardly chaotic poem, but full of wonderful evocations of the past and what Mr Wyndham Lewis calls 'grand granitic landslides' of translation, is an attempt to pay that sort of debt: a kind of personal anthology of the high moments in Greek mythology and in European, American, and Chinese history. Pound is not at all, like Mr Eliot whom he so much influenced, an essentially religious poet, though in his later *Cantos* there are some passages of 'natural piety' like this famous one,

> What thou lovest well remains,
> >   the rest is dross
> What thou lov'st well shall not be reft from thee
> What thou lov'st well is thy true heritage
> Whose world, or mine or theirs
> >   or is it of none?
> First came the seen, then thus the palpable
> >   Elysium, though it were in the halls of hell
> What thou lovest well is thy true heritage
>
> The ant's a centaur in his dragon world.
> Pull down thy vanity, it is not man
> Made courage, or made order, or made grace,
> >   Pull down thy vanity, I say pull down
> Learn of the green world what can be thy place
> In scaled invention or true artistry,
> >   Paquin pull down!
> The green casque has outdone your elegance.
>
> 'Master thyself, then others shall thee beare'
> >   Pull down thy vanity
> Thou art a beaten dog beneath the hail,
> A swollen magpie in a fitful sun,
> Half black half white
> Nor knowst'ou wing from tail
> Pull down thy vanity
> >   How mean thy hates
> Fostered in falsity,
> >   Pull down thy vanity,
> Rathe to destroy, niggard in charity,
> Pull down thy vanity,
> >   I say pull down.

On the whole, however, Pound's is rather a 'human' piety; he feels that there is a great ancestral wisdom of the past, that of Confucius, of Blackstone, of the American founding fathers, which we would be impious if we turned away from and rejected. And similarly we have a duty towards the great poetry, and music, and art of the past, a duty to keep it in use, fresh and fruitful for our understanding. Pound's status, if not as a poet, at least as a teacher of the young, has been badly damaged indeed by his personal eccentricities, by an occasional noisy arrogance or pretentiousness in his prose writing, by surprising schoolboy blunders in his nevertheless beautiful translations, and latterly of course by his conduct during the war when, though retaining his United States citizenship, he broadcast on behalf of Italy, a country where he had lived for very many years. But if men of action, according to Lord Acton, should be judged at their worst rather than their best, there is something to be said in taking the opposite course in regard to poets; for there, it is the best that will last. Certainly, if one were trying to instil into a young man, in our troubled times, a sane loyalty towards all that is best in our strange mixed inheritance – to instil into him, in fact, a balanced attitude to history, so that even in these bad times he would keep his courage up and not weakly or unnecessarily repine – one could hardly find better words than these of Pound's to do this in: 'What thou lovest well is thy true heritage.'

Thus we have seen that the sense of history in modern literature can take an almost incredible diversity of forms; but that nevertheless it is one of the most vital elements in very much modern literature; and that, when properly cultivated, it can be a source of moral strength in troubled times.

Section 3: Realism, Psychology, Experiment in Modern Novels

I am using 'realism' not in the narrow sense in which it is sometimes used to describe novels, like Zola's, which are based on an elaborate documentation of fact, and deal often with the rather more sordid sides of contemporary life, but rather in the way in which, in ordinary conversation, we contrast what we call a 'realistic' with an 'idealistic' attitude to life. That again is different from the technical fashions in which these two words are used in philosophy, and perhaps we might describe the 'realistic' writer as one who thinks that truth to observed facts – facts about the outer world, or facts about his own feelings – is the great thing, while the 'idealistic' writer wants rather to create a pleasant and edifying picture.

Thus Dr Johnson who, like most critics of the eighteenth century, had an 'idealistic' conception of literature could not bear to re-read the last act of Shakespeare's *King Lear*, because the death of Cordelia was too harrowing, and struck him as wicked and wrong. He preferred the version written by a Restoration hack writer in which Cordelia survives and so does Lear, to a happy old age under her protection. It would be no answer to his criticism of *King Lear* that, after all, wickedness often does triumph in real life; he would reply that it is the business of the poet to see that it does not triumph in dramatic poetry.

Though we can respect the tender feelings that lay behind Dr Johnson's criticism, we probably do not agree with it to-day; we feel about Lear, after all the torments he has gone through, with Charles Lamb and with Shakespeare himself, that

> he hates him
> That would upon the rack of this tough world
> Stretch him out longer.

We see that a 'happy ending' to *King Lear* would be a tepid and tedious anti-climax. Have we gone through so much, and only for that? . . . Thus the 'idealistic' critic, in his urgent desire for edification, may be blind not only to the outward truth of life but to what we may call the inner truth of poetry; to the inevitability of the highest tragic conceptions of a writer like Shakespeare. What I have called the 'realistic' attitude is one more bravely exposed not only to the outer shocks, but to the inner springs, of life.

The realistic attitude, in this wider sense, might be opposed to the eighteenth-century convention of decorum. In a neo-classical poem, like many of Dryden's panegyric odes, it is assumed that it is only proper for the poet to treat kings as if they were noble and gracious, and statesmen as if they were wise and prudent and far-sighted, and great ladies as if they were beautiful and chaste, and famous soldiers as if they were always brave and always successful, whatever actually may be the case; even though, in fact, as in the Restoration Court, everybody knows the case to be quite otherwise. The same tone of solemn official laudation may be seen in the funeral sermons of Bossuet. One cannot exactly call it flattery, for nobody was deceived by it; it was simply part of the routine of courtly politeness. But we can see the other side of the picture in works like the memoirs of Saint-Simon or Grammont in which what moves the writer is a curiosity, often a rather malicious one, about the real motives and actions of great men; and these works are much more 'modern' in tone, and can be read with much more pleasure, than the more formal sort of writing I have been describing.

That interest in people's real actions and real motives lay, of course, behind the rise of the novel. But where there was a formula for describing conventional 'heroic' actions, there was not one for what Fielding, attempting to describe the scope of the novel in his time, called the 'comic prose epic.' One way, which Fielding makes use of in *Tom Jones* was to take some of the formulas for the heroic poem, some of the neo-classical 'receipts to make an epic,' and burlesque them; and of course in Fielding's first novel, *Joseph Andrews*, he started off with an intention of pure burlesque. But the novel, after all, is not merely the comic antithesis of the heroic poem; Tom Jones is not Augustus or Alexander, as these might have been represented in a Restoration tragedy, but he is not a mere lay-figure of fun either. He is a young man, with his faults, but with his virtues, too, who in the end deeply engages both Fielding's sympathy and the reader's. He represents mixed, average human nature and it is with that, in future, that the novelist will deal. Fielding, however, has not found the final formula for the novel; George Moore observed that in *Tom Jones* there is no psychology and no description in the modern sense, 'no inner or outer world.' There is not, but there is perhaps a firmer grasp of action and character than in many later novels, like Moore's own, which are full of psychology and description. It was in these directions, however, that the novel was to develop. If we compare Dickens with Smollett or Fielding we notice how much more vividly he evokes the outer scene, and how much more definite a part atmosphere, the atmosphere of an old house, a city street, a lonely marshland, plays in defining the mood of his stories. His eye is open. He sees. The opening of the novelist's inner eye, on the other hand, his eye for the intricate workings of the human soul, its queer mixture of noble and base motives, can be traced more strikingly in French novels, like those of Stendhal, or Benjamin Constant's cruel and incisive piece of introspection, *Adolphe*. *Adolphe* in form is a conventional eighteenth-century tale. There is no more description, or real evocation of scene, than in *Tom Jones*; but the human heart is laid bare in a way that is new and frightening. Finally, in the massive novels of the later part of the nineteenth century, in Tolstoy's *War and Peace* or in George Eliot's *Middlemarch*, we begin to feel that the structure of the novel is as solid, and its texture as supple and various, as that of life itself. It seems able to include, within its capacious but still tidy limits, everything. It is not enough to say that such works are merely 'modern.' They are among the great achievements of the human spirit at any time.

But if the novel, as an art-form, had perhaps reached its peak with George Eliot and the great Russians, the urge to experiment with it, to make it more elegant or more flexible, went on. With Henry James, the great interest is in refining the construction of the novel, so that there will be nothing superfluous, no phrase, paragraph, or sentence which will not contribute to the total effect. His masters were Flaubert and Turgeniev. If he wished to avoid the superfluous, he also wished to avoid the implausible. He disliked, as many readers dislike, the way a writer like Thackeray perpetually breaks down the illusion he is trying to create by addressing his readers in his own person and confessing that it is all a story. He introduced the technique of telling the story from the point of view of some observer who is not necessarily a main participant in the story; but this observer's curiosity, and his success or failure in satisfying it, may nevertheless become the main theme. He introduced into the novel points of view so subtle, characters so reserved and refined, delicacies of motive so intangible, that probably no previous writer would have thought them solid enough for fiction. He makes all other English novelists, except Jane Austen possibly, look a little lumpish.

But James is not fantasticating; he is exploring a real world though a world sometimes, to the ordinary reader's sensibility, almost frighteningly airy and impalpable: a world in which through labyrinthine sentences we pursue a dangerous central precision. Such exhaustive analysis might, in itself, be too tiring for most readers. But it is carried along, on the whole, with light grace and charm. And James can evoke a scene when he wants to (like the New York of the first few pages of *An International Episode*) in a magical fashion, with a succession of light, delicate, almost ghostly touches that recall the nocturnes of his compatriot, Whistler. He is rather a special taste, but for those who acquire it (and it is often a taste acquired rather late) the taste of a lifetime.

The danger, however, of the novelist relying too much on the subtlety and delicacy of his impressions of mood, and scene, and situation, and on his careful unravelling of the strands that make up these impressions, is that he may lose the sense of architecture, of structure; as impressionist painting occasionally, when it dissolved into mere evocative blobs of colour, may be said to have done. James's basic care, however, was for structure, he planned out what he called the *charpente*, the solid skeleton, of his stories well in advance. But in writers like Dorothy Richardson, or Katherine Mansfield, or Virginia Woolf, who carry the impressionist technique further, who introduce into the novel so much of the traditional material of poetry – diluted, as Professor I. A. Richards has observed, or 'like gold to airy thinness beat' – there is the danger that the novel as a structure, as an architecture of character and action, will begin to float apart: Professor Richards also makes this criticism of James Joyce's *Ulysses*, but unjustly I think, for one knows of few novels more elaborately constructed, and few characters more solidly imagined than Stephen Daedalus and Leopold Bloom. It is true, however, that the *first* impression of *Ulysses* on a reader may be one of rich confusion, that it takes some time, and some effort, before the artistic, and above all the moral structure, of the story can be firmly grasped; and also that though the theme of *Ulysses* is in all conscience adequate and complex enough, the plot – one, not outwardly terribly eventful day, in two, not outwardly terribly significant Dublin lives – seems at a first reading rather thin to support the enormous, dense weight or atmosphere of observed detail. But a proper reading of *Ulysses* is more like *living* the events which the book describes than is the reading of any other novel; in no other narrative that I know is the pressure of life so thick, so dense, so that the reader has almost to cut his way through. Thus some modern critics have considered the book as the culmination of the possibilities latent in the novel as an art-form: the novel to end all novels. And certainly after Joyce, though one can point to many writers of wonderful talent, like Virginia Woolf, and even to one writer of genius, D.H.Lawrence – but with a genius, alas, impatient both of the disciplining of his intelligence and sensibility and of the shaping of his books as works of art – one cannot point, in the same way, to any major figure. And one notes a tendency to recapture a clear and obvious structure at all costs (in Graham Greene's symbolical melodramas, for instance, in Rex Warner's social allegories, in Christopher Isherwood's concise and economical fictional 'documentaries') even at the cost of losing the new and stunning *richness* which Joyce had given to the atmosphere of the novel.

We can see then that 'realism' is an elusive and complicated conception, and that new subtleties of psychological approach, or nuances of delicacy in description, which at first may appear to open out fascinating new country for the novelist may in the end so bewilder him with their vivid, disparate detail that he forgets what he was, in the first instance, mainly after – a morally significant fable.

One should mention, however, before leaving the subject, one other incidental innovation of Joyce's in *Ulysses* which can be also considered as in the direction of 'realism': a new frankness about sexual matters, which was an inevitable result of the acceptance of the 'stream-of-thought' technique. I do not know whether all the results of this emancipation from an old reserve have been wholly happy ones. In spite of the distinction which D. H. Lawrence, for instance, made between 'obscenity' (legitimate) and 'pornography' (illegitimate) in

26

the novel, I think it is true that young readers, in particular, may often derive an improper and unhealthy excitement from the detailed description of sexual episodes. I have not read an unexpurgated *Lady Chatterley's Lover*; and I do not find the expurgated version as moving or well-written as *Sons and Lovers*. Possibly the dogged puritanism which was one side of Lawrence's nature, the tendency in him to make almost a kind of religion out of sex, may have lain behind the failure; for it must be observed that the working of the sexual appetite in the human creature is often (as, for instance, Wycherley and Congreve knew) rather comic.

One might mention here, with a certain diffidence, but they are worth mentioning, some volumes published by the American expatriate, Henry Miller, in Paris, and unprocurable in an unexpurgated form (for perfectly sound reasons, too) in either London or New York. *Tropic of Cancer* and *Tropic of Capricorn* are perhaps less novels than fantasticated exercises in autobiography, but they have a verve, a style, and they convey the rich and complex impact of experience in a way in which it seems to me that no novelist since Joyce has done. 'At last,' said Ezra Pound, when he read *Tropic of Cancer*, 'at last an unprintable book that is fit to read.' Miller's books *are*, I am afraid, unprintable in Anglo-Saxon societies. He is not in the least *like* Joyce. He is perhaps a little like Rabelais and a little like Petronius, with more than a touch of Herman Melville and Walt Whitman. He has that perpetual rediscovery of the Absolute on every second page which is one of the grand contributions to the tradition of English writing of classic American literature.

At the same time, he is something like a permanent adolescent. Sex in itself, the machinery of sex, is wonderfully exciting when one is an adolescent, but as one grows older one becomes more interested in the permanent human relationships, at a moral level, which sex, like other human appetites and passions, subserves. I don't think Miller would do any harm to the right reader, but it would be quite a job deciding who the right reader might be. Also, he is a quite remarkably *naïf* writer, who pours out his words in a happy, uninhibited stream, as one might, over a few drinks, with intimate friends. He often writes sheer and conscious nonsense. There are expurgated selections from him, and books written specially for an Anglo-Saxon public, available in Great Britain and the United States, but these have to be studied rather selectively, for when he is off his favourite topic he is often not at his best. One might mention as a similar exercise in sexual frankness a semi-autobiographical novel, *The Black Book*, also only available in Paris, by a disciple of Miller's, the well-known poet Lawrence Durrell. This is more of a 'made' book, less spontaneous, full of beautiful passages of mannered prose, which recall, perhaps a little too obviously, Landor or De Quincey. Again, for all its imperfections of action and character, it has a richness and vitality lacking in most contemporary English fiction. But I feel, on the whole, that this taking of an impulse out for a ride is not after all 'realism,' in the sense in which I have been attempting to define 'realism' in this section; it is rather another, no doubt an exciting, mode of escape.

So, in so far as we are thinking of 'realism' as the pursuit of reality, it is hard to define it by outward characteristics. We might say that it is the opposite of evasion. But a striking sexual frankness, as we have seen, may be a way of evading social problems, and, more fundamentally, of evading moral problems. An elaborate technique for catching the flavour of every passing moment may be a way of avoiding a structural grasp of theme. A temporary rejection of experimental advances, as by many recent British novelists, may be a return towards the hard ground of reality at a more modest level. And there is a reality of beauty, of visions, and of dreams. All one can say finally is that the good contemporary writer, the novelist particularly, will have a firm respect for reality; but that everyone has to discover reality for himself; and from his own perspective and communicating to the account of his discovery the flavour of his own personality.

Section 4: Complexity, Allusiveness, Irony, Obscurity in Modern Poetry

It is, perhaps, more about poetry than about other forms of modern literature that people have a really sharp sense of what the 'modern' is, and whether they like it or not. It is hard to suggest a single and simple touchstone for the note of 'modernity' in world poetry (and may I point out again that much poetry of even the remote past strikes us as eminently 'modern,' while some good poetry of our own period seems to us not really contemporary with us?), but perhaps the nearest we can get to it is the presence, in a poem, of a feeling of harsh, unresolved complexity. Catullus for instance is very 'modern' when he says (I think the version I am quoting is Mr Jack Lindsay's, but since I cannot check the quotation, the responsibility for it may be my own):

> I hate and love.
> > You ask, how can that be?
> I do not know, but know it tortures me.

Robert Bridges, on the other hand, though he was alive, unlike Catullus, only a few years ago, does not strike one as at all 'modern,' when, in his beautiful ode on Purcell's bicentenary, he writes:

> Love to Love calleth,
> Love unto Love replieth –
> From the ends of the earth, drawn by invisible bands,
> Over the dawning and darkening lands
> Love cometh to Love.
> To the heart by courage and might
> Escaped from hell,
> From the torment of raging fire,
> From the sighs of the drowning main,
> From the shipwreck of fear and pain,
> From the terror of night.

The complexity of feeling between hate and love, harsh and tight in Catullus, has here been diluted and resolved. 'Love' in Bridges (an abstract personification, a poetical idea) is something very different from the personal '*I* love' of Catullus; Catullus's 'I hate' and 'I know it tortures me' are soothed away in retrospective images, a horror that has been *escaped* from,

> Escaped from hell,
> From the torment of raging fire,
> From the sighs of the drowning main . . .

The resolution is perfect. And the whole poem from which this passage comes is, if a trifle too long, exceedingly beautiful. But one sees the difference. Though Bridges disliked the poetry of the Augustan age, he was essentially, in his views of poetic propriety, a poet in the Augustan tradition; he shared with Dryden and Pope the cult of decorum. Catullus writes about human passion as, in his own immediate painful experience, he knows it really to be; Bridges personifies the mind's notion of what human love ideally *ought* to be. This is not to say that Catullus's way of writing is, by some absolute standard, 'better' than Bridges'. It is merely to say that it comes home more intimately to *us*. I would be giving a very mistaken impression, indeed, if I let it be thought that I considered the tone of 'modernity' in world literature equivalent to general literary value. The 'modern' tone is simply the tone that appeals to us in our situation. That situation will change, and so, therefore, will the associations of the idea of 'modernity' – that is an idea that can be defined to some extent for one's own period, but never defined in an absolute sense. In fifty years, if things settle down, we may see a revival of the cult of decorum, and it will be Bridges who will appear 'modern,' Catullus old-fashioned. Meanwhile for us, here and now, the 'modern' in world literature is simply that which appeals in a troubled time to our troubled hearts.

One reason why the best poetry of at least the last fifty years (and if we take in France, almost of the last hundred years) has been notably complex is that so, of course, has there been a growing complication in the organisation of our world. Society has ceased to be local and organic, many customs, habits, and traditions have decayed, and the poet has become a much more isolated person than he was even in the elegant and urban eighteenth century; he has lost the kind of *niche* and status that Pope had, and one might say that so far as the poet in the Victorian age remained a public figure – as Tennyson did, for instance – so his poetry suffered. Bridges, in that wonderful ode from which I have quoted already, seems to lament the inadequacy of poetry in his own day to the great public occasion,

> Lament, fair hearted queen, lament with me –
> For when thy seer died no song was sung,
> Nor for our heroes fal'n by land and sea
> Hath honour found a tongue,

but when he himself became Poet Laureate he steadfastly eschewed the poem on the public occasion, leaving honour to find a tongue for our heroes fallen by land and sea through the brassier Muse of Rudyard Kipling. Kipling's special kind of success and failure showed that it was becoming more and more difficult for the poet in our time to catch the common ear, without catching also a 'common' tone. What is remarkable about him is how the banjo-twanging, the drum-thumping, and the Cockney impersonations, so often fail, in the end, to prevent the result being true poetry; and the unobtrusive skill that could put across a difficult and tricky form like the sestina (Kipling must have been one of the first, after Swinburne, to revive it since Sir Philip Sidney's time) by doctoring and diluting the true poetry with the required dose of plebeian humour and sentiment:

> Speakin' in general, I 'ave tried 'em all –
> The happy roads that take you o'er the world.
> Speakin' in general, I 'ave found them good
> For such as cannot use one bed too long,
> But must get 'ence, the same as I 'ave done,
> An' go observin' matters till they die.

> What do it matter where or 'ow we die,
> So long as we've our 'ealth to watch it all –
> The different ways that different things are done,
> An' men and women lovin' in this world;
> Takin' our chances as they come along,
> An' when they ain't, pretendin' they are good?

That does not ring quite true. There is a very strange balance between a humoristic Cockneyism, and an old-fashioned poetic formalism, which Kipling perhaps felt he could not get away with in a 'straight poem': his Tramp Royal in real life would no more have said ''ence' than he would have said 'hence,' and this confusion between two manners reaches its climax perhaps in the first line of the coda,

> Gawd bless this world! Whatever she 'ath done ...

where the 'Gawd' and the ''ath' seem to cancel each other out. Perhaps the idea is that an uneducated man is aiming at a dignified literary diction. But the total effect is rather as if Kipling, too shy to express his own sentiments in his own person, had tripped on to the stage in the cloth cap and false moustache of a music-hall 'serio-comic.' So Kipling, too, is an example of a 'modern' writer which Bridges is not, his complexity taking the form of an artful *imitation* of simplicity. I think the time for a final evaluation of Kipling's work is not yet. He certainly did manage to bridge for a time the growing gap between poetry and public, but paying rather a high price. And his special road was not one that other poets cared to follow.

Nevertheless, Kipling's equivocal success like the high public status of Browning and Tennyson earlier on was a sign that the estrangement between poet and public had never become so acute in England as, for some important kinds of poet at least, it had become in France. Perhaps the historian of 'modern poetry' – in the sense of difficult, complex, abstruse poetry, poetry whose statements or whose attitudes puzzle the ordinary reader – might date its rise in England somewhere between 1910 and 1920: he would be thinking of the early work of Eliot and Pound, the realistic war poetry of Read, Sassoon, and Owen, the growing maturity of Yeats as seen in such a poem as *Easter, 1916*. He might mention Gerard Manley Hopkins, a poet of the 1880s who died fairly young, a Jesuit father, but whose poems were not published till 1919, as a 'modern poet' before his time; he might also allude to the work of Hardy, often gnarled and clumsy as to form, but impressive for its thought; and he might speak of some of the poets of the 1890s as 'modernising' influences, especially through their use of French models. He would say something about the Imagist movement and about early experiments in free verse, neither of which, again, go much further back than 1910. But if the same critic were to trace the 'modern' movement in poetry back in France, he would have to go at least as far back as Baudelaire. What is less than forty years old in England is more than a hundred years old in France. And one reason for this earlier development of 'modernism' in France was, I have suggested, an earlier and more complete estrangement of some important French poets from the tone and attitudes of the public life around them: not of all French poets – Lamartine and Victor Hugo are examples of poets who were deeply and actively involved in that public life. But they have not the kind of complexity that interests us to-day; they are not, as Baudelaire is, 'modern.'

It seems at first surprising that the estrangement of the poet from public life should have been more absolute, and should have become noticeable earlier, in France than in England. For in France literature has been generally a part of public life, and the man of letters a public figure, in a way that in England has not always been the case; but in fact the traditional values of much French literature – values of clear, rapid, sometimes superficial reasoning, of incisive generalisation, of dignified rhetoric and pointed wit, while real virtues in themselves were, as Baudelaire for instance noted, anti-poetic virtues. The whole tendency of French thought, after Descartes, was to exalt abstract reason as against concrete intuition; the tendency of French poetry after Malherbe was to exalt propriety and decorum of language as against an original and personal note; and the eighteenth century, though a very great century in French history, had been notable above all for its prose. In spite of the great triumphs of French romanticism, something of that anti-poetic tone lingered on in Baudelaire's time, and lingers on to-day, in French literature. The poet may not be merely a poet; he must justify himself at the bar of current opinion, which, in France, assumes always the airs of something final and absolute. Thus many French writers are busy to-day 'committing' themselves to various implausible and over-simple political creeds which the mere passing of time, and the changes of history, will make out of date and irrelevant in five or ten years – as the political creed of Victor Hugo, for instance, who *was* certainly a 'committed' poet is out of date and irrelevant now: something which has merely an historical interest, and which we put up with for the sake of a constant rhetorical, and an

occasional poetic, splendour. It might not be wholly unfair to say that
the claims of public life on the French poet have, since the early
seventeenth century, tended to turn his poetry into rhetoric; and that
there is a 'romantic' rhetoric (of which we have examples, too, in an
English romantic poet like Byron) which is quite as poetically false,
and much more garish and strident, than any 'classical' rhetoric; it is
the noisy pretence of being carried away by tremendously profound
and frightening thoughts and strange, tempestuous feelings. But the
thoughts and feelings seem, on a closer examination, rather 'worked
up' for the sake of the rhetoric; and the coherence of the one, the
sincerity of the others, does not bear much analysis.

The doctrinaire, in France, in fact, thinks either that he is the
superior of the poet intrinsically or that, even if the poet is a strange
and wonderful creature, still he needs sensible and well-informed men
to teach him what to feel and think; let him take what *we* are thinking
and make poetic eloquence out of it! Sartre, the latest fashionable
French doctrinaire, has (which is at least honest of him) announced
almost defiantly that his philosophy has no guidance or help to offer
poets; there is no doubt however that he considers himself intrinsically
the superior of the poet. Indeed, in his essays on the nature of literature,
he has made it clear that the purely 'literary' values of literature (let
alone the deeper poetic values) are the last thing he is interested in.
No, the questions he would ask the writer, rapping his desk like a
schoolmaster, are of another kind: 'What did you do in the last war?
What will you do in the next? What political party do you work for?
How do you stand in regard to the social revolution? What is your
line about the existence of a God?' This type of French intellectual
drill-sergeant has been satirised adequately, once and for all, by
Flaubert in his portrait of Homais. But no satire can destroy the vitality
and persistence of the type, and from Voltaire, through Taine, to
Sartre, the brilliant polemical popularising rationalists who have
dominated one side of the French mind in the last two hundred years
have been the enemies, conscious or unconscious, of true poetry.

With Sartre, indeed, that enmity is conscious. He has lately published
what he calls an 'existential psycho-analysis' – that is to say, a con-
jectural biography, insufficiently documented – of Baudelaire, with
the intention of proving that Baudelaire (whose unhappy personal
history, certainly, does demand all our forbearance and charity when
we consider it) was in the deepest sense a moral coward and intellectually consciously insincere. Baudelaire's own works, surely, are the

2

answer to that accusation. The truth of poetry is not something that can be faked: but it is the case, on the other hand, that if the poet is hemmed in too much by a hostile, probing intellectualism, he may retreat, in pure self-defence, to a greater and greater eccentricity of attitude, defiance of ordinary convention, and privacy of language. Faced with what struck him as a lack of understanding and a blank hostility, not only in the populace at large, but in intellectual circles, the French poet of the last century of Baudelaire's type adopted, with the militant chivalry of his race, an attitude of defiance. Baudelaire himself put on the mask of the dandy; it being his hope, as it were, to outstare the starers and by his own insolence to make the insolent drop their eyes. Gautier (determined that if the world was going to insist on the irrelevance of poetry, poets should insist on the irrelevance of the world) proclaimed the doctrine of art for the sake of art; an inadequate doctrine in itself but a useful shield, then and since, for poets who did not feel like becoming the tools of eager short-sighted reformers.

It was about this period, too, that there was invented (if I remember, in reference to Vigny) the famous phrase about the poet's 'ivory tower.' It might have been a more accurate metaphor to talk of the poet as the inhabitant of a besieged city: a city not strong enough to sally forth and destroy her enemies, but well provisioned, and with strong walls. But by the time of the later Symbolists, Mallarmé and his school, it might have been truer perhaps to speak of the city as that of the philistines with the poets moving about in it as spies, wearing a disguise, and communicating by a code, that made their presence unsuspected. Baudelaire still made enough direct impact on his age to have his masterpiece condemned for immorality. Yet Baudelaire is essentially a poet of Christian feeling; he shocked his contemporaries just because in the century of gas-light, of the railway, of the Great Exhibition of 1850, of an unheard-of expansion of manufactures, population, and trade, he insisted that the only true progress consisted in the diminution of the traces of original sin; and because he knew, all too intimately, what sin is, in what its attraction and its horror consist. His life, in which, as Sartre truly observes, he 'did' nothing (apart from creating his masterpieces), was as momentous and as morally significant as that other contemporary, apparently monotonous, empty, and idle, and dawdling life, the life of Kierkegaard. In a bustling noisy age both of these were capable of contemplation, capable of realising the vanity of the world.

Mallarmé, on the other hand, the spy in disguise in the enemy city, made no such direct impact on that city as Baudelaire had; merely unobtrusively gathering round him, from the ranks of the philistines, his small fifth column. Living the life of a poor schoolmaster, he seemed, to the large world around him, merely the leader of a set of faddists, the high priest of a precious cult that would pass. Yet Mallarmé it might be said, was more profoundly subversive than Baudelaire, if his work had been accessible to the common reader. He is even, at times, a more vividly and disturbingly sensuous poet than Baudelaire; I quote from Aldous Huxley's version of *L'Après-Midi d'un Faune*:

> I love that virginal fury – ah, the wild
> Thrill when a maiden body shrinks, defiled,
> Shuddering like arctic light, from lips that sear
> Its nakedness . . . the flesh in secret fear!

But we are not to take that literally, as we are to take, with a sad literalness, so much that is sordid or sinister in Baudelaire. Mallarmé is, as Baudelaire is not, consciously a symbolist.

Let me quote, on the general subject of symbolism, from one of our most acute young critics to-day in England, Mr Iain Fletcher: he is distinguishing between allegorical and symbolical poetry, and he says that if a poem is allegorical, 'it works out the details of something already given, something which has received prior justification as theology or political theory, an organisation of intuitions and judgments. Valuation of this will depend on the structure of the poem, on its music, its detail. With the poetry of symbol none of these things is of the first importance. A symbol has been defined as the expression of some otherwise inexpressible truth; and it is not on the verbal music, or on the incidental illustrations of the theme that judgment will depend, but on the insight which the poem accords into the life of the soul.'

What insight does Mallarmé accord into the life of the soul in these lines I have quoted? The faun and the two nymphs, seen remotely, as on a moving tapestry, have a meaning other than themselves: not, however, that allegorical meaning which can be tightly tied down, but the symbolical meaning that opens out in vague, endless suggestions, that conveys what could not be conveyed otherwise. Perhaps we think, when we read these lines, of the beautiful possible poem, with its ideal existence even before it has been written, that shudderingly resists the poet's hot desire to grasp and embody it. For if it is not an essential limitation of the symbolist method, as Mr Fletcher defines it, it does seem to be a limitation of it as Mallarmé developed it, that it becomes more and more shut in on itself, the subject of the poet being ever more narrowly confined to the nature of the poetic experience itself: poems being about poetry.

And the nature of poetry is perhaps something inexpressible, or something that can be expressed only through the symbols of particular poems. Let me quote my own version of one of Mallarmé's most famous sonnets, which will illustrate this truth: the terribly 'shut-in' nature of symbolist poetry, for all its beauty.

> The virgin, bright, and beautiful to-day
> Dare it now shatter with a drunken wing
> This hard forgotten lake, this ice where cling
> These flights of mine that never flew away . . .?
> Once was a swan, remembers it is he,
> Magnificent but hopeless in his strife
> For never having sung the realms of life
> When winter shone in bleak sterility.
> His neck in a white agony is shaken,
> Shattering the space that mocks him for his pride
> But not the soil in which his plumes are taken.
> Phantom mere brightness to this scene has drawn,
> Immobile in the cold, where dreams deride,
> Clothed in the useless exile of the swan.

It is of the very nature of symbolist poetry, as I have suggested, that it cannot be tied down to any single and simple interpretation, but, however much of its intention one may think one has dredged up to the surface, retains a residue of mysterious suggestiveness; so that the interpretation of such poems is almost as tricky, and as full of traps, as the interpretation of dreams. But I think that in this case we are at least not going very far wrong in equating

> This hard forgotten lake, this ice where cling
> These flights of mine that never flew away . . .

with the beautiful but almost entirely self-enclosed world of the symbolist poem itself; the poet is lamenting that it is his fate to be the poet, that is, to be himself, *only* in the poem, that is, in something other than himself, and other than himself in the most complete and hostile fashion; for one's own life is not and cannot be the 'life' as we call it, the 'order' as we perhaps ought to call it, of words upon a page. The most wonderful flights of the symbolist imagination cannot take it away from its merely symbolic mode of asserting itself: cannot take into reality, into life itself. The poet suffers, he is trapped like the swan (and the swan, in verse, is one of the permanent symbols of the poet) as a punishment for

> never having sung the realms of life
> When winter shone in bleak sterility.

The sterile bleakness of winter, the icy crystalline order of pure art, of the poem as something utterly self-contained, trapped and held that 'poetic' quality in Mallarmé's nature which should have flowed warmly, and perishably, out into life. The 'space' in which the swan's neck 'in a white agony is shaken' as well as being the perceptual space of the poem's winter landscape is perhaps the physical space of the outer universe, a space empty and meaningless to Mallarmé, who did not share Baudelaire's Christian beliefs. There was no God there, not even Baudelaire's harsh God of Justice. And we may remember the tremendous, frightening sentence of Pascal, battling with his own fears of atheism: 'The eternal silence of these infinite spaces frightens me.' The frosty soil in which the bird's wings are caught and trapped is that of the poem itself. It is only within the poem that poetry is now possible, the world outside has become unpoetical; yet that world 'outside' includes, of course, the poet's everyday self, and drawing no life even from that, the poem is acquiring a glittering and killing frigidity, which in the end will drive even the poet, or the possible poet, away. As poetry acquires more and more of a self-subsistent crystalline order, it becomes more and more difficult and painful for the poet to write it. So we are told in the last three lines that even the swan (that is, the poet as apart from the poem) has become an illusion:

> Phantom mere brightness to this scene has drawn,
> Immobile in the cold, where dreams deride,
> Clothed in the useless exile of the swan.

The 'brightness' of the ideal possible poem has drawn the poet rather as the brightness of a lamp draws a moth: but his death is a different kind of death, in the end the symbolist dream has become something too freezing and inimical to life for the poet to live in, or to live anything but a hallucination of life in. The poet is *elsewhere*, but his only proper place, as a poet, is inside this heartless, glittering, sterile poetic 'world.' So his 'exile' is 'useless,' since it is only in this world of poetry, which in purifying it so drastically he has now rendered uninhabitable, that he could have had his proper life. Thus the symbolist poet (like Mallarmé's disciple, Valéry, for many years) can cease to be a spy in the philistine city and become, to all outward appearances at least, for many years, a dutiful ordinary citizen; feeling that it is the poetic experience which matters and that the actual writing of a poem is in a sense a death and a profanation, an arbitrary and brutal limitation of an infinite and ideal world, the world of poetic possibilities. In the end is any actual poem as beautiful, or as suggestive, as a pure white page?

I have dealt with this one poem at great length because it seems a very handy model, indeed, of what I have called not only the complexity, but the allusiveness and the irony, of the typical 'modern' poem. The complexity is pretty obvious: but, as for the allusiveness, I have shown, I hope, that a reader can make no deep sense of this poem – no sense other than that of the beauty of phrases, the wintry brilliance of images, and the ghostly evocation of a landscape – unless he is on the look out for a complex set of allusions to the whole place of Mallarmé and his school in French literary history. And perhaps one must be a poet oneself, and also deeply interested in the history of poetry, to grasp immediately and intuitively that this, to put it crudely, is what the poem is *about*. I cannot see what clues and hints Mallarmé has given the ordinary reader, other than the use of that facile and common symbol (so unlike the run of his symbols) of the swan for the poet. The irony of the poem lies in the contrast between what it is and what it says. It is a strikingly beautiful poem (the reader will have to take my word for that, whatever he thinks of my own version): in its harmony, its brilliance, and its condensation it seems to embody almost a certain ideal of poetic beauty; and yet what it says is that it is impossible for the poet to go on writing the sort of poem it is. The winter images stand at once for an incredible bright beauty and for an atmosphere in which no life can persist. The price of the poem's beauty is the poet's death. With Mallarmé, indeed, we can think of pure symbolism as reaching its culmination, and making it necessary for subsequent important poets to free their wings from the ice and to find their way back, at whatever cost, to the 'realms of life.'

Strangely enough, one of the first results of this attempt by post-symbolist poets to bring art and life together again was not a new simplicity and clarity but a new confusion. Mallarmé is a difficult poet but it is doubtful whether he can be properly called an obscure one;

the difficulty of working out the meaning of such a poem as that which we have just examined is like that of solving a complicated set of equations; the symbols of symbolist poetry, like those of mathematics, offer us a severely coherent pattern of thought, held at some distance from life.

With Rimbaud, on the other hand, who may be taken as one of the main precursors of post-symbolist poetry, obscurity is intrinsic; for Rimbaud, unlike Mallarmé, does not know, or want to know, quite what he is doing. He speaks in a trance like a sort of inspired drunkard. He plunges poetry into life, and life into poetry once more, but at the cost of introducing into both a new element of bewilderment and disorder. Mallarmé led a life of sedate respectability. Rimbaud's life, during his short, dazzling period of creative activity, was one of drunkenness and vice; drunkenness and vice accompanied, moreover, by a savage and brutal violence of manner, a coarseness of language, which estranged from the young Rimbaud all the older men of letters, except the infatuated Verlaine, who might otherwise have wanted to help him. Yet it would be wrong to think of Rimbaud as simply a genius who happened to be a moral imbecile. He was rather a young man of sturdy peasant physique, of excellent intelligence (the best classical scholar in his country school), and of strong will who deliberately set out to disintegrate the normal patterns of life, to dislocate them, as Mallarmé had dislocated the normal patterns of language. The 'magical' world of poetry was, for Mallarmé, something that offered an escape from the drab emptiness of actual existence; but why, Rimbaud asked himself, should not the 'magic' be projected back on to existence, why should only poems, and not life, be 'poetical'? Why should one compromise ever with the prose world?

Rimbaud's excesses then were pursued not so much for their own sake, or for the sake of some delusive abstraction like 'pleasure,' as for the sake of an attempt at transformation and possession – an attempt to transform the matter of life into something magical, and to possess at every moment the feeling of tense, bewildering exaltation which belongs to a poet when he has completed a successful poem. Rimbaud would make no compromise with the outer world at all; in his writing, he did not start off from perceptions, but from self-induced hallucinations, from something like the state of delirium in which everything heard or seen is misinterpreted according to a momentary obsession. Through wallowing in excess and flirting with madness, he hoped to make himself a visionary, to reach a certain primal and primitive innocence of poetic awareness; even at the cost of moral suicide, for if we try to make life more intense by steadily increasing the doses of some stimulant, we either kill ourselves, or, if we are too strong for that, end in apathy. Rimbaud was too strong and he ended in apathy. He could not turn the real world permanently and successfully into the world of poetry after all. So he deserted poetry – that, perhaps, is more true than to say that poetry deserted him – became a merchant and an explorer in the Sudan and Ethiopia, wore himself out with his exertions, and died finally, back in France, in great pain, reconciled, perhaps, on his death-bed to the Catholic Church.

Rimbaud is the very type of the poet as rebel; not only against political orders and social conditions but against the very nature of human life, of reality, itself. He helped to inspire the French Surrealist movement, which, as its name suggests, refuses to reconcile itself to everyday reality; on the other hand he has very much influenced a great Catholic poet like Paul Claudel, who called him 'a mystic in the wild state.' The Surrealists on the one hand and Claudel on the other would be insulted by the suggestion that they have anything in common, but perhaps they have this, that they both seek to use words not merely to *record* existence but to key it up, for themselves and their readers, to a new pitch; they seek not merely to engage the reader's attention but to alter his life. By the power and richness of their language they hope to bewilder and overpower the reader, to drag him into their nets; it is a doctrine and a way of life and a means of persuasion that matter to them, not, as with Mallarmé and Valéry, the poem as detached from the poet, complete and perfect and crystalline in itself. Thus, it is almost hopeless to ask, as we have been asking with Mallarmé, what Rimbaud *means* by his poems. If to understand Mallarmé, we have to know the literary theories of his school, to understand Rimbaud we have to know every detail of his personal history; and the whole bulk of his poems can be taken as a single design, a sort of fantasticated autobiography, except that it is the fantastication, not the autobiography, that matters. Facts, what we call facts, are for this kind of poet nothing in themselves; they are merely a point of departure for imaginative transformations. Similarly, critics often discuss whether Surrealist texts of automatic writing, for instance, are 'meaningless'; and it can be pointed out that they have at least a clinical meaning, that they would give a psychiatrist many clues to the writer's obsessions, convictions, and general state of mind, but that clinical meaning is not what interests the Surrealists themselves –

rather what interests them is the delirium, the richness, the confusion, and the terror, of the sort of experience which the writing and reading of such texts (if one does not find them merely tedious) can evoke.

Such 'mad' poets would not exactly deny that they were mad, but would say that their 'madness' was a more alert and sensitive state, a state that gives a deeper insight into and a wider grasp of reality, than the state generally called 'sanity.' In England, and in the United States, poets are less likely to go all the way with a theory than in France; but a poet like Hart Crane with his dizzying use of language, in which the strict meaning of the sentences is irrelevant and everything depends upon the emotional associations of words and phrases; a poet like Dylan Thomas with his musical welter of dream images; a poet like W.S. Graham with his impenetrable personal syntax and his recurrent obsession with the sea,

> Very end then of land. What vast is here?
> The drowning saving while, the threshold sea
> Always is here. You may not move away,

are all in Rimbaud's tradition. The image of the sea which tends to play a major part in all poetry in this tradition has many possible associations and interpretations; but the most important for our purposes here, I think, is that the land is the surface on which we walk, as we think, safely – it is the waking conscious mind; the sea with its greater depth and density, in which we can drown under huge pressures and suffering unimaginable terrors, is the mind of sleep and the sub-conscious, as full of disturbing images as the sea is full of strange fish. We 'may not move away' from that in the sense that we must go to sleep every night and descend into this primitive part of ourselves. It is perhaps the larger and more important part, just as the real sea covers so much a greater portion of the globe's surface than the emergent patches of land. It is a part of which we feel a terror (the idea of losing consciousness, of being lost in the world of sleep for ever, is like the fear of hell); it is also a part for which we feel a certain nostalgia, a homing desire, for it was from the sea after all that all life first came – and just so, modern psychologists sometimes tell us, from the submerged, subconscious parts of ourselves come all the desires and impulses that move us in the waking world. Poets like Rimbaud should be thought of as the first explorers of this fatal ocean, its first explorers, at least, in terms of poetic art. We should not judge their lives, which so often seem, by the standards of the waking world, disastrous lives, too strictly. They are the first colonisers of a new realm, who may plant a flag or send home a report, but few of them indeed will ever return alive, to our ordinary world of surface consciousness, to tell in person, and from the perspective of final safety, their strange stories.

The most notable cause of obscurity in modern poetry is likely then to be this submergence of the poet in a sea in which he can no more account for his actions, or for his presence there, than any drowning or dreaming man. Yet poetry at the conscious level – or poetry, on the other hand, of what Mr Eliot has called 'the high dream' as opposed to the 'low dream' – has its own difficulties, too. The poems of Eliot and his fellow countryman, who influenced him so much in technique, Ezra Pound, avoid that dichotomy of art and life which may seem to have led the Symbolists on the one hand and the various explorers in the wake of Rimbaud on the other into so many difficulties. The idea of the work of pure art in abstraction from life is, as we have seen, and as Mallarmé saw, a finally sterile one; so is the idea of the utmost possible impurity, of vitality at all costs, for if many modern Surrealist verse texts are 'vital documents' in some sense or other – vital as witnessing the incoherence of our time – few of them are in any genuine or legitimate sense, and indeed few would really claim to be, 'poems.' Once the idea of a continual transformation of life into art, and of art into life, has been accepted from Rimbaud (as the Surrealists on the whole accepted it) as a mechanical formula, the quality of both art and life suffer; art deliberately assumes the untidy edges, the lack of beginning and end, the failure to fall into perspective, of life at its most tepid and insignificant, while life on the other hand assumes an element of unreal 'artistic' pose.

Eliot and Pound, however, like many Americans, were interested in the larger reconciling idea of 'culture'; for it is, after all, within the framework of the 'culture' of a human society that both life and art impact upon each other, and unless the 'culture' is of a fairly high quality, both life and art will be at a low ebb, while on the other hand we think of periods of 'high culture' as producing noble lives as well as noble art. For Americans, Europe as a whole is the ancestor of their culture, and they are therefore able to see the European scene in a broader perspective than the actual European, with his sharp sense of national differences, often can. The obscurity of Pound and Eliot comes not from any use of the subconscious dream material I have been talking about (they are both pre-Freudian poets) but from the

bewildering wide range of their cultural allusions, assuming in the reader
a knowledge of language and literature which he often does not possess.

In Eliot's later poetry the embedding of fragments from other
writers whole into his work has become less obtrusive, but in Pound's
later *Cantos* it has become more so: Chinese characters alternate with
passages from Greek, Latin and the Romance languages. This display
of erudition is sometimes irritating (more so in Pound than in Eliot)
but it should not be dismissed as mere ostentation. It enables the poet
to achieve most subtle effects of irony: thus when Eliot writes in *The
Waste Land*,

> But at my back from time to time I hear
> The sound of horns and motors, which shall bring
> Sweeney to Mrs Porter in the spring.
> O the moon shone bright on Mrs Porter
> And on her daughter
> They wash their feet in soda water,

we are to think both of Marvell's famous

> But at my back I always hear
> Time's wingèd chariot hurrying near,
> And yonder all before us lie
> Deserts of vast Eternity,

and of the less known poem which Mr Eliot cites in the notes, Day's
Parliament of Bees:

> When of the sudden, listening, you shall hear,
> A noise of horns and hunting, which shall bring
> Actaeon to Diana in the spring,
> Where all shall see her naked skin . . .

and so we are to contrast Marvell's grave seducer, for whom the
thought of death and judgment gives a finer edge to passion, and on
the other hand the simple lyricism of the Day passage (and yet Actaeon
will be torn to pieces by the hounds for his presumption) with the
slack immunity with which Sweeney, the modern unheroic equivalent
of Marvell and Actaeon, pursues his sordid 'love-life': Sweeney lacks
both the sense of sin and the sense of nemesis, and therefore he has no
bright awareness of beauty . . . the lines from an Australian popular song,

> O the moon shone bright on Mrs Porter
> And on her daughter
> They wash their feet in soda water,

mock his banal idea of 'glamour.' So there is not a line in this passage which has not been either borrowed by Mr Eliot, or suggested to him by another poet's line and adapted; and yet the passage is very distinctively in his own manner. And this use of allusion and concealed quotation enables him to set the present and the past in perspective, and to exhibit ironically the decay of past standards in present-day life.

We have run over, then, some of the main qualities which poetry, written in whatever age, that strikes us as having a specifically 'modern' ring, is likely to possess; and we have seen that when we know something about the poet's relation to his age, and the particular contemporary problems that happened to obsess him, we become less bewildered by 'modern' poetry. I think much modern poetry *is* very difficult, and that it does not always repay the labour involved in working it out. There are times when we all fall back for refreshment on poetry that is *not* modern. For the qualities of simplicity and clearness are permanently valuable qualities in literature, as perennially refreshing as pure running water is. Complexity, however, has its proper place in literature; human life is a complex phenomenon, and in the last hundred years or so its complexity has been more and more heavily borne in on all of us; and a false, or affected, simplicity is a detestable thing.

Section 5: 'Modernity' in the Drama

This can be a very much shorter section than the ones which precede it. For one thing, there is a sense in which absolutely *all* great drama (Sophocles, Shakespeare, Racine, or Ibsen) strikes us as modern in spirit; and for another thing, in an age which has been notable for innovations in form by novelists and poets, dramatists, the better dramatists particularly, have been remarkably conservative about form. Thus Tchehov's best plays of fifty or sixty years ago, like Ibsen's of seventy or eighty years ago, do not seem to us, when we see them performed, the least old-fashioned.

It is true that neither Ibsen nor Tchehov any longer appears to us, as they may have done to their contemporaries, strictly 'naturalistic.' I have seen a performance of *The Cherry Orchard*, in fact, by Oxford undergraduates, in which an excessive emphasis on some of the technical mannerisms of Tchehov, combined no doubt with an immature response to his deeper themes, turned that melancholy, complex, and profound comedy into something like farce. Tchehov's technical device, by which his characters do not directly answer each other but

44

carry on vague soliloquies which they allow others to interrupt, is just as much of an 'artificial' convention as, for instance, the excessive logic and coherence of the interchanges in French classical tragedy; it is intended to underline the isolation of individuals, just as the opposite convention is intended to underline their interrelation; it is very typical, in fact, of the way in which self-absorbed and absent-minded people do talk; but Tchehov's characters can become, in the hands of all but very skilful actors, mere 'humours.' Ibsen's middle-class Scandinavian backgrounds have for us – and had even for his non-Scandinavian contemporaries – an irrelevant appeal of grotesque local colour; and his use of physical properties, like the wild duck in the attic, as symbolic centres for his plays is faintly disturbing just because such a profoundly poetic way of thinking underlies such a deliberately drab and gritty prosaic surface. There is a sense, though it is a shallow one, in which both these great dramatists may be said to lead us into fantasy worlds; the surface reality is rather superficial, fantasy lies close underneath it, and the fundamental reality of the human grasp has to be sought deeper still. In this, they might be compared to a writer like Dostoevsky who likes to give his narration and his conversations a surface air of the humdrum and the matter-of-fact; just under that surface, there is wild melodrama; under the wild melodrama, once more, there is tragic wisdom. It might be said, in fact, that one great achievement of 'naturalism' both in the nineteenth-century novel and the nineteenth-century drama was to make the tragic impact, the deep poetic perception, possible again, by rescuing it from the faded graces of an outworn literary style. But the non-literary approach can now itself be recognised as just another, though more cunning and inclusive, literary convention.

Tchehov and Ibsen were brilliant innovators, certainly; but their successors – even though these successors include men of genius, like George Bernard Shaw – have simply taken over their inventions, without adding to them, and without perhaps even making the fullest possible use of them. Shaw certainly differs from both of them in making a much wider use of the drama to air his views on current topics: so much so that Robert Graves considers him as not a dramatist in the proper sense, but rather a writer of satirical dialogues like Lucian, a 'philosopher turned demagogue'; and there is something in this, for the beautiful scene, for instance, between Don Juan and the Devil in *Man and Superman* is almost never acted in performances of that play, though for the reader it is the most exciting part of it. It is not acted, because it contributes nothing to the action; and it is the *action* after all of a play (and not any incidental ornaments of that action, like stray felicities of diction or fine set speeches) which is properly dramatic. On the other hand, if what Shaw adds to Ibsen and Tchehov is not properly dramatic, something that he fails to take over from them is. He took over from Ibsen the idea that real and serious themes of contemporary life could be handled on the stage; and in *Heartbreak House* he took advantage of Tchehov's technical invention of making characters in a play no more attend fully to each other than they do in real life, nor directly answer each other, but instead mirror in their dialogue their own continuing preoccupations. (And this, after all, was not a completely new invention, for it is basically the same idea as that of Ben Jonson's 'comedy of humours.') What Shaw failed to take over from Tchehov and Ibsen was their ability by the use of some piece of symbolism – the shot sea-gull, the cherry orchard that has to be sold, the wild duck in the attic – to give their plays, behind the flat prose surface, the third dimension of poetry. These symbols stand for some aspect of a situation that cannot be made fully explicit at a conceptual level, but Shaw always thinks that every situation can be made explicit, and therefore poetry escapes him; and the history of English prose drama in the last fifty years is that partly of the gradual exhaustion of the original inspiration Shaw provided – it *was* exhaustible, simply because of that lack of poetic depth in it – and of attempts to tap the roots of poetry elsewhere: in Irish peasant life by Synge, in Dublin slum life by O'Casey, and lately, in writers like Mr T. S. Eliot, in efforts to resuscitate and make contemporary a tradition of English poetic drama that has been moribund since the Restoration.

Shaw's successors in his own or a broadly similar vein – one might mention Galsworthy, Granville Barker, J. B. Priestley, James Bridie – have sometimes a closer feeling for everyday atmospheres, and a more warm and instinctive sympathy with the 'ordinary man,' than Shaw himself, but they are lesser men: and they also lack poetic vision. I would say that Sean O'Casey in his early plays of Dublin life was perhaps the only dramatist, domiciled in the British Isles, and writing in English, of this century who had gone afresh to Ibsen and Tchehov to learn their lesson of 'poetic realism': but since he has jettisoned the realism in his later plays in a German expressionistic style, and become more consciously 'poetical,' his poetry has gone bad on him. I would say the only hope for the English drama at the moment is a genuine revival of the verse drama tradition: but apart from Mr Eliot, and perhaps Mr Christopher Fry, one can only point there to a crowd of promising young writers, mostly true poets certainly, but mostly also with everything still to learn about the theatre.

The novelist and the poet can, of course, experiment as they please, if they can find some publisher to print them. But the dramatist requires a theatre, and somebody willing to risk paying the rent of that theatre and the salaries of the actors and the general cost of the production. So he cannot, as the poet and the novelist can, give the public twenty or thirty years to catch up with him: he must, however original his views, be ready to compromise with the conservative tastes of the 'big theatre' audience and the even more conservative standards of 'big theatre' actors and producers. That is why the history of the drama is so oddly different, in England certainly, but also I think in other European countries, from the history of any other kind of literature. Periods of high excellence in the drama tend to be short and to peter out towards the end, and then it takes a tremendous effort to get the drama started again. One reason for this is that, once a dramatic period *is* established, new dramatists tend to imitate not so much the life around them as the work of established elder dramatists. The plays of Beaumont and Fletcher, for instance, are full of this sort of literary imitation, and mark the decadence of Jacobean drama. One cannot say that Congreve actually marks the decadence of Restoration drama but, like all his contemporaries, he goes on writing in terms of the wits and rakes of good King Charles's golden days in a much more refined and respectable period; for he is the contemporary, after all, not of the wild Lord Rochester but of the smooth and pious Joseph Addison.

What seems 'natural' and 'realistic' dialogue, in fact, to actors, is not dialogue which catches the tones of contemporary speech, but dialogue which reminds them of what they are used to hearing and speaking on the stage. This applies not only to dialogue but to atmosphere and properties. The sort of typical bland comedy, for suburban middle-class consumption, which still makes a periodical mild success in the London West End, shows a spacious living-room with French windows, a comic servant dusting, and pleasant, leisurely people who most of them do not seem to have to work for a living. The middle-class audience in England to-day, which still enjoys these plays, is suffering from a housing shortage; finds servants both very difficult to get and beyond the ordinary person's means; and has, as a legal duty, to be doing useful work of some sort, even if it were feasible for it to live on its dividends. The audience on the whole would rather have an

47

idealisation of a kind of life it once lived, or hoped to live, than a sharp and disturbing picture of the kind of life it is living now.

Thus the drama, because of this imitativeness of actors, and this tendency in audiences to acquiesce in what they are used to, again and again in English history simply runs to a dead stop. Then it has to be started again on almost completely fresh lines. The intervals between the starting and stopping can be very long; after the petering out of the Restoration impulse, around 1700, there are no English plays which have at once literary and theatrical value (with the two exceptions of Goldsmith's and Sheridan's comedies) till the 1890s. The Victorian age, one of the great periods in English life and literature, contributed nothing at all to the drama till it was almost at an end. And for the last fifty years we have been living on a double impulse, a brisk push, given by Shaw and Wilde – the one to the comedy of ideas, the other to the comedy of pure entertainment – but the balls they started rolling have come to a standstill. Perhaps Mr Eliot will give a new ball a new push; but certainly it does seem to me that in spite of the contributions of three Irish dramatists of genius – Shaw, Synge, and O'Casey – the history of the drama in the last fifty years makes a rather thin show compared to the history of poetry or the novel. There have been plenty of clever and successful playwrights like Mr Somerset Maugham and Mr Noel Coward; but even their plays in the last twenty or thirty years have begun to 'date' rather badly, and to look like what they are: extremely skilful contributions, but without a deep inner life of their own, and lying somewhere just on the other side of literature.

There has been experiment, of course, in what we call in England the 'little theatre' as opposed to the 'big theatre,' but it is doubtful whether these experiments mark a genuine progress. The techniques of German expressionism, for instance, which have been used in differing ways both by Sean O'Casey and by Auden and Isherwood, seem to me retrogressive in relation to the drama; instead of characters you get types; instead of situations in depth you get flat simplifications of topical issues: the direction is away back to the morality play and when you have the rare gift, which O'Casey has, of putting flesh and blood people and actual situations on the stage, and letting the poetry of reality speak for itself, it seems a pity to start writing in terms of the propaganda cartoon. With Auden and Isherwood, flippancy and cleverness, a gift for charade and pantomime, enable them to dodge the sweat of grappling with real drama; they are edifying and amusing, and they produce pieces of genuine entertainment like *The Dog*

48

Beneath the Skin or sincere uplift, like *The Ascent of F6*, but they never at any time give one the illusion of reality. And the illusion of reality matters; it is what makes a play. Many other so-called 'innovations' or 'experiments' in the theatre in our time similarly seem to be essentially retrogressive. Mr Eugene O'Neill has a device by which you not only hear what his characters say, you hear what they think; but if they were adequately conceived you should be able to guess their thoughts from the tone of their conversation; and this is really a reintroduction of that hammiest of all devices in 'realistic' drama, which writers otherwise of little moment like Pinero are praised for getting rid of, the 'aside' or the soliloquy spoken aloud in naturalistic prose, which the actor delivering it has to get off his chest without looking as if he had gone mad, while the other actors have an equally embarrassing time pretending they do not hear him. And one should remember this when one criticises dramatists of our time for their failure to experiment radically; so many of their experiments have been failures, and have made one see the real merits of the conventional thing, even of ideas which we all learned to jeer at when we were schoolboys, like the unity of time, place, and action. Mr Shaw writes *Back to Methuselah* which takes one several nights to see and has much more talk than action in it: and one begins to see the point of insisting that a play ideally should present a unified action within a certain limited space of time. Whatever pleasure *Back to Methuselah* gives us, it is not essentially a *dramatic* pleasure. Similarly, in a recent American play which has been a great success in London, *Death of a Salesman*, we get an application to the drama of the loose, flexible construction of the novel or the film, there are flashbacks, soliloquies, narrative commentaries, changes of scene made possible by having several sets ready on the stage at once and lighting up one or the other as it is needed. It is very ingenious. But is it really what we want from the drama? Is our idea of dramatic pleasure not really rather the idea of the rich implications that can be drawn out of a tight and strict construction?

To sum up then, let us repeat that all really *great* drama strikes us as essentially modern; but that our own period, in England, has not been so notable for the production of striking plays as for that of striking poetry and fiction. In reading nearly all contemporary plays in English (with the exception of perhaps half a dozen of Shaw's, which would include *Heartbreak House* and *John Bull's Other Island*, two or three of Synge's, which would include *The Playboy of the Western World*, but

49

probably not the unfinished *Deirdre*, perhaps one or two of the later short plays of Yeats, particularly *Purgatory*, O'Casey's early Dublin tenement tragedies, perhaps Mr Eliot's *The Cocktail Party*, perhaps Joyce's *Exiles*, perhaps Stephen Spender's *The Trial of a Judge*) we are too obtrusively aware of the rapidly dating 'period' quality in the play: aware of its diction, sentiment, and character as belonging to a particular time and place, and unreal from the point of view of our own time and place. When we have this 'period' feeling about a play, we can be sure that it is not a great play. Thus when we read Beaumont and Fletcher, however much we have enjoyed a facile grace of style and a fertility in the invention of episode, we are never for a moment in doubt that this is something rather cold-bloodedly and very skilfully confected to hit the taste of a particular audience; and we do not have that feeling about Shakespeare. We have that feeling, again, of something specially trimmed to the audience in the comedies of Mr Somerset Maugham and Mr Noel Coward; not in Wilde's *The Importance of Being Earnest* or in Congreve's *The Way of the World* where we feel that a fine artist is incidentally delighting us in the course of delighting himself. The meretricious, or commercial, or essentially imitative product can be detected, in fact, quite easily, by the lack of that note of inner delight in it – and by an inescapable touch of the jaded or the shoddy in its use of language.

On the other hand, when we read Shakespeare, or some of the few genuinely great plays by his contemporaries – say, to take some of Mr T. S. Eliot's choices, *Volpone*, *The Revenger's Tragedy*, *The Changeling* – we forget about the element of 'local colour': about how much the moral attitudes, the manners, and the ways of speech of men in the early sixteenth century differed from our own: we are caught up in an intense illusion of reality. In fact, this illusion is more intense even in the mere reading of a great play (let alone the seeing of it adequately performed) than in the reading of a great novel. We take up *War and Peace* and lay it down again; the illusion is again and again broken. We read *Macbeth* or *The Wild Duck* at a sitting. Again, when we read a novel, we are in a sense passive: the novelist with his descriptions and analyses does much of our work for us; we have not to co-operate with him, merely to watch and listen. But we co-operate with the dramatist even in reading a play to ourselves in solitude. We become the characters; we recite their speeches to ourselves; we feel our muscles tensing with their emotions. Thus the drama at its rare heights – which always, as I say, seem to precede and usher in long periods of decadence – does seem to me (with the possible exception of some kinds of long narrative poem, *The Iliad* or *The Divine Comedy*) the great literary achievement of the human race (and for our own period the long narrative poem, anything in verse on the heroic scale, seems an impossibility).* For if one compares the great dramas even with the greatest novels, there is a sense in which the latter look like loose and extended scenarios for a possible drama (Henry James felt this very strongly). There is a sense also in which we could consider many lyrical or meditative poems as having their place ideally, and explaining themselves perfectly, in some drama of the poet's life of which only these eloquent fragments have been written. And the drama is our model in all kinds of writing when we want to cut out these passages, perhaps vividly and charmingly written in themselves, which contribute nothing to the total effect; it gives us our idea of *construction* in literature. And the best advice one can give, often, to a young writer who is not a dramatist (who writes stories, or poems, or even essays on general themes) is: 'Dramatise, dramatise!' That is to say: 'Do not be loose, and dawdling, and wavering, and expansive. Concentrate, eliminate. Space out, and weigh, and measure your important effects, so that you may be able to bring them home with the most obvious brutal strength.'

But the high ages of drama are few and far between, and it does not seem to me that our own is one of them. It is an age of good plays rather than great plays. There is too much drift and too much anxiety for the finest drama; there is not that easy inner confidence, that feeling of possessing an assured style of life, that belongs to such different places and times as the England of King James, the France of Louis XIV, classical Athens and early seventeenth-century Spain; and which in a completely independent civilisation belonged to the Japan that produced the Kabuki and the Noh plays. Since this book is so largely concerned with the qualities and achievements of 'modern' writing, it is well to emphasise that the typically 'modern' attitude seems incapable of producing really great drama. That will keep us humble. We shall avoid the mistake of thinking that literature 'progresses' just as science progresses; we shall realise that there are some basic inadequacies in our 'modern' attitude, and we shall look back with reverence to our ancestors, our inferiors no doubt in technical knowledge and range of information, but able to excel us

* But see my remarks later on Ezra Pound's *Cantos*, whose ultimate significance is perhaps that of a tremendous *failure* to write an 'heroic poem' in an unheroic age.

in some things: the writing of plays among them. We shall realise too that the 'modern' attitude, with its emphasis on harsh, unresolved complexities, is essentially a transitional attitude: and that some future society, more settled in its ways, and more happy about its assumptions than our own, may be able to produce a serene, objective art of a kind which we cannot possibly produce, ourselves, now; but can only long for and wistfully imagine.

CHAPTER TWO

THE NOVEL

Section 1: Two Ancestors

We can trace, I think, the immediate ancestry of the modern English novel back at least as far as the 1890s, to the work of two novelists who were at opposite poles in their conception of the novel, its form and its function, but who nevertheless felt a half-reluctant admiration for each other. These two friends were Henry James, then in the full maturity of his powers, and H. G. Wells, then making a brilliant beginning. I have said something already about James's high idea of the novel as an art-form; it is doubtful whether Wells ever regarded it primarily as an art-form or as anything but a vehicle for popularising his ideas. In his fascinating *Experiment in Autobiography*, Wells describes a conversation in which James reproached him for his lack of artistic conscience, in relation to a novel of his called *Marriage*. In this novel, a 'novel of ideas,' more important from Wells's point of view for the ideas discussed in it than for the story or characters, the hero and heroine at one point disappear into a country lane and emerge three hours later engaged. Wells gives no hint of what they were saying or doing during this long period, and Henry James hinted to him that this was because he simply did not *know*; and this for James, with his strict view of the rules of the game of novel writing, was just cheating. Wells, who had a very lively social conscience, but hardly any artistic conscience at all, could not see what the fuss was about. 'The Novel,' he writes, 'was not necessarily ... this real through and through absolutely true treatment of people more living than life. *It might be more and less than that and still be a novel.*' It would be 'more,' in many cases with Wells, in that it would include long discussions of, and digressions about, current social topics that struck Wells as urgently important; it would be 'less' in that these discussions would often not specially help the story along, and that the 'treatment' was often not 'through and through absolutely true' nor the 'people more living than' (nor, even, often, as living as) 'life.' Wells as a novelist simply hurried carelessly over what did not immediately excite him. Yet all that Wells writes has a certain vitality, and that came, as James noted, from the odd and perhaps irrelevant way in which he conveys, through a perhaps ill-constructed and implausible story, his own genuine excitement. 'The ground of the drama,' James wrote, 'is somehow most of all the adventure for *you*. . . .'

All life was a genuine adventure for Wells and what gives his vast uneven production in fiction and so many other fields a genuine if intermittent vitality even to-day is the fashion in which he does convey his oddly engaging personality; a personality bubbling over with hope, eagerness, and impatience; warm and irritable; given to the grandiose gesture but given also to humorously puncturing its own self-importance. Wells is a genuine artist in his early scientific fantasies and in such realistic studies of his own early environment as *Kipps*. He was also, in the field of ideas, a genuine liberating influence, especially for his own class – for the great new reading public, literate rather than educated, which was coming to the surface in the 1890s as a result of the growth of the population and the gradual spread of compulsory education during the Victorian age. Wells grew up at a time when Darwin and Huxley were turning the brighter young men of his class away from traditional religious beliefs and when their own ambitions were making them rebel against traditional social standards. They looked to science to transform the world – it was the time of the first telephones, gramophones, automobiles, even the homely bicycle seemed a revolutionary invention, and men were dreaming of the possibilities of heavier-than-air flying machines; science was going to transform the world, and literature, in comparison to science, was something of minor importance. That explains Wells's odd, humorous patronising air in his autobiography to friends and acquaintances of his, James, Conrad, Hueffer, Gissing, who took the art of the novel at all seriously. The novel for him was nothing in itself, it was a vehicle for more important matter; a sugaring of the pill of scientific and social instruction for a large new eager audience that could not yet be expected to read a serious book unless there was 'a story in it.' Wells felt that he was speaking for those who had been kept in their 'places' by their 'betters' long enough, and who must now have their own say; thus he was instinctively hostile to convention, formality, restraint, of any kind, which had helped to keep these underdogs in their 'places,' and that helps to explain his odd indifference (an indifference so strangely combined with a genuinely creative imagination) to the idea of 'art' as such; for art is based on convention, formality, restraint. Wells's god was science; his wish as a writer was not to produce masterpieces that might last for ever but to be an increasingly effective populariser of scientific ideas, especially in their relation to social change.

And Wells did achieve his ambition. From the point of view of pure literary criticism, he might be thought to have squandered his gifts. An early fantasy of his like *The Time Machine* is a real work of art; a later 'serious' and 'thoughtful' novel, like *The World of William Clissold*, is so much dead bulk. But Wells was, what he wanted to be, a liberator. It is easy to say now that one of the effects of the various emancipations for which he worked all his life has merely been to release untidy emotions from a traditional discipline; to make many people discontented with a necessary subordination in society and a necessary routine; and, in relaxing old codes, to destroy a sense of style. What we do with our new liberties is not the liberator's fault, and we should always honour liberators. Let us admit that Wells was an artist who often scamped his work and a thinker who let his emotions lead him astray. What is important is that he sought truth to the best of his abilities and that he loved his fellow-men; and in his hopes and fears, his enthusiasms and errors, he was more genuinely one of them than any other writer of his time. He might have said with one of his heroes, President Theodore Roosevelt: 'I am only an average man, but, by George, I work harder *at* it than the average man.' And if the modern novelist looks to James rather than to Wells for a model of scrupulosity in his art, he is none the worse for having a touch of Wells's eager, aspiring spirit.

The intellectual nourishment which Wells wished the novel to carry in panniers on its back, for James would have to be fully digested into its supple body. James writes novels on momentous themes; but he does not allow his characters to discuss these themes in an abstract way and still less does he interrupt his story to discuss them himself. He is one of the most 'intellectual' of novelists, but not, in Wells's sense, a 'novelist of ideas.' 'Ideas' in abstraction, by themselves, mean nothing to him; what interests him is how out of the proper handling and grasping of a 'story' there rises, in both writer and reader, an awareness of the 'grand theme,' of the informing design, 'the pattern in the carpet.' But the 'theme' is never wholly separable from the 'story'; it has its concrete weight and relevance in relation to the story, just as the story has its dignity, is raised above the status of mere anecdote, in relation to its emergent theme. Thus James *shows*, rather than *says*, what his novels are about; it is in an indirect and symbolical way (James's use of material properties in his stories to embody human attitudes has something in common with the symbolism of Ibsen and Tchehov) that he exposes and resolves the tensions and predicaments of civilised human life. His thinking is not (as too often in Wells's case) a kind of stucco plastered on the surface of his novels, but is built into their stone. That is why no novelist more quickly exasperates lazy readers; and even the most alert and attentive readers are likely to be kept upon the stretch.

The task, on the whole, of the novelist in our century has been to recognise that the foundations of the world he walks on are dangerously shifting, that we are living in a time of rapid and disturbing change, so that we can neither say with any precision *when* some new pattern of relative stability will emerge, nor *what* sort of pattern it will be; and yet, since the human heart hungers after permanence, to project into his own work some image of that aspiration: to give his novels a coherence, that is, either moral or aesthetic, that will hold together against the shocks of time. To attempt merely to 'keep up with things,' with every passing fashion in expression or thought, is fatal to the novelist; 'he that runs against Time,' as Dr Johnson said, 'has an antagonist not subject to casualties.'

It may be, in fact, that the conditions which make the writing of really great novels a possibility include the existence of that relatively stable background, to which we only to-day aspire; and it may be that the most suitable literary narrative form for the present and the immediate future is something other than the novel. Behind the great novels of the past, it might be said, there was the novelist's awareness of an established order which he might judge to be in the main a good or in the main an evil order, but which was in either case reliably *there*; and human acceptance of the order, or rebellion against it, had a constant significance. There is nothing of that sort to-day, it might be said, for us either to accept or rebel against. All arrangements have a very provisional air, and the marks of the time are uncertainty and anxiety. The individual to-day is exposed not only to petty humiliations and frustrations, as Wells's early hero Kipps was, but to mortal dangers – from wars, from revolutions, from slumps; he may have the luck to escape all these dangers, and if he does escape them, he may find a wider range of social opportunities open to him than Kipps did.

But Kipps felt that within limits he controlled his own life, and that is what it is becoming harder for the individual to feel to-day. Unless he is a person of very strong character, he is likely, therefore, to drift through life without any very passionate purpose or any very definite belief.

One of the greatest of modern novels in English, James Joyce's *Ulysses*, is concerned largely, as we shall see later, with just this sense of drift. Other novelists refuse to accept drift as something ultimate and desperately seek in their novels to find some belief or some purpose by which men can give meaning to their lives. The novelist like Joyce who appears merely to give a detached portrayal of drift is in the tradition of Henry James; he has a moral theme, but he allows that theme to emerge naturally from his story, he does not seek to abstract it from the story, and to draw the reader's attention to it as something separate. In this, he is aesthetically in the right; one is often asked, for instance, by people unfamiliar with modern poetry to tell them the 'real meaning' of some difficult poem, and they are disappointed when one says to them that the 'real meaning' is not something separable from the poem itself. For instance, one may be asked if the 'real meaning' of *The Waste Land* is that contemporary civilisation is in a state of crisis and decay; but that is only a drastic simplification of the 'real meaning.' Other 'real meanings' are that civilisation is always and everywhere in a state of crisis and decay and yet that the time is always redeemable. There is a true message of hope and a true message of despair in the poem; and the point of the frequent comparisons between the past and present in the poem is not necessarily merely that the past was noble, that the present is sordid, but probably also that, stripped of the illusions of the past, we are perhaps to-day more nakedly in touch with a timeless human predicament. The true waste land is not so much our culture, mechanical and meretricious as that is, as the proud and barren human heart that needs to obey a super-natural command and to be touched with a supernatural charity; and from that other side, from eternity's side, one time is much like another. All are unredeemed, and all redeemable . . . Even when one has said all this, one has not given the 'real meaning' of the poem; one has merely provided the reader with a slightly fuller set of rough clues. Similarly with a book like *Ulysses*: such great works of art without an obvious 'moral' in one sense, are far more 'moral' in another sense, than books with an immediate purpose of practical persuasion. Their morality is in their structure.

Artists of the type of Joyce, James, and Eliot, who can build their thinking *into* their work, are, however, at all times rare. The novelist like D. H. Lawrence, or Aldous Huxley, who uses the novel to propound, to advocate, to discuss some 'philosophy of life' is in the tradition of H. G. Wells; however strongly he may disagree with all, or some, or most of Wells's own extraordinarily varied and inconsistent set of philosophies. He may not rank so high as Joyce or James from the point of view of pure art; but he shows a commendably urgent concern with the immediate problems of his fellow men. If he never succeeds in arriving at a complete aesthetic coherence, the moral coherence of his work may nevertheless for a long time resist the dissolvents of social change.

Section 2: *Indian Summer*

In the years following the death of Queen Victoria, the sense of effortless moral and practical superiority which had been one of the marks of English history in her reign was replaced by a new uneasiness and doubt; there was doubt about the rights and wrongs of the Boer War, about the validity of the doctrine of free trade as an immutable economic truth. The growth of German industrial competition popularised the doctrine of Protectionism, while Germany's increasing military and naval power pointed the way to conscription, which was against all Victorian liberal traditions. There was uneasiness too about the problem of Irish Home Rule which had been shelved but not solved and about Mr Lloyd George's budgets and his National Insurance schemes, which meant the beginnings of State interference with the individual for the individual's own good.

There seemed to be also, in these years immediately following the death of Queen Victoria, a perceptible diminution in national grandeur and vitality. The politicians had still the same dignity but seemed to be on a smaller scale (Asquith compared with Gladstone, Balfour compared with Salisbury) and to lack the old fire of the Victorian giants. There was less, too, of that invigorating Victorian atmosphere of perpetual debate between Evolutionists and Bishops, between Protestants and Catholics, between Biblical Critics and Fundamentalists, between Hegelian and Utilitarian philosophers; there seemed to be no longer any broad and important intellectual issues which deeply divided the public and even the burning political topics of that day, tariffs or free trade, and national insurance, look from our present (certainly not intrinsically more enviable) point of view comfortably parochial. Even the early Fabians were becoming rather a *clique*, from which the livelier and more exploring mind of H. G. Wells would presently detach itself.

Nevertheless, if the Edwardian age was a time of plain thinking, it was also, for those reasonably comfortably situated, a time of high living. If the Victorian sun had set, it still left an afterglow; a fading splendour and a dying warmth still gilded the scene. The Edwardian decade and the years of the reign of King George V up to 1914 must have been for the larger part of the British people their last glimpse of 'normality,' of what they expected easy, ordinary everyday life to be. It was comfortable and jolly, after all, for so many people to be agreed, on a vague basis of sentiment, about so many things. Social barriers were gradually being lowered. The country houses of the aristocracy of birth which, in the latter part of the Victorian age, had been gradually opened to the new aristocracy of wealth were opened now to the still newer aristocracy of talent. H. G. Wells, the son of the lady's maid, the fervent radical, found himself chatting at dinner to Arthur Balfour or exchanging ideas and finding he had a good deal in common with a progressive Imperialist like Lord Milner. In fact the greatest of the new Imperialists, Joseph Chamberlain, had started off life as a radical, like Wells, and retained a great deal of the radical to the end; the new Unionist Party which had been formed when the anti-Home Rule Liberals left Gladstone was a much more capacious and tolerant body than the old Conservative Party had been, if also, perhaps, a body without such clear and definite principles. And the gradual rise of the Labour Party was pushing the Liberal Party, on the other hand, farther to the right. The leading politicians on the Liberal or Unionist side, whichever happened to be in power, kept up the old custom of 'dining with the Opposition'; and indeed perhaps the weakness of both Balfour and Asquith as leaders, from the point of view of their more eager followers, was that they lacked partisan zeal.

Thus in essence (in spite of furious rows occasionally in the House of Commons usually centring round Home Rule, Mr Lloyd George's still genuine and combatant radicalism, or Liberal threats to force their measures through the House of Lords by creating new Peers) the two great traditional parties were growing closer to each other. Nor was the working man being slighted or ignored. While the Fabians were happily busy at their ant-like labours of compiling exhaustive statistics about everything, a new small Labour Party, which had little connection with the Fabians, but represented rather the power of the Trade

Unions and the long traditions of English Noncomformist radicalism among the working classes, was feeling its way and getting its feet in the House of Commons. Apart from that, the working man had his new popular newspapers and Mr Kipling paid him the compliment of writing many of his poems in what he assumed to be the working man's spoken tongue. It was to him, too, or at least to the lower-middle-class layer of clerks, shop assistants, typists, who felt themselves just a little higher in the social scale, that Wells's novels of ideas made their great appeal. The common people were, at least, being 'kept in the picture'; and in spite of a number of serious strikes shortly before the outbreak of the Great War, Marxian Socialism among the workers was not, except in Glasgow and parts of Wales, a force yet seriously to be reckoned with.

On the whole, however, we shall not go far wrong if we think of the years from 1901 to 1914 as the great age, in English cultural and political history, of the middle classes. The working classes were not yet a major force in British life; the old aristocracy of birth were ceasing to be so (in the last decade of Queen Victoria's reign, two Prime Ministers, Salisbury and Rosebery, were peers, but in the present century all our Prime Ministers have been commoners). Thus, the most typical novelists of the Edwardian age were John Galsworthy and Arnold Bennett, and their novels epitomise this middle-class predominance. The picture of life which they give us, in fact, is a narrower picture than that of the great Victorian novelists; for it is a mark of the middle classes in nearly all societies that they 'know their place' in regard both to their superiors and inferiors, and tend to 'keep themselves to themselves.' What Galsworthy and Bennett give us, therefore, is not a complex picture of the Edwardian world as a whole, but rather a close view of a single very important section of society.

Galsworthy's world was that of the commercial upper middle classes, of large overfurnished houses in the suburbs, offices in the City of London, family ramifications, solemn dinner parties, the patient accumulation of wealth and the steady honouring of a code. Religion, philosophy, art, scholarship, even politics in any expert sense, lie outside the boundaries of this world. It is 'respectable,' that is enough, it does not want to be 'clever' or 'smart.' Galsworthy's most famous series of novels, *The Forsyte Saga*, is a study, at first with harsh satirical undertones, but latterly more and more warm and tolerant, and finally almost sentimental, of this world. In the first novel of the series, *The*

Man of Property, Galsworthy's chief male character, Soames Forsyte, has a sense of property which extends to his wife as well as to his house so that he breaks into her bedroom when she locks the door against him. Irene, who for Galsworthy symbolises the disruptive effect of beauty on the ordinary routines of life, then runs away with another man, and, once Soames is deserted by her, Galsworthy's attitude towards him, which has been very harsh at first, gradually softens. Starting off as something like the villain, he becomes in the end something like the hero of the long tale. He is a dry, rigid, limited person, but he is consistent, and he has his own code, and in the general dissolving of standards after the Great War Galsworthy came to feel that any code, even a stupid and limited one, was better than no code at all. So Soames becomes for him a symbol of sturdy and inarticulate English virtue, with a dignity and pathos of its own – it being part of the pathos, no doubt, that Beauty, as symbolised by Irene, instinctively flees from it.

The Forsyte Saga and its successor, *A Modern Comedy*, do therefore reflect a real change over the years in the temper of Galsworthy's mind; he begins by attacking those who cling too hard to tangible things but becomes in the end relieved that there *are* things, both tangible and intangible, to cling to. For the great quality of Galsworthy's mind was a sort of human piety, a respect in particular for the virtues of loyalty and self-restraint. The defect of his mind was a lack of curiosity or anxiety about ultimate things. His code was inherited and fundamentally unquestioned, for his questions, even when he appears to be a satirist, are not about the validity of the gentleman's code in itself but only about how honestly it is being applied. He had the nonsense knocked out of him at school and somehow at Oxford he failed to have, in Max Beerbohm's phrase, the nonsense put gently back again. He was incapable of mental playfulness, scepticism, irony. So he fails in humour and falls short, in his more intense passages, of a truly tragic note: achieving in the stead of that a kind of muffled sentimentality. It was thus inevitable, in spite of his early leanings towards Socialism, that he should have become the favourite reading of middle-class ladies in suburban and provincial circulating libraries. His attitude to life was fundamentally the same as that of these ladies: a quiet, decent, well-mannered conventionality mitigated by an earnest but rather impracticable humanitarianism. His world is a solid but a rather grey one; we rarely glimpse the blue heavens above and hardly ever at all pierce down to the 'accepted hells beneath.'

Arnold Bennett had nothing of the high moral dignity, the vague but real distress about the injustice and unkindness of the world, which make Galsworthy such a very attractive figure in spite of his limitations. He was, however, more naturally and completely a creative artist, but an artist crippled, at least in the latter part of his career, by accepting the standards of vulgar success. There are critics who consider Bennett's *The Old Wives' Tale* the greatest English novel of this century. It is a novel in the French tradition, the tradition of Flaubertian realism. The life he describes in this book, the life of the English provincial lower middle classes in the pottery towns of the Midlands, Bennett knew intimately and all his best novels and collections of stories, such as *The Card* or *The Matador of the Five Towns*, have the Midlands as their background and their theme. If he had been a conscientious artist he would have continued to write about this gritty, humorous, provincial scene he knew so well, but he discovered that the sense of construction and depth he had learned from his French masters did not arouse any more applause, or make any more money, than his hastily written popular farces and romantic novels. He could produce works of ephemeral entertainment more rapidly and more profitably than works of art. He became famous and wealthy; he began to lead an expensive and gay life and to acquire a taste for the outward trappings of wealth, his yacht, his cigars, his wine, the deference of head-waiters. But the cost of becoming a popular figure in London society – and writers so different as Sir Osbert Sitwell and H. G. Wells have borne witness to Bennett's poise, and charm, and gaiety as a social lion – was a loss of touch with his dour provincial roots and the squandering of his gifts on literary journalism in the popular papers and on a steady production of potboilers.

It was Bennett's misfortune to have all the gifts of an honest artist, and to achieve his first successes in that Edwardian decade in which (in reaction against the 'art for art's sake' doctrine of the 1890s) almost nobody was judging, praising, or discussing literature from a purely aesthetic point of view: the literary journalism of Wells, and Shaw, and Chesterton was all about 'ideas.' Like many fine natural storytellers, Bennett had no 'ideas' to speak of; so there was thus nothing at all in his surrounding atmosphere to sustain him against the temptations of facile success. He wrote a really good novel or two, to show he could do it, and then settled down to enjoy himself. It was, in a sense, the lack of a philosophy that ruined him, but he also lacked a sense that any philosophy is necessary. Thus, even in his best books, one is wearied after a time by a lack of any deep curiosity on Bennett's part about the inner workings of people. He depicted minutely and exactly the hard surface detail of life, the appearance, behaviour, and speech of his Midlanders, the streets they walked in, the rooms they lived in, without suspecting that any mysteries might lie under that surface. Yet with all its limitations the world of his best books is solid and true and living and, all in all, one of the most accurate descriptions of English provincial life that has ever been made.

Of the other novelists of the Edwardian decade who have a moral or artistic interest, one of the most important is Joseph Conrad, a Pole, who, after an exciting career as a sea captain in the English Merchant Marine, settled down in England and wrote novels in the English language. Dr Leavis of Cambridge has recently stated in his book, *The Great Tradition*, that he considers Conrad one of the major English novelists. This is an interesting judgment, but it has to be questioned how far Conrad really belongs to the English tradition at all. He was a Pole by birth and a Pole in all his fundamental habits and loyalties; that is to say, an extravagant, brave, chivalrous man with a very sensitive 'sense of honour.' There is a story, for instance, that he once felt himself insulted by Shaw and wanted to challenge him to a duel. As a merchant skipper, the Englishman he knew best was the sort of man whom he met in distant ports, in outposts of the Empire, with a lingering touch of the Elizabethan adventurer about him. The qualities he loved in the English character were its courage, its capacity for self-sacrifice and for staunch silent endurance, and for a high, noble vision never articulately expressed. He was out for the heroic, wherever he could get it; he was one of the genuine 'last romantics' because he had lived romanticism as well as dreamt about it.

Thus many of his novels and short stories have a poetic quality, and they have been favourite reading among English poets of this century. Mr T.S. Eliot's *The Hollow Men* has an epigraph from Conrad's wonderful long-short story, *Heart of Darkness*: 'Mistah Kurtz – he dead.' This story is remarkable both for its evocation of the African jungle and for its parallel glimpse – of which the jungle, in a sense, is the symbolic prelude – of the possible depths of corruption in the human soul. Mr Kurtz is the agent of a trading company in a lonely African outpost and, carried away by drink, by loneliness, by a growing megalomania, he has made himself a tyrant over the natives around him more cruel and bloodthirsty than their own savage chiefs. They regard him with superstitious awe. In the story, we see him dying of fever and oppressed by hallucinations and bad dreams. It is his own diseased mind that is taking its revenge on him, not his victims. Eliot's very title, *The Hollow Men*, is probably suggested by Conrad's story since the narrator suggests that it was some inner emptiness, or hollowness, in Mr Kurtz, that allowed his lusts and fantasies to take possession of him. *Heart of Darkness* is a vision of evil, of evil in the heart of nature that has run riot without human discipline, and of evil in the unchastened heart of man; and perhaps the suggestion of the title *is* that the heart of darkness, the very core of Satan's kingdom, is not anything solid, but exactly a hollowness, an emptiness, a great gap around which everything living has rotted away. Thus Conrad at his best thinks, as a poet does, in grand symbols. He is by no means always at his best. Sometimes he writes what is not much more than a boy's adventure story, but dresses it up in an English too florid for his purpose. His style, indeed, never has an English ease, has always a foreign tang, sometimes beguiling, sometimes estranging; it reads often like a beautiful but not wholly idiomatic translation from some wonderful French original; and to the end of his life Conrad *spoke* French more easily than English.

One might mention, along with Conrad, Rudyard Kipling, whose view of life and whose range of subjects were not wholly dissimilar. Like Conrad, he very much admired strong, brave, silent men but, unlike Conrad's, his is the slightly wistful (and therefore slightly sentimentalised, slightly false) admiration of the intellectual, who has wanted very much to be a man of action, and never succeeded in becoming one. It might be said of Kipling, even more than of Galsworthy, that his attitude to life was never that of the adult, fully educated man but always that of the very clever and very plucky schoolboy; not, in Kipling's case as in Galsworthy's, the decent, worried, tolerant prefect, but rather the bookish boy who is shortsighted, dirty, and awkward but who very much admires dash and courage among his companions, the Stalkies and M'Turks, even if that is accompanied by ruthlessness. There was some streak in Kipling's character that made him respond sympathetically to ruthlessness, when accompanied by gusto and style; but it is far too easy to exaggerate that side of him, as also to exaggerate the touch of morbid obsession with horror (which made Andrew Lang say, when he read Kipling's terrifying early story, *The Mark of the Beast*, that the author of it would die mad before thirty). Kipling has written certain stories, like *Mary Postgate*, and certain poems, like the war-time one with the lines

> When Time shall count from the date
> That the English began to hate,

which, intended to shower hate and shame on England's enemies, are themselves hateful and shaming. But on the whole, apart from these occasional distressing lapses into a venom quite untypical of the English character, he was a genuine and honest patriot, and not necessarily of a diehard sort. He was, on the whole, for his time, up to date in his view of the responsibility of Empire, and his heroes, men like Rhodes, and Chamberlain, and Milner, were men who looked forward, not men who looked back. He could be chivalrous, as he was, on the whole, in his poems about the Boer War: compare his tribute to General Joubert,

> With those that bred, with those that loosed the strife,
> He had no part whose hands were clear of gain;
> But subtle, strong, and stubborn, gave his life
> To a lost cause, and knew the gift was vain,

with the appalling pomposity, frigidity, and falseness of Robert Bridges in one of his fortunately infrequent attempts at patriotic verse,

> Full thirty moons since unwilling enmity,
> Since daily suspense for hideous peril
> Of brethren unrescued, beleaguer'd,
> Plague-stricken in cities unprovided,
> Had quencht accustom'd gaiety from the day
> When first the Dutchman's implacable folly,
> The country of Shakespeare defying,
> Thought with a curse to appal the nation . . .

Kipling knew and understood the multifarious peoples of India with a deep and instinctive sympathy, which comes out in his one successful long narrative (one can hardly be certain whether it ought to be called a novel or not), *Kim*, and in many of his best short stories. But he had no sympathy for Indian, any more than for Irish, aspirations after independence. He saw the British as being, like the ancient Hebrews, a chosen people. Those whom they were called to rule, as well as their rivals in Europe, were 'the lesser breeds without the Law.' Nevertheless with all these limitations, it must be said that Kipling is (with the possible exception of D. H. Lawrence, in a quite different style, but not, I think, in his heat and suddenness, with a wholly dissimilar temperament) the best short-story writer in English of this century; and if he

3

could never manage a 'proper' novel, *Kim*, whatever it should be called, does call up the strange atmosphere of India to the senses and the imagination as does no other book in English about that great subcontinent.

Kipling is one of our great masters of prose, as he is one of our great masters of verse. His gift of style, his extraordinary mastery of language somehow sanctifies and excuses his lapses of taste, his stridencies of sentiment, even his moments of hysterical cruelty. If he can in every sort of way on occasion jar on our nerves, there is also in some of his stories a vision of the inner hearts of men, of trouble, of suffering, and of the possible supernatural consequences of earthly error, which astonishes one by its air of authority; especially when one contrasts it with what is crude, blatant, of too cheap and brassy an effectiveness, in other stories. Kipling in fact is a writer who must be rediscovered from time to time and who, when the quarrels in which he so furiously engaged himself are forgotten, will be remembered for a passionate exactness of language and for disturbing moments of deep vision that every now and again break, with the most startling effect, through the compact and jaunty surfaces of his verse and prose.

On the whole, however, it is probably not to Kipling or to Conrad that the more sensitive Edwardians turned for a lucid insight into the everyday problems of their own lives. The novelist who has best crystallised that age for us, and who has exposed its predicaments with the most delicate insight and sympathy, is Mr E. M. Forster: a novelist still living, still writing (though in the last thirty years he has written no more novels), still generally read, esteemed, and imitated. Mr Forster, unlike all the other novelists I have been dealing with in this section, enjoyed the advantage of having received that combined stimulation of the intellect and broadening of the emotional perspective which is the great gift to a favoured few in our country (not to all those who go up to Oxford and Cambridge but to those who make the most of their time there) of our ancient universities. Mr Forster had studied at Cambridge (he is now an Honorary Fellow of King's College, Cambridge) and had come under the influence of wise and humane thinkers of the type of Lowes Dickinson and G. E. Moore. Dickinson had given him an interest in the classical background of Western culture, in that amenity, suavity, tense but graceful balance between competing ideas and passions, which is the achievement at their highest of the ancient Greeks; Moore may have taught him that the assumptions of common sense are not so simple as they seem and

that the most ordinary personal preferences and decisions may conceal
all sorts of intellectual confusions, and will become clearer to us in their
implications if we train ourselves to analyse them out.

In Forster's novels, therefore, we feel as we do not feel in Galsworthy's
or Bennett's, or in Kipling's and Conrad's either, that a philosophical
mind is at work. Forster is interested in human behaviour in so far as
it presents us with moral problems; not with problems which can be
solved in an obvious and heroic way, by embracing a cause, or joining
an army, or going to some distant country as a missionary, but with
the problems of everyday life, such problems as whether we have been
kind and understanding enough to our neighbours, whether we are
judging them by the same standards as we judge ourselves, and also
on the other hand whether, in our wish to keep in with our neighbours,
we are perhaps being unfair to our own ambitions and desires.

Mr Forster wrote very few novels – five in all. The first, *Where Angels
Fear to Tread*, appeared in 1905, the last, *A Passage to India*, in 1924. In
1924 Mr Forster was still a comparatively young man (he is a gay and
active figure even to-day) but he realised, I imagine, that the curtain
had risen on a new scene, that the world after the war was not the
world he had grown up in, and that he could not write with his old
mastery about a shifting society of which he was no longer intimately
a member; so in the last thirty years, though he has written some
charming books of criticism, essays, and memories, he has produced
no fiction.

Even in his productive period he was, in comparison with Galsworthy, Bennett, Conrad, or Kipling, or even with a perfectionist like
Henry James, a remarkably sparse and cautious writer. In the nineteen
years of that productive period he averaged just one novel every four
years. Some of these novels, moreover, are short and perhaps none of
them is, on the surface, what looks like a 'great' novel. They deal with
pleasant, ordinary English middle-class people, just, usually, but no
more than just on the 'upper' side of the great divide between 'upper'
and 'lower' middle class. They are written in a smooth, tidy, sometimes just slightly precious style which has a touch of Cambridge
preciseness about it and just a touch, also, of maiden-lady delicacy.
Mr Forster, in fact, writes about 'nice' people in a 'nice' manner, but
what makes him an important and disturbing writer is that his great
interest is a critical examination of whatever it is in the atmosphere of
English life that so often makes 'nice' people behave nastily. He is a
critic, one might say, of that English passion for respectability and for

correct behaviour at all costs, which makes so many English people afraid of passion, but, even more than of passion, of the sudden critical disloyalties of thought. Mr Forster's characters will go to quite unscrupulous lengths sometimes to prevent any unsettlement of their code, but to Mr Forster this tends to prove that there was something sadly inadequate, something smug and self-protective to say the least, about the code in the first place.

Thus, in Mr Forster's third novel, *A Room With a View*, the question at issue is an apparently trivial one, whether a nice, pretty, good-natured, rather ordinary girl should or should not marry a very nice young man who is genuinely in love with her but who is 'not quite of her class.' It is not a matter of 'class-warfare,' as we understand it to-day – or of any real broad or to the outside observer terribly perceptible gulf to be bridged; it is a matter of almost invisible distinctions of manner and behaviour between two of the almost innumerable segments of the English middle class. English people have a very strong sense of the exact social group they belong to, of its customs, its taboos. This is not an articulate sense; one would rather say that when two English strangers meet each other they sniff at each other like dogs, and see if the smell is a familiar one. If these imperceptible barriers are absurd, they are none the less real, and to break them down even on a small front, in the name of individual responsibility and initiative, has something mildly heroic about it.

This theme of the individual, the individual's own response, his own sense of responsibility, his own sense of reaction towards and trust in a 'stranger,' for which he must sacrifice 'tradition,' is really Mr Forster's main theme. In an early novel, *A Room With a View*, he treats the theme in a vein of genteel, almost ladylike comedy, but in his last novel, *A Passage to India*, it has become tragic. Now it is no longer a matter of gaps, barriers, misunderstandings between different sections of the English middle classes; it is a matter of gaps, barriers, and misunderstandings between the British in India and the native educated Indians. The story is that of a friendship between a native Indian doctor and an English official which has to stand the test of a false accusation against this doctor by an English girl that he has made indecent advances to her. The girl is not consciously insincere; she has been in a nervous state, the climate is telling on her, and while the Indian doctor is showing her round some local caves she has a kind of hallucination. Her accusation, however, has a very bad effect on both local communities, British and Indian, a terrible atmosphere of tension and hysteria is worked up. The girl is a lumpy, ordinary sort of girl but she has real intrinsic decency (Mr Forster does not go out of his way to make his 'good' characters necessarily glamorous ones) and before the Indian doctor is brought to trial she has plenty of time to think things over. At the trial, she confesses that she has been suffering from an hysterical delusion. The British community drop her, her young man breaks off their engagement, while on the other hand the Indian community show no gratitude for her courage and magnanimity but indulge in rather mean and vindictive demonstrations of triumph. She has ceased to be a 'person' in the views of both communities and has become a mere symbol of the tensions and the bad feelings that hold them apart.

The Indian doctor, of course, is let out of gaol, and his English friend has stood loyally by him throughout this crisis, but they have both felt the pressure of group opinion on them, and, now that the crisis is over, they begin to drift apart. The mere habits of their lives, different circles, different routines, separate them; yet they meet once again much later and, in spite of the fact that the Englishman has now married and is therefore tied very much more to his own community, and in spite of the other fact that the Indian is now much more bitterly nationalist than he used to be, they have a frank, friendly conversation as in the old days. Both sense that it will be for the last time. The moral of the story is that individual sincerity and loyalty are possible, but that the pressure of group life, and of accepted social conventions, works very hard against them.

Though Forster is a great master of social comedy there is in all his novels this tone of sadness which comes from realising how every individual, even the most liberal and tolerant individual, is weighed down by even the stupidest conventions of the particular group he belongs to. One might say that Forster is the best modern English novelist of the liberal tradition, the tradition which says it is up to every man to choose his own friends, his own job, to arrive at his own convictions. Forster realises the almost tragic inner struggle that is involved in living up to this ideal. Apart from that, however, he has a strong sense of how many of these virtues of the liberal tradition are inherent in the British character at its best. They are inherent especially in the upper middle classes, in British administrators and professional men and scholars, whose very mode of education is traditionally called a 'liberal education': that is an education (as opposed to a 'mechanical education') that will enlarge and humanise the mind and not merely prepare a man to earn his living at some particular trade. But on the other hand Forster knows how the mere code of manners of these classes, who are the custodians of the liberal tradition, tends to fence them off from other classes in the community. Foreigners, if they find Englishmen shy and awkward, might learn from Forster's novels what an honest struggle lies behind the British effort to be fair. It is not for the British a matter of having a given tradition of warm friendliness between all classes and communities. There is rather a tendency (partly due to shyness) to erect these barriers which Forster writes about. But there is also a strong puritan conscience at work in the British professional and administrative classes which makes them feel that any principle, which they apply to their own group, ought ideally to be applied to all groups, that discrimination is unfair; and it is from this basis, from the uneasy conscientiousness, the high principles, and the refined sensibilities of our traditional ruling classes in Great Britain that our present democratic order or system has partly evolved; there has also, of course, been pressure from below. But British democracy is not a democracy which has been achieved by violence or revolution; it has evolved rather through the fact that various social groups, deprived of advantages belonging to more privileged groups, have demanded a reasonable share in these advantages; and the more privileged classes, because of their honesty and conscientiousness, have had to recognise the justice of the demand. Forster then is a novelist not only of isolated individualism but of a tradition of moral independence in the individual which has helped in the past to secure for Great Britain social justice and peace.

Section 3: The Time of Transition (1910–1920)

The decade of the First World War happened to coincide with a very important period of creative experiment in English literature. The War was not in itself the cause of the new movements, which were mostly well under way before its outbreak; and some of the most notable innovators, like T. S. Eliot and Joyce – the one an American citizen domiciled in Great Britain, the other an Irishman exiled in Trieste – did not serve in the war; nor did another American domiciled in England, Ezra Pound, important both as an organiser of new movements and as a publicist for them. Joyce had been working on his great novel *Ulysses* and on his earlier *Dubliners* and *Portrait of the Artist as a Young Man* for years before the outbreak of the war; so, in France, had Marcel Proust been working for years at his immensely long novel,

A la Recherche du Temps Perdu, and the appearance of the first volume merely happened to coincide with the outbreak of hostilities. Percy Wyndham Lewis, the painter and polemicist, the founder of the magazine *Blast* and the soul of the Vorticist movement, did serve in the War, but never wrote about it at any great length. His influential first novel, *Tarr*, written in three weeks, was about bohemian life in Paris. New techniques of vivid imagery, and 'free verse' were used effectively by a war poet, like Herbert Read; but they came from Imagist movements, encouraged by Pound, and Richard Aldington, and Ford Madox Hueffer, which antedated the war by several years. What was happening, in fact, was a general and rather violent break-away by young writers from the contented attitudes, and the slovenly techniques of writing, that had been, as we have seen, so typical of the Edwardian age. The new novelists looked perhaps to James and Conrad, not exactly as models to be imitated, but as examples of artistic integrity. The new poets violently rejected what they regarded as the insipid decadence of contemporary British verse, and the smugness of the Victorian poet, and the soaring vagueness of the Romantics, and looked for models in other countries (in nineteenth-century France), in other ages (mediaeval Italy and Provence), even in other cultures (ancient China and Japan). There was a desperate desire to freshen up an atmosphere that seemed to have grown mawkish and stale.

The experimentalism of this decade can be compared, then, to the revolt of the Pre-Raphaelites, and even to the revolt of the 1890s, against the complacencies of Victorian Liberalism; but history itself, as the Great War showed, was *also* revolting against these complacencies, and therefore Eliot, and Pound, and Joyce, and Wyndham Lewis, and T. E. Hulme were not simply making a gesture but announcing, prophetically, the advent of a newer and harsher age. The reading public did not take to them at once; but in ten or in twenty years they were to seem to a new generation of young readers tremendously topical and in thirty or forty years, now in the middle of the century, they have almost the status of modern classics. The war unsettled society as their sharp, disturbing insights had earlier unsettled them.

The war unsettled society in two ways. It had, on the one hand, what a novelist like H. G. Wells, who clung all through it to his expansive optimism about the future of human society, would have called a 'liberating' effect. It hastened on that emancipation of women, political and social and sexual, which had in any case been making great strides since the beginning of the century. If women could serve as nurses or in the auxiliary armed forces, were they not also capable of exercising the vote? As women engaged in war work, and mixed more freely with men, their manners also became less lady-like and formal, more slangy and direct, more free and easy. The war also did something to promote that merging of social classes which had been already under way at the beginning of the century. Many young men from humble social backgrounds did well in the Army, became officers, came home with new ambitions and a new sense of dignity. Young officers from the upper classes, on the other hand, like Siegfried Sassoon or Robert Graves came home with a new questioning attitude towards their inherited code.

But this 'liberation' was also an undermining. The First World War destroyed a deep subconscious social confidence (based on the fact that since 1815 the existence of the British Empire had not really been at stake, nor the effort of the whole nation engaged, in any major conflict, and based also on a century of more or less peaceful expansion of wealth and population and imperial strength) that, whatever disasters might happen in the outer world, life, for the British, a 'business people,' would go on 'as usual.' Great Britain, it was felt up to 1914, was a 'going concern,' immune both from revolution and decay. The war, accelerating many social changes, good and bad, disrupting old habits of life, destroyed also that old, easy confidence.

When the war first broke out, indeed, it was greeted by many older writers, and also by young poets like Rupert Brooke, with eagerness. Perhaps Great Britain had been too long at peace, become slack and fat, and the war, for her young men, would be a heroic invigorating experience. What nobody foresaw was the squalor and monotony of trench warfare, its terrible costliness in life and, more profoundly, in the unhappiness of survivors. Soon the poets were ceasing to write the war up in romantic terms, but were instead, like Sassoon, Owen, Graves, and Read, giving vivid and terrible pictures of what actual war was like; and in the prose accounts of their experiences which many of these writers published after the war – often five or six years after – we can see the whole experience exploding in their imaginations, rending their nerves once more, like a bomb with a delayed-action fuse. Behind and beyond the actual fighting also, great social upheavals were taking place; of which the most important, the Russian revolution, gave a provisional and tentative appearance to all the rearrangements of Versailles. After the Armistice, the founding of the

League of Nations did arouse some idealistic hopes in persistently optimistic writers like H. G. Wells. For younger men, the years of the war, and the years immediately after it, were years of doubt, uncertainty, confusion. The young poets who had entered the Army in a mood of eagerness came out of it in a mood of disenchantment; and the old, easy, comfortable, thoughtless hopefulness of the Edwardian decade never really came back again as a main factor in English life or literature. Instead, both about human hopes and about human actions, there was a 'new realism' – a tendency to look facts, however unpleasant, in the face and to think, as T. E. Hulme thought, of man no longer as a giant figure striding to perfection but as a limited creature, who could know perfection, but who was necessarily imperfect; yet who with a harsh discipline of himself might achieve a certain decency.

A very famous novel of this decade, James Joyce's *Ulysses*, is symptomatic both of the new experimentalism and the new sad, realistic attitudes towards human society. *Ulysses* deals with the events of a single day in the life of its two heroes, in Dublin, at the beginning of this century. The two heroes are Leopold Bloom, a Jewish advertising agent, who stands for Ulysses in the Homeric epic; and Stephen Daedalus, a young poet, who stands for Telemachus. All the incidents of Homer's poem are elaborately paralleled, or parodied, in Joyce's novel; but the ordinary reader's enjoyment of the novel is not much enhanced by having these parallels pointed out to him; they were useful rather to Joyce himself, in forcing him to impose a complex outer structure on what might otherwise have become a mere flux of inner monologue. It is for the same reason, to give himself an outer framework, that he works out the itinerary of the story so elaborately; mentioning so many Dublin shops, offices, public-houses, back streets, low quarters, that his novel is almost at moments like a guide-book to the city, though not to its beauty spots. For most of his action does go on either inside the mind of Bloom or inside that of Stephen (though there are glimpses of the 'inner workings' of minor characters too, and at the very end of the book there is the torrential monologue of Mrs Bloom, who seems to stand for a kind of eternal feminine principle, passive but tenacious, a principle of eternal renewal and acceptance). Mrs Bloom's monologue at the end, uninterrupted by outer action, does show to what a shapeless fluidity this 'stream-of-thought' technique might lead; and therefore Joyce perpetually interrupts and deflects Bloom's inner monologues or Stephen's with impingements from the outer world; and he has one passage (that in which he parodies in succession all the most notable historical styles in English narrative prose) in which he steps outside the characters and discourses *about* them in the old style.

Thus Joyce's great achievement in *Ulysses* is not simply his use of a subjective method, but his success in building this up into an objective framework. We get inside the minds of Stephen and Bloom but we do not simply *identify* ourselves with them. Joyce enables us to put them into a wider perspective than they put themselves.

So much is this the case, in fact, that these two characters, individualised though they are in more elaborate detail than any other two characters in fiction, nevertheless have a large and general symbolic value, too. Bloom, a vulgarian in his attitude to the arts, blankly indifferent to religion, a timid but persistent sensualist, obsessed by sordid worries about his wife's faithfulness, is nevertheless generous, warmhearted, full of inquisitive alertness about science and politics; hoping that the world will be transformed by technical improvements and by the substitution of a new internationalism for the old, narrowminded nationalism. In a sense, in his general attitude to life, Bloom is like a typical Wells hero (or almost like Wells himself) seen from another point of view. To Stephen Daedalus, who represents the despair of the poet in a cultureless, commercial world, all Bloom's ideas are nonsense. But Bloom is not ridiculous to Stephen in himself, nor, indeed, to Joyce; and the spirit Bloom stands for is not ridiculous. Again and again (as in the episode, modelled on that of the Cyclops' Cave in Homer, where Bloom just escapes from being beaten up by a bigoted Irish nationalist) we see that Bloom stands in Joyce's mind for a human, a civilised, a rational attitude in contrast to native barbarism; for Joyce, if he was not a naive liberal progressive either, was far from being an Irish nationalist himself. Bloom is the sort of well-meaning Jew who, because of his liberal attitudes and his imperfect assimilation to a local culture, is the predestined victim of Fascism. He is a pathetic and comic figure in many ways, a compendium of many common human weaknesses, and with a touch, indeed, as Mr Percy Wyndham Lewis has noted, of the comic Jew of the music halls. But he is, as Mr Wyndham Lewis has also noted, a distinctly amiable figure, and even, perhaps, in many ways his middle-aged creator in disguise (as Stephen Daedalus, a frank piece of autobiography, is his youthful creator *without* disguise). Bloom, with all his faults, is the largest and most sympathetic *human* figure in *Ulysses*.

James Joyce himself said, emphatically, that he intended Bloom to be 'a good man.'

Bloom then is partly the symbol of that social optimism, based on a firm belief in science, which was so influential a creed in Joyce's own youth. It was partly the creed of one of Joyce's own masters, Ibsen. Stephen Daedalus, on the other hand, represents the cult, not exactly of pure art, but of art as 'the eternal affirmation of the spirit of man.' The acceptance of that cult is a common result of losing one's religious faith and of not finding in any merely practical social purpose an adequate substitute for it. It is not so much that Stephen despairs of society as that he cannot make a religion of society. Like T. E. Hulme, he sees the hopeless imperfection, and imperfectibility, of men in most of their practical relations; yet he knows too that man hungers for perfection, and can at once express that hunger, and perhaps on rare occasions satisfy it, through poetry and music and art. This is a very isolating position, and where Bloom on the whole is a morally strong character, Stephen is an extremely weak one. He has to pursue his dream of beauty hampered by hunger, and bad teeth, and family claims upon him, and his own uncontrollable adolescent lusts. He has always to be resisting appeals to his sympathy that strike him as irrelevant to his vocation, and that makes him seem conceited and peevish. One particular grief gnaws often at his heart, which is that, when his mother is dying, he refused to pray for her, because he thought that, after the loss of his faith, prayer would be hypocritical; and also because he was afraid that praying might revive his faith. Essentially, Stephen is a young man in search of a father – of a father to guide and help him (his own father, a drunkard going steadily downhill since his wife's death, is no use); and Bloom is a middle-aged man with no son (his only son died in infancy) who needs a son to give him confidence in his manhood; for, though gregarious, Bloom is lonely, his life is a shabby failure, none of his dreams has come true or is likely to, and he knows that his handsome, musical, sex-obsessed wife, Marion, is perpetually betraying him.

Though the theme of *Ulysses* is so momentous, the construction of the book so intricate, its atmosphere so dense, there is, nevertheless, in the working out of the plot, in the old-fashioned sense very little 'story.' Bloom, going about Dublin on his day's work, pausing now and again to attend a funeral, to stare at a girl, or to eat a meal, worrying about his money, his wife, his sexual needs and his digestion, but with an alert, inquisitive ear cocked, nevertheless, for what is going on around him, runs into Stephen (wandering pointlessly and later drunkenly around) once or twice, observes him with fatherly care, and late in the evening is able to rescue Stephen from a drunken brawl outside a brothel which they have both been visiting; to sober Stephen up; and to persuade Stephen to come home with him. For both Stephen and Bloom, the meeting is something momentous, though both would find it hard to explain why. Each perhaps has a sense, through the chance meeting, of having achieved human recognition, and so of having enhanced his dignity. What is sad and ironical is that these two people, who so much need each other's trust and affection, have no common language. (And here we might have a kind of allegory of the need in our time for, and the difficulties that lie in the way of, a marriage of science and art.) It is impossible, in fact, for Bloom and Stephen really to communicate with each other, but they can convey good-will. Stephen is strengthened in his sense of vocation, and Bloom draws enough courage from the encounter to assert himself mildly with his wife. So much for the main shape of the book: what of its conclusion, which might seem irrelevant to that shape, the long interior monologue, in a state between dream and waking, of Marion Bloom? That is to be taken, as I have already suggested, as a symbol of a total, uncritical acceptance of life which lies beyond the scope of both Stephen and Bloom, and perhaps beyond the scope of the masculine human animal as such. Both Stephen and Bloom are idealists; Stephen lives for perfection, and Bloom for improvement. But Mrs Bloom stands for an impulse which has more to do with keeping the race going than any ideal – for the blind and greedy, but eternally creative, principle of life itself. It is only superficially that her monologue seems a sordid record of a vulgar woman's erotic fantasies; it is really a speech by an earth-goddess. Men discriminate and complain, they are always after something better; it is because women discriminate less, and complain less, because they will always be satisfied in the end with what they can get, that life goes on.

The atmosphere of *Ulysses* has the thickness, the almost stifling density, of our sensuous and emotional experience of the 'real world.' To many readers, when first published, the book, because of the frankness that was inherent in its use of the naturalistic interior monologue, appeared unbearably depressing; to-day we are more likely to be struck by Joyce's wisdom and compassion, by his deep understanding of and pity for human nature at all levels, by his sense of the goodness that underlies Bloom's vulgarity, the poetic vision that underlies Stephen's weak and peevish self-conceit, the affirmation of life that underlies Marion Bloom's gross fantasies, than by any undue emphasis on the sordid side of life. Rather we feel that Joyce 'sees life steadily and sees it whole' and that his attitude towards all his characters is one of comprehension and forgiveness. In one sense, the book *is* a tragic one, for it depicts a society in which the 'best men' – and both Bloom and Stephen represent the 'best men' – have lost the faiths and habits that make life in a society real and noble. It is because the reality of Dublin falls so far short of what it should be that Bloom and Stephen are both such uncompromising idealists. But if the picture of Dublin life is depressing at least we do see in Bloom and Stephen a kind of essential human nobility asserting itself, with however little practical effect, against discouraging circumstances. And Joyce himself, of course, accepts Dublin far more completely than they do; he is like Mrs Bloom in that respect. Shabbiness and failure and genteel pretence and undergraduate brutality and the smells, and the smoke, and the clanging trams, and the crowded bars of a great city have all their own poetry for him. He conveys that poetry through the ear rather than the eye. He was a very shortsighted man, who saw the world around him through a blur or haze; he was also a singer, with a wonderful ear for music, and before he turned to prose had written some very slight but exquisitely singable lyrical poems. He uses his sentences, with their elaborate musical cadences, to call up impressions which are often all the more emotionally concrete for not being visually hard and precise. We are immersed *in* his world, not seeing it from a perspective. He had a wonderful 'ear' in another sense; just as he could mimic or parody any style in English prose literature, so he could catch in writing the pitch and rhythm and idiom of anybody's speaking voice. We do not always see his characters very clearly, but we can always hear *their* voices (and not, as so often in novels, some version of the author's *own* voice) while they are talking.

A friend and contemporary of James Joyce was Percy Wyndham Lewis, whom I have already mentioned. If Joyce was above all a musical writer, a writer whose appeal is to the 'auditory imagination,' Lewis, his primary genius that of a draughtsman, is a writer whose first appeal is to the eye. Towards the end of the decade we are considering, Lewis published a striking first novel, *Tarr*. All the important characters in *Ulysses* are seen, to a great extent, from the inside (though as I have suggested, by his care for 'grand structure,' Joyce also establishes an 'objective' view of them). In *Tarr*, and in Mr Lewis's subsequent novels, everything is seen from the outside. Lewis is not interested in the feelings and sensibilities of his characters; he is interested in their appearance and their behaviour, as that might strike a brilliantly acute outside observer, lacking in sympathy with the people he is describing, but not quite 'clinically' detached, since he has a bent towards satirical humour. For Lewis, the human animal in general is something rather pretentious and absurd, about whom it would be ridiculous to have strong feelings, one way or another; but one may permit oneself to laugh. The scene of *Tarr* is Paris, and the characters are a set of down-at-heel Bohemians, would-be writers, would-be artists, social pretenders. None of the characters is very likeable, but where Joyce would have found the side of them that was human and touching, for Lewis they are like a set of silly and clumsy automatons. The book, too, is full of episodes of violence: but Lewis refuses to exploit melodramatic possibilities. The main character is a neurotic German called Kreisler, who rapes the hero's mistress, kills an enemy with whom he is having a duel after the duel is officially over, finally kills himself. Kreisler is in his essence rather like a Dostoevsky character, 'wild' and 'tortured,' but for Lewis he is simply a silly, violent creature who destroys himself (like most human creatures, from Lewis's point of view) and therefore as 'good for a laugh,' or for a cold, satirical sneer, as anything else. This was a novel view of satire – satire directed not against some particular social class, some opinion or belief, some current folly, but against human existence in general. Lewis either lacked that natural sympathy with our fellow creatures which most of us feel, or was able, for the sake of a special artistic effect, to freeze that sympathy at its source. His book was admired, but, given this attitude to life of his, could never be widely popular. Some later satirical novels – particularly *The Apes of God*, a satire on many of his literary and artistic contemporaries – have made him more unpopular still, with the result that a brilliantly original philosophical fantasy of his, *The Childermass*, and many interesting general books on a variety of topics, have not had the success they deserved.

In these later books of his, however, Mr Lewis was to perfect his peculiar style. Just as every sentence in Joyce's prose has a musical cadence, a hint of the hidden lyric, so every sentence of Lewis's calls up some harsh, definite, frightening or absurd picture to the eye. This is not to say that his prose is *displeasing* to the ear; it has an explosive emphasis and a jogging mechanical force. Nevertheless, Lewis, in his works of fiction at least (his philosophical or critical works are another matter) is a hard writer to read. The reader feels like a punch-ball receiving thud after thud; he is never allowed to rest. One might say, perhaps, as a general criticism of Mr Lewis that he specialises too much in the exploitation of negative emotions. He shows up every kind of human activity as mechanical, or false, or meaningless, or hateful; the reader begins to wish that he were offered something to love and admire. Sometimes he is offered something; it is the notion of the lonely and persecuted 'great artist' or 'great man' among a ridiculous crowd of gibbering submen. Unfortunately this noble figure, free at last from all the frailties which so disgust and amuse Mr Lewis in the generality of the race, looks far too much like, in most cases, a projection of Mr Lewis himself. And 'the standpoint of genius,' from which Mr Lewis sometimes claims to write, is not the standpoint of genius in general; it is the standpoint of *a* genius (Mr Lewis is undoubtedly that) who has never been able to regard *himself* in a critical light, who gives as much weight to his passing furies as to his permanent insights, and who has never thought fit to fetter himself by any sort of schematic consistency. In the sour dignity with which Mr Lewis faces a world which has certainly never quite given his genius its due there is just a touch of Shakespeare's Malvolio; and one might hazard a guess that, like Malvolio, he is 'sick with self-love.' Joyce was a greater, not a smaller, writer for loving his fellow-men.

These two writers I have mentioned in this third section because they were both of them innovators of genius in a way in which at least two of the writers I am to deal with in the next section – Aldous Huxley and Virginia Woolf – were not; though Huxley was a writer of comprehensive intelligence and Mrs Woolf of the most exquisitely charming individual talent. D. H. Lawrence, the third of the writers I am to deal with in the next section, was a man of genius, but he was also an exasperatingly uneven writer who sacrificed, too often, his conscience as an artist to his mission as a prophet. The very originality of a man of genius often prevents him from having the immediate influence on the public of a writer who does not so much originate, as adapt originality for public consumption. One may find in Mrs Woolf a certain dilution of Joyce's inventions and in Aldous Huxley a certain softening and civilising of the satirical impact of Wyndham Lewis. And this would not be a matter of imitation but simply of new literary possibilities of a given period which the writer of genius carries, from the point of view of the general reading public, too far. and the writer of talent just far enough. Certainly Aldous Huxley,

Mrs Woolf, and D.H. Lawrence influenced the mood, and formed the taste, of the intelligent reading public in the 1920s to a far greater degree than Joyce or Wyndham Lewis. Lewis, in fact, had so much the sense of being pushed into a corner, of being deliberately chosen for the role of 'odd man out,' that in defiance he assumed the role of 'The Enemy': which for literature was not immediately a loss, since he has a great gift for satirical attack, but which may well have been a loss, from a longer perspective, in that it hindered the maturing of his personality and the deepening of his sympathies. There has been a natural tendency because of the undeserved neglect of him, for young writers to 'rediscover' him periodically and perhaps to pitch his standing too high. I am a very great admirer of his gifts myself, but I have tried to indicate here what I feel to be a human lack in him.

Another writer, not English, who should be mentioned here for his influence on English fiction in the 1920s is Marcel Proust. Proust's great theme is what the French call 'recueillement,' which means more than the English 'recollection'; it is the regathering of all the threads of one's life. Life is always flowing, yet it is easy enough for a man to go over in his mind the main incidents of his life. It is more difficult for him to relive them, to recapture the sense of what past time was like before it flowed away. It is more difficult still to get that recaptured and revived awareness of the past into perspective with the present. And finally to shape all this fluid material into a kind of crystalline unity of contemplation is very difficult indeed. Yet these are Proust's achievements. He is neither a novelist of the ear, of the musical cadence and the living echo, like Joyce, nor a novelist of the eye, of the bitter and incisive visual cartoon, like Wyndham Lewis. His long sentences certainly call up image after image and move generally with a graceful and undulating – if sometimes with a cumbrous and confused – motion, but what they are after is neither picture nor music for its own sake but the translation of experience into thought. Proust had at once the temperament of a woman and the mind of a philosopher. As we read him, we seem to be sinking into a glaucous and submarine, yet fluttering and excited landscape, in which the morning sun bleeding through the shutters of a hotel bedroom, the faces of pretty girls passing like figures on a frieze along a beach, the powdered hair of a flunkey on the stairway of a great mansion, the monocled mask and booming voice of some dandy at a party, the possibility of being smiled at, at the theatre, by a duchess, a small boy's hopeless need for his mother before he can sleep, and a young man's half romantic and half perverse craving for the nearness of a cold-hearted flirt, these, and more sinister images, make up a confused and flowing tapestry of personal impressions. We are not sure that we want to be so completely submerged in the warm and viscous depths of somebody else's life; we become oppressed at having to surrender, again and again, to all the temptations and vices that beset a young man of weak and yielding sensibility, but then we find this sensibility controlled by a persistent will and a powerful analysing intellect. The material, however questionable in itself, is being shaped towards some generalisation about love, about selfishness and insincerity, about possessiveness, about man's experience of time, which will have the validity of mathematics. So out of the material of erotic elegy, material which by its very nature tempts the writer to sentiment, to falsification, to a flattery both of himself and of those whom he loves, Proust gradually and patiently erects a structure of pitiless objective truth.

Thus Proust, like so many great French writers of the past, like Rochefoucauld, La Bruyère, or Vauvenargues, was essentially a 'moralist': a 'moralist' in the French sense of one who seeks out the laws of human conduct, rather than in the English sense of one who lays them down. It was just because he was a moralist in this sense that he dealt so often with what, to English tastes, are 'doubtful' subjects; for men's secret vices and follies do, in fact, afford us more subtle clues, often, to the springs of their conduct than the respectable fronts which they put up to the world. There is much that is perverse in the feelings Proust analyses, and much that is trivial and vulgar in the world of high society he describes; nor is he at all sparing to the weakness of his own character. The noble values, heroism, chastity, loyalty, might seem, apart from a few attractive figures like the narrator's grandmother and his friend Robert de St Loup, to have almost no place in Proust's world. But then Proust's devotion to his art and his eagerness to arrive at the truth within the limits of his own experience of society (an 'exclusive' and interesting, but not wholly typical experience), these are heroic and chaste and loyal.

Proust's novel was translated into magnificent English prose (it is said that the English version is a finer piece of writing than the French original) by the Scottish poet and scholar and soldier, Charles Scott-Moncrieff. This translation is certainly one of the most wonderful pieces of English prose produced over the last thirty years; it might be said that no original piece of English writing, brought out during the same period, has such poetically moving and such exquisitely elaborate evocations of landscape. And here a debt is being paid back to England, for Proust learned how to describe architecture and scenery, and how to suffuse such descriptions with personal feeling, through reading and translating Ruskin. The style, the mood, the manner of Proust, as transmuted through Scott-Moncrieff's version, had a profound and far-reaching effect on English writing in the 1920s – on the prose of Virginia Woolf, for instance, which like Proust's often seems to be seeking to translate experience into thought, and, from the descriptive side more especially, the side of Proust's *bravura* accumulations of detail, on the styles of Mr Sacheverell and Sir Osbert Sitwell. It was asserted, however, by some critics, that the mood of Proust's novel, its feminine and yielding mood, had a debilitating effect on the morale of English writers during this period; that was a point, for instance, which Mr Wyndham Lewis frequently and bitterly made. Proust was certainly a great writer and a great man, but he was not exactly an influence on English literature that made for blunt directness or for manly briskness.

A novelist of much less importance than any of these, but one who also set a fashion, and who was attractive and individual as a man, was Norman Douglas. A descendant of Deeside lairds on his father's, of German noblemen on his mother's, side, educated largely in Germany, Douglas as a young man entered the British Foreign Service, served in Russia, and travelled in India. By birth and background he belonged to an international ruling class; and a good deal of the cast of his mind, his lifelong interest in such subjects as geology and botany, and his elaborate scholarship in topographical literature, was typically German rather than English. After he left the Foreign Service, his life became that of a wandering bohemian, with many friends in most European countries, but with no close conventional ties. He was sometimes in funds, but often, especially during the years of the First World War, beset both by shortage of money and by bad health. He remained, however, indomitably cheerful; his aristocratic background, combined with his mixed experience of life, made him feel as much at home drinking coffee in a Paris railway station with an urchin who had stolen his coat as dominating the conversation at a fashionable dinner party. He was well served by the strenuous and athletic constitution he had inherited from his ancestors; though his books sometimes seem to propound a rather dangerous gospel of pleasure, he found his own great pleasures in long walks, in sight seeing, in simple meals in remote Italian inns. He was never drawn into purely literary circles, and was neither a social nor an intellectual snob. He could enjoy wealth, but he could also endure poverty; an unconscious vein of stoicism in his nature corrected his epicurean philosophy, and kept him on the whole both healthy and happy during his long life. *South Wind*, his most famous novel – indeed his only 'straight' novel – set a pattern for Mr Aldous Huxley's *These Barren Leaves* and, with a more exact following, for Sir Compton Mackenzie's *Vestal Fires* and *Extraordinary Women*. The rather thin thread of the story has to do with the impact of relaxed Mediterranean morals on Anglo-Saxon respectability. But what is memorable about the novel, as about Douglas's travel books, is the gently mocking commentary on things in general, the fantastic historical digressions, and the vivid evocations of landscape. Douglas at his best wrote as good prose as any author of his time. He is not always at his best, but even at his most tiresome he has his own characteristic flavour. In his impatient individualism, his amusing old-fashioned anti-clericalism, his passionate interest in the details of 'natural philosophy,' his bluff, hearty, enjoying temperament, and his rather simple-minded belief in sensuality as the cure for most human ills, he belonged neither to our own age or the last, but to the French eighteenth century. His gift for mockery is based on a firm limitation of interests not typical of the complex, uneasy modern mind; and his gay rebelliousness on a social assurance equally, to-day, untypical. And the occasional touch of spleen or brutality in his writings recalls the eighteenth century, too. *South Wind*, which is by no means the best of his works, appeals sometimes to an appetite in immature readers for rather facile sophistication. Douglas was too much of an egoist to have the objective interest in character and situation a novelist needs; but his travel books, where he himself is frankly at the centre of the picture, are another matter, and are probably the best written in English during this century.

Section 4: The 'Gay' 1920s

One can think of the 1920s as a decade in which the English people as a whole were recovering from the shock of the First World War and hoping desperately that things would get back to 'normal': to the material comfort and moral security of the Edwardian age, to the old Victorian confidence in the steady march of human progress. For the fighting soldier, on the other hand, as we can see from the war memoirs of Siegfried Sassoon and Robert Graves, the war had left something like a permanent scar on the mind, and they would never be able to believe in the illusion of 'normality' again. And to clever and sensitive people, even if they had not been through the war, the 'contemporary situation' seemed a hopeless muddle, and they sought for diversion and satisfaction rather in the interests and pleasure of the private life. At a popular level this attitude often led to a cheap hedonism, a cheap cynicism, and an equally cheap sentimentalism. There was a good deal of cant in the 1920s; cant in particular about 'freedom' (meaning especially freedom in sexual behaviour), about 'youth,' and about the 'old men who led us into the war.' 'Youth' became so very much of a cult that even to-day reviewers in English papers generally refer to us as brilliant representatives of the younger generation until we reach the age of fifty when, if we are sufficiently distinguished, we may gradually mature into respected elder figures or even, if we are lucky, grand old men. This cult of youth was satirised, with his usual pungency, by Mr Wyndham Lewis in *The Apes of God* and *The Doom of Youth*: he saw behind it a cult of immaturity, which he felt was being encouraged by sinister interests for ends of their own. For apart from all the other and more romantic and attractive characteristics of 'youth,' two obvious ones are that it is credulous and docile; the violent movements of our time, as well as many of the merely silly ones, have gained half their adherents at least from the young, the emotionally and intellectually immature, and a good proportion of the other half from older people who jealously preserve their immaturity or 'refuse to grow old.' As for the new sexual freedom, it was sometimes seriously defended, but often treated as a natural result of the war. Mrs Viveash, in Aldous Huxley's *Antic Hay*, is excused for breaking many hearts because her own heart was broken when the man she 'really' loved was killed in the war; and the war is often also brought forward in the fiction of the 1920s as an excuse for unmannerly or neurotic behaviour by young men. It was too convenient an excuse altogether for all kinds of personal weakness, and the more popular types of 'advanced' writing of that decade are vitiated by a soft streak of silliness and self-pity.

It would be wrong, however, to dismiss the whole decade as a period of rather brittle frivolity and of rather damp moral, or immoral, exhibitionism. The more vulgar and blatant symptoms of the age's unrest did, in fact, point to a general unease which was felt, at a deeper level, by wise and sensitive people. There was a lack of anything very stable outside the individual for him to hang on to. The social background was no longer a comforting, protective enclosure; the writer was flung back on his own sensibility – his anxieties, his curiosities, his pleasures and his dreams.

In the best novels of the 1920s, what we must look for therefore, is not a broad and comprehensive picture of society but rather an individual attempt at preserving personal coherence of attitude against a social background that is fragmentary and confused. The novelist of the 1920s, we might say, is not looking through a window at the world, he is seeing his own face and the faces of others in a mirror; the foreground is very clear to him, the background blurs away. Thus it could be said, even, that the three most distinguished novelists of the 1920s in England, Virginia Woolf, Aldous Huxley, and D.H. Lawrence, are none of them typically novelists: Huxley being essentially a philosopher, Mrs Woolf a poet of mood and sensation, D.H. Lawrence the prophet of a new and personal religion of dark emotional drive. Moreover, each of these novelists speaks not for the whole man but for a separate layer of the human structure; Huxley for the intellect, Mrs Woolf for the sensibilities, and Lawrence for the emotions. It is as if one could only think, the second only sensitively perceive, the third only express the most massive impulse of the moment. This is not to say that these are not good and improving writers. Aldous Huxley and Virginia Woolf have both very distinguished gifts, and Lawrence has genius; though we may doubt whether that genius ever found adequate formal expression.

Reading Mrs Woolf, we must not be chiefly interested in the active clash of character or the intricate working out of plot. What she does convey with almost unequalled delicacy is the complicated 'sensation of living,' of living from moment to moment, each moment having its own distinctive complexity of colour, texture, shape. Her characters do not engage other characters in overt dramatic conflict; rather, they wander through the park, looking at the play of light on leaves and grass, observe the dogs and nursemaids, the banana peel on the gravel path, the crinkled face of a bedraggled old man on a bench, while some tenuous but profound *inner* conflict plays itself out within their own selves in terms of this pattern of sensation. What bounds the human creature for Mrs Woolf is not the edge of his skin but the outer limits of his perceptions; and thus it is harder for her characters, each tightly if impalpably closed in an exquisite world of his own, to communicate or to come into any sort of collision than for characters more crudely conceived. For my view of the sunset does not communicate or collide with yours.

Perhaps the most solid and real of all Mrs Woolf's novels is *To the Lighthouse* where she used the experiences of her own childhood. She was the daughter of the great Victorian mountaineer, rationalist, critic, and scholar, Sir Leslie Stephen, and thus a member of one of these great families of the Victorian intellectual aristocracy – the Huxleys, the Stracheys, the Darwins, the Haldanes are others – which, generation after generation, have produced an extraordinarily large number of brilliant and public-spirited men and women. In the liberal atmosphere of Victorian England this kind of intellectual aristocracy had established itself almost as deeply in the country's life as the old aristocracy of blood and certainly more deeply than the new aristocracy of money. Thus, in everything she writes, Virginia Woolf is inescapably a scholar and a gentlewoman. Behind all her subtle and exact sensibility to shades of mood, there is, moreover, the background of her father's sturdy agnosticism and of the firm, if rather sad, rationalism of the Cambridge school of philosophy. She was one of a group of writers – Lord Keynes, Roger Fry, Clive Bell, were others – who were all influenced to a greater or lesser degree by the brilliant work of the Cambridge philosopher, G. E. Moore. Moore is a philosopher of great technical importance, whose work I have not the time, nor for that matter the competence, to analyse here, but his importance as an influence on these writers (the Bloomsbury group as they were often called, since many of them at one time or another had flats in that agreeable district of London) was that instead of emphasising some belief about God or some theory about history he tended to emphasise the importance of good and pleasant states of feeling in the individual human life. In all the writers who were influenced by him there is a passionate striving towards a clarity of good-will and understanding, and towards a perception of the passing but real beauty of the world. The good is to be found in individual experience and, though men and women are mortal, the good is not less real.

This refined and difficult but by no means sentimental philosophy gives the work of this Bloomsbury group its own dignity and pathos. They accepted the death of the individual as a final death and yet it was in the experience of the individual that they looked for what values there are in life; the values being *really* there, not merely a projection of individual feelings; this gave them a rigorous and stringent attitude towards all kinds of stupidity, unnecessary failure, and general sloppiness in human living. It robbed them perhaps of that charity which accepts failure as part of the essence of the human condition. There is not exactly a lack of warmth in their writing, but there is sometimes a rather frightening assumption that most human living is mere muddle and waste, and that only a few successful lives, those of intellectuals and artists, of truly 'civilised' people in short, really 'count': though of course at the same time the lives of 'outsiders' may, *for* the civilised people, have a value of pathos or comedy. At the same time, most of these writers, perhaps all of them, were humanitarian in their social attitudes. Their humanitarianism did not spring, however, from any self-identification with the struggling and suffering masses of the people, but rather from an impatience with what seemed to them irrational and untidy and destructive in ordinary life. Their pity was real but it was a little cold.

In Mrs Woolf's *To the Lighthouse* there is, as I have said, more warmth and body than in any of her other novels, because it is based on strong and deep memories of the sense of community in the family; and a sense of community of that sort, great as her gift for friendship was, was not something that she was ever really to find in any later setting in which she moved. In other novels of hers, one is too much aware of her condition as a brilliant solitary, guessing rather than grasping at the reality of other human lives. Thus in her brilliant experimental novel, *The Waves,* the characters present themselves not through conversation or action but through a series of soliloquies intended to give the essence of their histories and the key to their natures. But all the characters have too much the voice, too much the attitude, of Mrs Woolf herself; one feels that the book is a long monologue and that it would have been better as a straight piece of poetic introspection.

In spite of all their beauty and charm, the atmosphere of Mrs Woolf's novels is often rather a sad one. What she is most deeply aware of is what a contemporary poet, Mr Louis MacNeice, calls 'the loneliness,' the 'incommunicableness' of life. The moods and feelings which so obsess her characters are never, for reasons that I have already tried to explain, adequately communicated to the other characters; each lives in a lovely but almost completely self-enclosed world. She made one attempt, however, at a straightforward fictitious narrative in the traditional sense, the novel *Orlando.* This is a kind of affectionate parody of the historical biographies of her friend, Lytton Strachey. One might take the book at first for a straight historical biography until one realises, with a start, that the hero, an adolescent at the beginning of the book, has still hardly grown any older though we have covered the reigns of Queen Elizabeth, King James, and King Charles I. This scheme enables Mrs Woolf to give a brilliant picture of English social and literary life through three centuries and to indulge her peculiar, pungent sense of gaiety and fun – a side of her which does not get sufficient scope in most of her 'straight' novels. Perhaps indeed her essential gifts were not so much those of a novelist as those of a poet, a meditative and yet alertly observant poet, for whom mood and scene are one, and those of a literary critic with a wonderful power of bringing the past to life again. She was one of the fine stylists of her period, a wonderfully delicate and exact mistress of a just slightly mannered English prose. A sense of the changing and coloured flow of life was given form in that prose, by a wry, sad irony and a gift for implying, without expressing, passion; regret and longing were always held beautifully in check by an English gentlewoman's sense of decorum. Yet though Mrs Woolf will be read eagerly in years to come, she will not be read exactly for the picture she gives of ordinary English life, but rather for the revelation of her own rare and very beautiful personality. One feels that she writes fiction because, in her own period, the sort of poetry that she would have wanted to write was no longer a real possibility; she expresses a personal vision, and she expresses it in a poetical way.

Aldous Huxley is a much more uneven writer than Virginia Woolf, sometimes a rather flat, tiresome, didactic writer. Possibly his earliest novels, *Crome Yellow*, *Antic Hay*, *These Barren Leaves*, are his most charming. They are full of wit and sadness and a zest for caricature and an extravagantly youthful display of learning. The world they depict is in one sense a narrow one, the world partly of English country houses, and partly of London's literary Bohemia. Nearly all the characters are people with large unearned incomes, or artists, or writers; nobody appears to have a routine job to do, and thus everybody has leisure for endless discussions that make many pages of these novels read less like ordinary fiction than fragments from a philosophical debate. These early novels at least of Mr Huxley's are not, however, by any means so arid and abstract as such a description might suggest. They have the interest of satire. What Mr Huxley likes to show is how people's ideas and principles somehow fail to square with the actual lives they lead. He displays very amusingly various types of intellectual pretension and looks sharply about him for insincerity and falsehood. Some of his novels, particularly *Point Counter-Point*, have a considerable historical interest in that they offer us hardly disguised portraits of contemporaries such as D.H. Lawrence and John Middleton Murry. In his handling of tragic or violent incidents (of which he becomes much fonder in his later novels), Mr Huxley tends to be melodramatic and not nearly so convincing as when describing bright chatter at literary parties. He is the sort of man who understands people through their ideas but who is rather at a loss when he has to deal with the more direct and simple feelings and emotions and the tense situations that can arise from them.

The theme of many of these novels of his, perhaps the one essential theme of all of them, is the search for a workable faith in the bewildering world we live in to-day. In some of his novels, for instance, in *Point Counter-Point*, he seems to be trying to believe in a creed rather like that of D.H. Lawrence – the creed of what he calls a 'life-worshipper.' But Rampion, who stands for Lawrence in *Point Counter-Point*, is on the whole an unconvincing figure (Lawrence thought so himself), and more naturally and sincerely Huxley seeks salvation in a mystical attitude, one involving the renunciation of ordinary human appetites and passions and especially involving the renunciation of ordinary human egoism. The self is the great enemy and a state of non-attachment is the thing to be aimed at. That is Mr Huxley's present position.

It has been arrived at, however, after a long and difficult journey. Mr Huxley's novels express his own personal dilemma, as a man with a destructive sense of irony, and an extremely sceptical and critical intellect, who nevertheless feels very deeply the need for something to ground his life upon. Because he is so pre-eminently an intellectual, whatever faith he finally accepts must be one justifiable by logical argument; not merely by appeals to feeling or tradition. Mr Huxley in fact is so exclusively an intellectual that he has a certain squeamish horror of whatever lies below the level of the intellect, of the body with its needs and appetites, of the feelings and emotions in their raw state. This horror reflects itself in his picture of a scientifically planned society of the future, at once hygienic and inhuman (a Wellsian Utopia seen from another point of view), *Brave New World*. Because of this horror of the flesh, even the more or less settled religious attitude to life which Mr Huxley has now arrived at seems a somewhat joyless and pallid thing. One feels sometimes that he finds it easy to love God just because he finds it difficult to love men.

From a purely literary point of view, it might be contended that Mr Huxley has written too much – too many novels, essays, discursive travel books – so that he has not conserved his talents as he ought to have, and that in his later writing especially one is too obtrusively aware of repetitive stylistic mannerisms; there is a touch in a good deal of what he writes of the schoolmaster wagging a finger and pointing at the blackboard and making at regular intervals little propitiatory jokes – not always terribly good ones. Yet at its best Mr Huxley's writing expresses the temper of an urbane, civilised, and honourably serious mind. And in his earlier writing particularly he is often a genuine wit.

It is much more difficult to give a contemporary judgment on D.H. Lawrence than on either Mrs Woolf or Mr Huxley. There is power in his writing, undoubtedly, but power put to disturbing uses. Let me quote a passage from a short story:

> At a certain moment the men who are really living will come beseeching to put their lives into the hands of the greater men among them, beseeching the greater men to take the sacred responsibility of power . . . At last the masses will come to such men and say, 'You are greater than we. Be our lords. Take our life and our death in your hands, and dispose of us according to your will. Because we see a light in your face, and a burning on your mouth . . .' Ah, but my chosen aristocrat would say to those who chose him: 'If you choose me, you give up forever your right to judge me. If you have truly chosen to follow me, you have thereby rejected all your right to criticize me. You can no longer either approve or disapprove of me. You have performed the sacred act of choice. Henceforth you can only obey.'

That shows Lawrence's prophetic power (he is not speaking through his own mouth, however, but through that of a character in one of his stories); he is prophesying what the *morale* of a movement like National Socialism in Germany will be; and the passage is beautifully written, with power and simplicity – almost too beautifully, in fact, for Lawrence fails to realise not only that what he is prophesying will prove hateful but that there is something hateful in the motives of his hero, the German aristocrat Count Psanek, who prophesies it. He recognises a strong and sincere emotion, yields to it, and refuses to make judgments about good or evil, right or wrong. Or rather it is only the strong and sincere emotion (and an emotion, so very often in his stories, involving either the will to hurt or the will to dominate) that is 'good' to him. Thus from any more complex or more balancing point of view he is objectively 'wrong' in all his practical attitudes.

Lawrence's social background was very different from that of Mrs Woolf or Mr Huxley; where they came from the English mandarin class. Lawrence was the son of a miner, his mother being of a slightly higher social class than his father, who resented her 'refinement'; so that he was brought up in an atmosphere of struggle for dominance between man and wife, with his sympathies tugged sometimes towards his father's rowdiness and sometimes towards his mother's hymn-singing. His mother's Noncomformist piety gave him that serious Puritan streak which remained with him all his life, his father's humiliations and brutalities made him return again and again to the theme of the man of little education, of few words, who dominates a more subtle and complex woman by the dumb force of his masculinity. More generally, it can be said that the English lower classes have much less of that reticence and reserve which we think of as typically English than the middle classes; they are more direct and passionate in their expressions of love and hate, less likely to be argued out of a prejudice, and that directness and that obstinacy come out in everything Lawrence wrote. He felt a coldness and lack of true contact in English middle-class life, particularly but not exclusively where sexual relations were concerned. *Lady Chatterley's Lover*, the frankest of his novels from this point of view, is by no means his best one. Indeed, it is perhaps his worst. But it was by no means a pornographic book in Lawrence's own intention, but rather a passionate plea for honesty and frankness in the relations between men and women and for the recognition of the body's dignity and its needs. For Lawrence, the most important thing in life was something in people far deeper, less conscious, and less controllable than their outward attitudes and personalities; in a letter to Aldous Huxley, he once explained how he was interested in human beings at the elemental level – at the level, so to say, of the basic carbon that can be formed by different kinds of pressure into coal or diamonds, not at the level of the final complex product itself. Not, 'What have you made of yourself?' but, 'Of what sort of fundamental stuff are you made?' is the question he would ask about people. Surface personality or 'attitude' he thought of as being largely pose or a matter of social convention; what he looked for were the deep drives, and therefore he instinctively disliked invalids and cripples, in whom he felt that these drives have gone sick, and perhaps rather romanticised gamekeepers, miners, all kinds of healthy in-articulate men, in whom the expression of their emotional and physical need is direct.

He wanted, that is, people to be more 'primitively' themselves than they can be, really, in a civilised community; and he spent much of his life looking for the sort of simple life he wanted, in places like Sardinia, and Sicily, and Mexico, but probably never quite finding it. The wisdom he was looking for was no wisdom of the mind but what he would have called a 'wisdom of the blood,' and because of that deep sensibility of his to what is instinctive and natural no English writer of our time has been able to describe animals, or children, or natural scenes, or the basic drives of love or hate between persons, with so much power. But, though he is undeniably a writer of genius, he is also a strikingly uneven writer. In a tedious way he shovels into many of his novels conversations, scenes, personalities, taken from his private experience, with little regard for the shape of the book as a whole. He rants at the reader, he harangues him. The special vocabulary in which he expresses his deepest convictions, the vocabulary of the wisdom in the blood and the impulses in the solar plexus and the ganglia, is, to a reader of my own generation at least, at once philosophically absurd and poetically unconvincing. For all that, Lawrence's ideas are not to be dismissed in a hurry any more than his art is. He has perhaps only one novel which is completely satisfactory from the point of view of structure as well as texture, *Sons and Lovers*, but the short story was less of a strain on his powers of construction, and many of his short stories are masterpieces; so are his travel books *Sea and Sardinia* and *Etruscan Places* and his one critical book, *Classic American Literature*, very oddly indeed as it is written by the conventional standards of literary criticism, is enduringly vital and suggestive. His poems, from a formal point of view, are rough and unfinished, like, as Mr. T. S. Eliot has suggested, pages from the rough working notebook of a great poet; but his genius shines through them. As for his philosophy, in spite of the stridency of his manner and the claptrap of his vocabulary, there is something to be said, after all, for his belief that if the deepest natural impulses are habitually thwarted the whole superstructure of civilisation that has been built on them will gradually go wrong. His weakness as a thinker was in not allowing enough place in his scheme of things for the intellect; which, after all, *is* part of the human complex; and in supposing that in our world to-day we can really get on without it. The power of human reason has often been perverted to wrong ends, but for all that man is a rational as well as an appetitive, a passionate, and an imaginative being. The kind of animal harmony of which Lawrence dreamt is not something ultimately compatible with the dignity of the human condition. We must restrain our appetites and passions, we must cultivate self-control, and seek self-knowledge. Lawrence is full of energy; he has perhaps more energy than any other writer of his generation, but it is too often a blind energy. Sometimes it leads him to a wonderfully acute and tender perceptiveness, sometimes it makes him bang his head angrily against a stone wall. Nevertheless, in his own exasperating, untidy way he is perhaps the greatest and most significant prose writer of these troubled ten years.

Three other minor but still very significant writers of the 1920s should not be passed over in silence. One of them represents the extreme development of that dandified and disconcerting frivolity which was one aspect, for instance, of the early work of Aldous Huxley; the other two, in their different ways, represent firm reactions against that cult of the 'amusing.' The first of these three, Ronald Firbank, was the grandson of a railway magnate who had sprung from the working classes, and the son of a typically conventional middle-class Tory M.P.; in three generations, Firbank himself had somehow managed to acquire the appearance and attitudes of a decadent aristocrat. He had a lean, bony, exaggerated face, out of which still started the same masterful nose that had looked out from between the broad cushiony cheeks of his grandfather and that had given some dignity to his father's air of vapid complacency. Firbank's face, with its slightly Red Indian look, has been preserved by Augustus John and Wyndham Lewis, and his high thin voice, his hysterical giggle, his pathological shyness, his wriggling walk, and the mixture of brilliance and inconsequence in his conversation have been evoked by acquaintances like Lord Berners and Sir Osbert Sitwell. For a limited circle, those who frequented the Eiffel Tower and the Café Royal – London's wealthier Bohemia, in fact – he became something like a public figure, a mascot of the decade, without apparently ever making an intimate friend. Younger writers like the Sitwell brothers found him extraordinarily amusing, but only for the first ten minutes; his incoherence, his inability to conduct conversations except at a series of tangents, then became tiresome. Most of the descriptions of him suggest a high-grade mental defective with a streak of genius. He was a profoundly solitary person. He seems to have thought at one time that the Roman Catholic Church held the answer to his problems, but nobody in that Church seems to have worked for his conversion or watched over his morals; just as, though apparently he was an alcoholic who hardly ever ate, none of his acquaintances seems to have thought it worth while to bully him into going into a nursing home. He died at last in solitude in an Italian hotel, using what was left of his money to ward himself off from these human contacts which at once frightened and fascinated him.

Firbank's life was one of self-absorption and unhappy vanity; the saving elements in it seem to have been his deep affection for his mother and his genuine and fantastic sense of the absurd. The limited range of his experience helps to explain the peculiar quality of his novels. He retained his precarious balance by concentrating with an almost religious earnestness on the 'amusing'; in his world, to be obvious and to be serious were equal solecisms. His characters are seen neither in action, in profile, nor in depth, but in teasing fragments, through a haze of cocktail chatter. His pages are full of the oddest snatches of conversation, impossible clues never to be followed up. The smart dresses, the overheated rooms, the expensive bric-à-brac are on the same plane as the people, contribute as much to the total atmosphere, and show the same magpie-like collector's instinct as the scraps of fashionable recorded slang. The tales are fantasies but they spring from a deep feeling for what is really brittle and trivial in life. The heroes and heroines of the tales are, like Firbank himself, victims of a Narcissus complex, projecting fantasies, and automatically rejecting the fantasies of others. Everybody talks 'brilliantly,' nobody listens; beneath the high, thin giggling, there is the pathos of profound isolation. In spite of a life which seemed calculated to destroy him physically and morally, in spite of a perverse and cold schoolboyish fondness for equivocal subject matter, Firbank retained to the last an odd innocence of vision; his stories really belong on the same shelf with *Peter Rabbit* and *Through the Looking Glass* rather than in the case-book of some pathologist of literature like Professor Mario Praz. Like the books Alice liked, they are 'full of conversations' and the narrator wanders through them with an open-eyed Alician alertness. But for the more philistine reader, Firbank's puritan concentration on the 'amusing' soon becomes a strain; the writing, like the talk, is wonderful for about ten minutes at a time. Then life begins to leak away; one becomes tired as when, at a very bright and noisy party, one realises one is not going to get to know anybody any better.

The novels of L.H. Myers provide a kind of indirect commentary on Firbank's world. The best known of them, those collected under the title *The Root and the Flower*, are set in the India of the Moguls. They are not historical novels in the strict sense, though based on profound historical knowledge. Their theme is the spiritual life and how far, if at all, it can be adequately embodied in social institutions.

Myers's very unpleasant portrait of the great Mogul's degenerate son, Daniyal, and his court of buffoons and flatterers, 'the Camp,' devoted to art, gossip, trivial sensuality, mild malice, and amateur theatricals, is a criticism of the kind of aesthetic 'civilisation' for which Firbank lived and died. The frivolity of this mode of life, which refuses to make a choice between good and evil, seems to Myers more corrupting than the sincere choice of evil itself. There are, he feels, worse things than brutality. But serious power politicians are also treated harshly, and it seems to have been Myers's feeling that spiritual insight is denatured or deformed when embodied in institutions, and the representative of spiritual wisdom in his book, the Guru, is the enemy of institutional religion. The Guru's belief is also in original goodness rather than in original sin. It is interesting to learn, from an excellent article by Mr Walter Allen, that Myers had both a certain sympathy for Communism, a movement through which he felt a fresh wind of the spirit might be blowing, and an intense dislike of the Anglo-Catholicism of Mr T. S. Eliot. It is with spiritual rather than ordinary social problems that Myers is concerned. His characters are princes or courtiers, free from ordinary immediate frustrations, and the central problem for him is what, for the man who has the opportunity of a full and rich experience, is the good life. It seems, for Myers, to involve renunciation, but a renunciation that may be very long delayed. More generally, he is more impressed with the fertility of the basic human impulses than with the instability, which he is also aware of, of human institutions; his historical philosophy might be described as a kind of optimistic fatalism, and does in fact seem to apply better to Indian history than to the modern industrialised West. He is a writer who gives a general impression of wisdom, but whose wisdom may seem rather to lack particular relevance to our own affairs.

T. F. Powys resembles Myers, at least the Myers of *The Root and the Flower*, in that his books are essentially tracts or allegories; they have been described by Mr Empson as Buddhist death-plays with Christian imagery. Their setting is always rural, and the texture of the prose rather consciously recalls both Jane Austen, a little superficially, and more profoundly Bunyan. The characters tend to have Bunyanesque names, like Lord Titball, and to embody like Bunyan's a single personified human drive, often an unpleasant one, such as lust, stupidity, cruelty, or greed. The good characters, who are sometimes clergymen, are usually hated because of their goodness and come to a bad end. If one took these novels as realistic descriptions of country life in our day, one would feel profoundly relieved that one lived in town, but the unpleasant subject-matter is balanced by a gentleness of attitude, a tenderness for the rural scene, and a sincere if melancholy mysticism. Thus in *Mr Weston's Good Wine*, the wine is death, and we drink it to escape from this vale of troubles. Mr Powys is an excellent but minor artist. He has not Miss Austen's actuality; and the religious attitude which he expresses allegorically is not, like Bunyan's, that of the social group he realises for us but that of himself as an isolated and untypical observer. His mild insistence, moreover, on the brutality of rural life, pungent at first, becomes a mannerism, and lends itself to parodies, like that of *Cold Comfort Farm*. Yet he has created a world of his own; and, at his own level, he is one of the most genuine artists whom the history of the English novel can boast of in this century. It is not his fault that his art springs from his sensitivity to the life of a rural England, no longer proud and self-confident as in Bunyan's time or Miss Austen's, no longer central to the general life of the country, but in moral decay.

Section 5: The 'Serious' 1930s

If the 1920s were a decade when a writer tended to turn away from the everyday problems of social living and political choice, the circumstances of the 1930s forced his attention back in that direction. In 1929, there was the great Wall Street slump with its disastrous repercussions everywhere in Europe. Unemployment and distress, as well as militant nationalism, helped Hitler to power in Germany in 1933. His policy of rearmament put the Germans back to work but threatened the peace and the liberties of Europe. Later in the decade, the Spanish Civil War and the Italian invasion of Ethiopia forced writers and intellectuals to take definite political sides, divided their sympathies, aroused their passions, as no comparable set of political events in the 1920s had done. On top of all this, there was, as these ten years progressed, a gradually growing and intensifying and, alas, only too well justified fear that the Spanish episode, the Ethiopian adventure, the fighting in Manchuria, were perhaps mere preludes to a Second and more disastrous World War. Thus the typical and important literature of the 1930s is a literature of topical urgency, reflecting a feeling of tension and an awareness of crisis.

Since 1917, Russia had been very much isolated from the Western World. Her very isolation, the little that was known in any exact or reliable detail about the working of her new system of government was likely, on the principle of *omne ignotum pro magnifico*, to engage and tantalise the imagination particularly of the young. A young man growing up in Great Britain in the 1930s, with no certain prospect of a job in front of him, and an all too possible prospect of being caught up in another great war, with many instances of social distress brought sharply home to him by such incidents as the Hunger Marches, was likely to have his confidence in the British gift for 'muddling through,' in the virtues of compromise and improvisation, generally, rather badly dented. He would find himself thinking with interest and curiosity of this large country, Russia, in which, in however ruthless a fashion, the problems of preserving full employment and keeping production swinging upwards did seem to have been solved. Very few English writers in the 1930s actually became members of the Communist Party and those who did remained, usually, members for only a short time. But it could at least be said that just as the Roman Catholic Church in the 1890s provided a kind of focus of attraction for writers who in the end may have never taken the final step towards conversion, so, in the 1930s, did various versions of Marxist doctrine provide this kind of focus for many English intellectuals.

A well-known London publisher, Victor Gollancz, founded the Left Book Club, which besides publishing a magazine for its members sold them every month a book on some aspect of Socialist, or at least militant anti-Fascist, politics. If many young men of middle-class, or even upper-middle-class or actually aristocratic upbringing, were driven towards the extreme Left in these years, the same unsettlement and discontentment was driving others to the extreme Right. Sir Oswald Mosley's British Union of Fascists copied the Black Shirts of the Italian Fascisti but propagated, following a rising tide, the ideas rather of German National Socialism. A wider reaction than any of these was, as a natural reaction against the Fascist and Nazi glorification of war, a passionate but rather sentimental pacifism. This could be seen in the growth of the Peace Pledge Union, whose members were committed to taking up, in any future war, the position of conscientious objectors, but the same people who joined the Peace Pledge Union were often, misled by the amiable confusion of their enthusiasms, those who called most loudly for the carrying out of a policy of Collective Security and the imposition on Italy, in connection with the Ethiopian episode, of 'sanctions' (given the limiting condition, naturally ineffective sanctions) 'short of war.' Political meetings in these ten years in Great Britain had a more violent and dramatic flavour than is common in

British politics. Brawls between Fascists and Communists, and the beating up of interrupters at Fascist meetings, were common. The outbreak of the war itself, which pulled the British people together into one team again, as perhaps nothing else would have done, showed to what an extent all these domestic episodes were mere froth on the surface. But the young man who clung (as I, for instance, remember clinging myself during these years) to the old middle-of-the-road attitude, to the faith that Great Britain would in the long run solve her own problems in her own way, and did not need to borrow any foreign cheapjack remedies, still felt the emotional tug of these more melodramatic, more vividly coloured, and fundamentally of course infinitely less sane and humane policies of the extreme Right and Left. It seemed, in a sense, weak and old-fashioned of the intellectual to refuse to adopt bitter and drastic attitudes.

It might be said that two English poets, Roy Campbell and John Cornford, who fought in Spain in these years on opposite sides (Campbell as a Carlist, Cornford as a Communist) represented in their different ways the *same* response to the troubles and anxieties of the period – the response of a fierce radicalism, whether of the Left or Right, that wanted to be rid for good and all of what seemed old-fashioned, inefficient temporising. And of these two, it should be noted, Campbell, who had worked all his life with his hands, as cowboy, fisherman, farmer, was much more genuinely the 'man of the people' and Cornford, the son of a famous Greek scholar, much less so. For theoretical Marxism did, on the whole, tend to make its appeal rather to intellectuals themselves. Theoretical Marxism appealed to a sense of guilt in these upper middle classes: that sense of guilt sprang from a feeling, among young men like Cornford, that they ought not to be able to lead comfortable and satisfying lives while so many of their fellow-countrymen were condemned to poverty and insecurity. Thus those who, in the 1930s, accepted the myth of the revolution were not those who would have made the revolution, had there been one. The English Labour movement, in so far as it is a genuine working class movement (which it basically and centrally is) has always been moderate, slow-moving, sure-footed, and cautious.

Thus, we can say that the best English novels of the 1930s reflect a state of social tension. They can be divided, perhaps, into four main categories:

1) There is firstly what one may call the symbolic melodrama, or literary thriller. Novels of this sort use the mechanism of the old-

fashioned tale of crime and adventure to bring across to the reader a vivid sense of the insecure, frightening, dangerous state of the contemporary world.

2) Secondly, there were what one might call 'documentary' novels, novels in which the writer made use of his own personal experience and observation of various social situations to underline, usually in a rather quieter way, that same lesson of the world's insecurity and the need for some positive and constructive political faith.

3) Thirdly, there were what one might call novels of social allegory, novels in which a simple, sometimes fantastic tale was used to state and illustrate some troublesome contemporary problem, such as, for instance, that of the correct relation between the idea of tradition and the other idea of making society completely over anew, starting from scratch, or, if not exactly from scratch, on the basis of some doctrinaire notion either of how social change ought to take place or of what a truly 'rational' society would be.

4) Fourthly, there were novels written superficially in terms of comedy or even of farce, but with an underlying very disturbing note of bitterness which emphasised the ruthlessness, the nerviness, the unhappiness, the lack of purpose and the lack of love, in much contemporary British life.

Let us take these four types of novels in order.

The great master of the novel of symbolic melodrama was undoubtedly Mr Graham Greene. Greene divides his novels into what he calls 'serious' performances and 'entertainments,' but both kinds have a similar basic pattern. Both kinds are exercises in the very old narrative theme of the hunting down of a man: but the story is not seen, as in the ordinary detective novel, from the point of view of the hunters, but from that of the hunted man. Greene's 'entertainments,' like *Stamboul Train*, *A Gun for Sale*, or *The Ministry of Fear* are, as far as the plots go, plain, old-fashioned thrillers, full of spies, and secret documents, and chases in the dark, and murders. His mastery of the thriller form, and his ability to give it a wide significance, can be seen in his excellent scenario for that fast, gripping British film, *The Third Man*. On the other hand, in a fairly recent 'serious' novel, *The Heart of the Matter*, there is no violence but merely a study of the chain of events which leads a devout and good man, out of an excessive regard for others, first to commit what he regards as mortal sin (he commits adultery partly out of compassion for a lonely woman, and then takes communion without going to confession, so that his wife will not be upset by suspecting his adultery) and secondly, as a way out of what seems to him an utterly hopeless situation, to commit suicide thus cutting himself off completely, according to Catholic doctrine, from the possibility of a final act of contrition. The poor man is driven down to hell in fact by his excessive desire to do always 'the decent' – that is, the obliging, the unobtrusive, the self-surrendering – 'thing': though Greene, of course, points out that the mercy of God is infinitely mysterious and that we do not know whether it may not be stretched to cover even this odd case. But if it were possible for a man to decide to damn himself by rule and method, Greene's hero has almost done so. Yet he is an intrinsically 'nicer' person probably than most of those who read about him.

For Greene, in fact, who is a convert to Roman Catholicism, the ideas of 'good' and 'evil' (understood in some absolute, final, almost mystical sense), are much more important than the ideas of 'niceness' and 'decency' or even of 'right' and 'wrong.' Right and wrong for Greene are matters of social decorum, or of some traditional code accepted without thinking, but the choice of good and evil is a terrible, significant, and final choice presented to the individual soul. Good and evil, moreover, have nothing to do with respectability or success. Thus, in one of Greene's best novels, *England Made Me*, the powers of goodness, or rather the difficult final choice of the good, are represented by two weak and ineffective characters, Anthony, the hero, and his friend Minty.

Anthony is the sort of typical black sheep of a shabby-genteel English family, whose great preoccupation throughout his boyhood has been 'keeping up appearances.' Tragically, that has become Anthony's preoccupation, too. He has drifted about the world, from one job to another, and he has lost job after job through petty dishonesty (so that he can have money for drinks and cards, and take his place in the local community), or for boasting or lying (pretending to have gone to an important public school that he has not gone to, or to know people he doesn't know, or to have seen military service that he hasn't seen). He is handsome and quite attractive but essentially rather ordinary and his whole life has been an attempt to compensate for his ordinariness by trying to appear more socially important, more of a 'gentleman,' more of a 'man of the world' than he really is. He is a pathetic product, in fact, of English snobbery which will not allow him to be honestly, decently, rather drably himself. He has an essentially weak will and few assets other than a good appearance, a rather feeble cunning, and an undoubted sex-appeal.

Minty is not even a real black sheep. He comes from an excellent family, he has been to a good school: but he is a misfit and an eccentric, insignificant in appearance and slovenly in dress, the sort of person who just does not fit into the social pattern, who cannot 'do' anything effectively, and who is a constant source of embarrassment to his family and friends. He is physically a weakling, incapable of earning a living; with a mixture of prudence and heartlessness his family have provided him with a small pension so long as he lives in a Scandinavian city and does not come home to bother them. He is the typical 'remittance man,' but with none of the remittance man's traditional vices. He is not a man of scandalous life, he is merely irritating and futile. Naturally he is very lonely, mildly resentful of his social ostracism (he rather maliciously keeps up contacts with the British Ambassador in this Scandinavian city who, as an old schoolfellow, and in any case the representative of the interests of the British community there, can never quite finally 'drop' him). He is also pathetically eager to make friends and opens his heart at once to Anthony. The great consolation of Minty's life is, however, not his earthly friendships but his religious faith. Even his devoutness, however, expresses itself to the outward eye in a finicky old-maidish fashion and nobody takes it very seriously. Minty, nevertheless, is, we discover as the plot develops, an almost wholly good man; without self-will, without any deep in-grained malice, a man almost totally devoted, in spite of his weakness and insignificance, to a genuine vision of goodness, and at the same time a man with a terribly acute and painful intuition of evil. He is a kind of crippled saint – a man whose real goodness can never find adequate outward expression, because of the terrible sense of inferiority which crushes his spirit and makes him miserable.*

Anthony, in the story, when we first meet him, has not yet made his final choice between good and evil. He has come to the Scandinavian city where Minty lives because his sister, who has always dominated him, is living there, too. A very rich, powerful, wicked, and un-scrupulous financial magnate is in love with her and wants to marry her. She does not care greatly for him (she is a cold, capable, self-centred woman, her one great love being for Anthony) but she is willing to

* Few modern 'serious' novelists tell a story in a more straightforward way than Mr Greene, but one's interpretation of the story will be affected by one's point of view. I once heard a British Council lecturer describe the character of Minty as a terrible study of degeneracy and evil – and he is, of course, the sort of Englishman abroad whom official circles find embarrassing. But neurosis, though it may be even more of a nuisance, is not wickedness.

accept his advances, if, in this way, she can help her 'little brother.' The magnate gives Anthony a job as a kind of secretary and is friendly and nice to him for a time, and Anthony for the first time in his life enjoys that sense of wealth and social importance which he has always hankered after. But he has not reckoned with his own conscience. Some of the jobs that the magnate asks him to do strike him as rather dirty jobs, and finally when he is asked to behave very brutally to some poor man whom the magnate has ruined, and who is demanding an interview, he protests. It is not, he says in his weak but definite way, the decent thing to do. The magnate is angry, though he conceals his anger. He is deeply in love with Anthony's sister and he is in any case jealous of her affection for Anthony and the time she devotes to him; but especially he is not the sort of man who can put up with somebody always around him whose mere presence implies a perpetual moral reproach. So the magnate has a henchman of his push Anthony into a river on a foggy night. Minty guesses that a murder has been committed, and lets the murderer know that he guesses, but can do nothing about it. Thus, in this story we see evil triumphant in the world, and yet the story is not wholly a story of mere loss, because good in the end has been triumphant in Anthony's soul – he has taken his stand for righteousness – and that is more important to Mr Greene, who thinks in terms of eternity, than the mere passing successes of the wicked in this life.

Mr Greene does not heavily underline the moral implications of his stories, as I have been doing here. His novels are written in a brisk, unpretentious, sharply visualised style (so that one remembers many scenes, but perhaps no sentences): and there is quick cutting from one episode to another as in the cinema, there are no long, dull, ruminative or padded passages. This technique, which assures that the reader is never bored, has nevertheless perhaps something a little mechanical about it. The words are almost too transparent and I am not sure that one really loses much by seeing one of Mr Greene's stories as a film instead of reading it, always supposing that, like *The Third Man*, the film is adequately made. One tends to think of Mr Greene, in fact, along with the great directors of cinema thrillers, like Alfred Hitchcock, rather than along with other novelists. He has Hitchcock's wonderful sense of atmosphere – of the atmosphere, in particular, of what he calls 'seediness,' an almost untranslatable English word which conjures up a composite feeling of the shabby, the homely, and the sinister. Greene loves, in fact, to set his most melodramatic episodes in the most homely surroundings, the cheap restaurant, the shabby newspaper office, the furnished room where the tasteless furniture fills one with a sense of spiritual emptiness, or the great railway station with its atmosphere of nervous waiting, tightness at the pit of the stomach, and uneasy departures towards unnamed dangers. He has a lively sense of that feeling of *deprivation* – the lack of style, or flavour, or roots, or manners – which is so typical of megalopolitan civilisation, but to the stripped, deprived, peeling backcloths of his urban scenes he manages to give a positive and exciting tang. He will describe in his first few pages some commonplace scene, introduce some dimly ordinary character; but we know that we are in a world that we too often ourselves live in, a world that is full of pockets of moral evil, just as, down its dark alleys, it is full of musty smells; and it is an exciting world, because it is a world in which we feel from the start that 'anything' (meaning probably something violent and unpleasant), 'anything at all can happen.'

So much for the symbolic melodrama. The documentary novel, on the other hand, our second kind, tends less to emphasise the melo-dramatic aspects of life than the quiet and homely and ordinary episodes which always make up most of the texture of the individual human life even in times of the utmost tension and crisis. For tension and crisis are the headlines in the morning paper, and the lingering nasty feeling in the mouth and the diaphragm, but they cannot fill up every minute of the work and the leisure of one's day. We have to 'go on living' even in a conquered city or after an earthquake or a devastating bombing raid, or after what seems some final blow to all our political hopes, and to some minds this wonderful obstinacy and staunchness of the individual in perpetually picking up the splintered fragments of his life will always seem more interesting than the grand catastrophe itself. Thus, one has heard that during the war refugees and exiles were happier if they could carry with them an old battered kettle or a patchwork quilt, some trivial object, however shabby, which symbolised to them 'the old home,' and if the pathos of this is almost unbearable from one point of view, from another point of view one is encouraged when one thinks of the strength of the human impulse for continuity. Shaken, battered, deprived of all that seems to make life worth living, human beings still refuse to drop the threads.

Thus, Christopher Isherwood's two books about Berlin before the rise to power of Hitler, *Good-bye to Berlin*, and *Mr Norris Changes*

Trains (published in the United States as *The Last of Mr Norris*) are very largely concerned with the small everyday adventures of the narrator, whose experiences and attitudes are very largely those of Mr Isherwood himself, as a young man teaching English in Berlin to private pupils, living in cheap boarding houses, casually making friends at many social levels, and talking with his friends. *Good-bye to Berlin*, in particular, could be taken as a mere series of pleasant, rather slight sketches of a random sample of the Berlin populace. But the deep theme of both books is the decay of a civilisation, the decay of tradition, and its tragic, or stultifying, or sometimes absurd and ridiculous, effects on individual human lives. We are not given a lot of abstract argument about how Hitler rose to power or about the moral implications of Nazism. We are merely shown, sitting in the kitchen, drinking tea with their friends, visiting flashy night-clubs, enjoying their holidays, a wide range of persons who have not only lost most of their traditional faiths but who, having failed to get any solid intellectual grip on the deteriorating world around them, are in the end easy meat for (or, in the case of the romantic young Socialists and the sophisticated middle-class Jewish or half-Jewish liberals, predestined victims of) the unscrupulous demagogue. There is, however, in all this demonstration, no tone of moral superiority. Isherwood nowhere suggests that, in the place of his Berlin friends, he, or anybody else, would have behaved more effectively. They are trapped, the poor among them by hunger and insecurity and the need for something positive and exciting to believe, to live for; the rich by their almost over-civilised isolation, by the gentle rhythm of their lives that makes it hard for them to imagine, and impossible for them to cope with, violence. Instead of any patronising tone, there is instead in these books of Isherwood's a great charity and a detached and penetrating good-will, so that even where Isherwood depicts a real scoundrel, like his Mr Norris, he manages (while conveying his own disapproval very clearly) both to make us laugh at him and feel rather sorry for him, too.

The actual writing in Isherwood's novels is much more interesting and distinctive than that in Greene's. Greene's clipped, vivid sentences make us see what he wants us to see, but they do not convey the deeper resonances of judgment or personality. Isherwood, on the other hand, has style; any competent writer could get hold of Greene's techniques (and, in fact, many have) but the special and inimitable note of Isherwood's writing springs from his personality. The style is the man. It looks easy and simple, it is exactly like somebody talking to us, and Isherwood never seems to be taking any special pains with his writing, but at the same time there is no waste; the deceptively casual-looking sentences create the impression, convey the idea, hit the exact tone, that Isherwood is aiming at. This complete lack of wastage gives Isherwood's books, which are all rather short – a rapid reader like myself can get through any one of them in an hour – and all smooth, easy reading, a density which they do not at first appear to have. One knows many longer and more ambitious-looking books that are far less packed with genuine *matter* (that is to say, with what has genuinely been felt, observed, correlated) than these two short books about Berlin. The air of easy, careless, modest charm in the writing disguises a tense economy of structure. Isherwood's earlier novels, *All the Conspirators* and *The Memorial*, have the same grace of style and give one a similarly tight, exact picture, this time of the troubles and anxieties of English middle-class life in the 1920s. Since the outbreak of the late war, like his friend the poet W. H. Auden, Mr Isherwood has been in the United States, chiefly in California, where he writes film-scripts. Like so many of the leading writers of the 1930s, he has to-day moved away from his old tendency to interpret life chiefly in political terms, and has taken up a more or less religious attitude. He has published nothing in fiction since the war apart from a rather slight *nouvelle* – not up to his best standard – about the film industry in England in the 1930s. He has however written a lively and amusing, if sometimes rather superficial, travel book about South America called *The Condor and the Cows.* His style is as lively as ever, if sometimes (what is natural, perhaps, in a travel diary) more relaxed. It will be a great pity if he never writes any more novels though the atmosphere of Hollywood, where he spends so much of his time, is perhaps likely to baffle the talent of a novelist whose great gift is not the notation of garishness but the conveying of fine, and gentle, and subtle differences of shade and tone.

Let us turn now to our third type of novel, which I have called the 'social allegory.' The most important writer of this kind of novel (if novel, in the strict sense, it should be properly considered) in the 1930s was Rex Warner. Warner was a classical scholar, who in that decade was a master in a public school, teaching Greek and Latin, and who is now an official of the British Council. He was head of the Council in Athens for some time. He was a friend of Auden and Isherwood, and their group, and is also known as a translator, a critic, and a poet. His two best-known allegorical novels are *The Aerodrome* and *The Professor*. Both deal, though from slightly different perspectives, with essentially the same theme.

The setting of *The Aerodrome* is a small, sleepy, rather backward and out of the way village in the south of England, on the outskirts of which the Air Ministry decide to erect a large new aerodrome for experimental purposes. In charge of the aerodrome is an Air Vice-Marshal who is a man of great intelligence and driving ambition. It soon becomes obvious to the reader that the village is not an ordinary village, and the aerodrome not an ordinary aerodrome. The Air Vice-Marshal takes charge of village life and starts to dominate and organise the local inhabitants in a way which would be inconceivable in real life, and if we take the story as a true story, we are likely to find it thin, implausible, and fantastic. But the allegorical meaning is not difficult to grasp. The Air Vice-Marshal represents the radical planning, organising mind, the mind that wants to build society anew from its foundations and that is more interested in social efficiency than in individual happiness. Indeed, according to theories like the Air Vice-Marshal's it is not good for society that the individual should be too happy, too comfortable, too much at his ease. He will become lazy then and will resist necessary change. He must be kept 'on his toes.' It is a theory of military discipline applied to civil society. If the Air Vice-Marshal represents such radical anti-traditional movements as Communism, Nazism, or Fascism, the village, on the other hand, stands for habit and tradition, for man's accustomed ways of doing things, which may not be ideally either the best or the most effective ways, but are the ways he is used to and feels warm about. The village, in fact, stands for whatever forces those are in human life that make men, rightly or wrongly, resist change. The Air Vice-Marshal is clever and strong, the villagers, taken individually, are mostly either weak or stupid, but, in spite of the Air Vice-Marshal's dazzling and ruthless tactics, it is the village that triumphs in the end. The Air Vice-Marshal is defeated and killed and his plans for taking over and reorganising not only the village but the country come to nothing.

It is the great weakness of the Air Vice-Marshal (who, though in one sense he is the 'villain' of the novel, is a man with certain heroic and attractive qualities) that he does not make enough allowance in his grand schemes for the dignity of the individual human personality and particularly for the ties of local loyalty and of family love and affection. Yet we are not left feeling that there is nothing *at all* to be said for his point of view. The village itself is not idealised. It is a backward place.

Many of the villagers' cottages are insanitary, many of their pleasures are brutal, many of their traditional habits are crude and unpleasant. They are used to the life they lead, and they have an inner warmth that the Air Vice-Marshal lacks, but the life they lead is often a muddled and thwarted one, by no means corresponding to one's highest notions of what human life might be. What Mr Warner is perhaps driving at is that we cannot live either wholly by habit and custom, on the one hand, or wholly by abstract reason on the other, that we must find some working compromise between the two, and some compromise too between a fanatical and ruthless devotion to some abstract ideal, like the Air Vice-Marshal's, and a mere complacent jogging along in our old ruts, accompanied by a bland indifference to all larger issues. Mr Warner seems to suggest that the way for us to find this working compromise between reason and tradition – and there is a tradition of reasonableness in human affairs, after all, and also a reason for there being traditions – is by having respect and affection for each other and therefore a receptive and tolerant attitude towards each other's points of view.

The Professor is a rather sadder story, in which in an imaginary country a professor, who is a great scholar and a great believer in liberal ideas, is invited to form a government at a time when tension between the extreme Right and the extreme Left – say, between the Fascists and the Communists – is threatening to plunge the country into civil war. He hopes to found a government of liberty and order which will rally to its side, on a patriotic basis, men of goodwill in all classes and in all parties, and bring a new idealistic spirit into public life. In point of fact, he is used as a tool by extremists – extremists of the Right in the story, though recent history suggests that it might as easily have been by extremists of the Left – and in the end swept from power, put in prison, and put to death. He dies in great moral loneliness, for if the Right sweep him ruthlessly aside, for the Left he is the foolish dupe who has betrayed them to their enemies and destroyed all their hopes. The professor does represent the spirit of rationality, modified by goodwill towards his fellow men and by a respect for tradition, which Mr Warner seemed to be advocating in *The Aerodrome*, but in this case that high spirit of love and reason seems much less strong than the crude passions of class-hatred. On the other hand, the Professor, even though he completely fails, does manage to retain a moral dignity which the more forceful and successful characters in the book lack. There is something very fine in his refusal to countenance cruelty and hate, whatever the refusal may cost him, and in the dignity with which he meets his death. One thinks almost of the death of Socrates and one feels that the spirit of reason will, in this as in that case, long survive the momentary triumph of the crude passions that destroy its representative.

But there is more to be said than that. The tone of the book implies not only Mr Warner's sense of the tragic dignity of the Professor's predicament, but a certain ironical criticism of the practical inadequacy of the Professor's attitude. The Professor is a noble, heroic figure, but it cannot be denied that in his view of life and politics he is a little unreal and bookish. He has thought all his life too much in terms of abstract ideas and has not grappled enough with the complex world of men. The Professor's mistress, whom he loves very deeply, is secretly the lover of an exiled Fascist leader, and there is a suggestion that this man, morally so far below the Professor, has a certain coarse vitality and strength about him, a 'manliness' in the crudest sense, which the Professor lacks, and is the less effective for lacking. So the lesson of *The Professor* may be that though political leaders certainly should have high purposes and should not betray those purposes, still they should have, too, a realism about human nature, and that they should have enough of the earthy and the common in them to be able to arouse a response in – to guide, and to check the earthy, common material they are dealing with – average human nature, with all its prejudices, interests, and passions. With a little more hardness and a little more scepticism in his nature, the Professor, not pitching his immediate hopes so high, might have at once ridden his storm and postponed the immediate defeat, as well, perhaps, as preparing for the ultimate victory, of his own high ideals. Mr Warner may have been thinking of such a figure as President Wilson, who, by insisting too narrowly at Versailles on his own ideals, in abstraction both from the reality of the situation in Europe and that of the situation in the United States, in a sense betrayed these ideals by his very eagerness to impose them; by yielding more, by a greater resilience, he would probably in the end have gained more of what he was actually after. And again, as in the Air Vice-Marshal's case, it is never *one* man who imposes his ideals on history, but history is shaped rather by the concurrence of many factors of sentiment, opinion, and interest, and by the co-operation, and competition, of many diverse minds. The Professor had great strength (as President Wilson had before he came to Versailles) as a symbolic figure; but nothing is more fragile and transitory than this symbolic strength, which comes from accidentally embodying many vague and perhaps contradictory aspirations, and no politician should rely on it when he steps down off his pedestal into the dust and heat of the arena.

Whatever puzzles of interpretation there may be about the details of these two books, one can, however, say with confidence that they deal with a debate between innovation and custom, as also between an idealistic and a realistic view of politics, which was going on in many intelligent people's minds in the 1930s, and is indeed still going on now. One may say that the Air Vice-Marshal betrays his ideals, and even formulates them wrongly in the first place, by being too ruthlessly 'realistic' about his way of achieving them; the Professor betrays them by not being realistic enough. The Air Vice-Marshal is so obsessed with the efficiency of power, that he forgets that power is of the order of means, that it must subserve justice; the Professor is so obsessed with the beauty of justice that he forgets that justice, such imperfect justice as is achievable in this world, if it is to have a firm base at all, must be based upon power.

The fourth type of novel that I mentioned was the farcical comedy with bitter undertones. The most successful writer of this kind of novel, in the 1930s, was Evelyn Waugh. The pattern of Evelyn Waugh's novels will recall to many readers that of the earlier novels – say *Antic Hay* or *These Barren Leaves* – of Mr Aldous Huxley. There are the same parties, the same casual love affairs, the same sense of a glimpse at an inner circle, the same endless buzz of witty or amusingly fatuous conversation. But Mr Waugh's characters belong less to the intellectual world than Mr Huxley's and much more exclusively to the world of high fashion. They are the young men and women whose handsome or horse-like faces, flushed a little sometimes with surprise or indignation that the flashlight photographer should direct his lens at them, we may trace week by week through old numbers of *The Sporting and Dramatic* or *The Tatler*. The clothes of the women, and the furniture of their rooms, have a quiet and tasteful expensiveness that comes from a thorough study of *Vogue*. Mr Waugh's characters, in fact, are what journalists of his period called 'the bright young people.' They go in one's mind with horses, and long rakish cars, and spats and bowler hats, and Mayfair and St James's Street. Moreover, Mr Waugh's attitude to this fashionable world is much more ambivalent than Mr Huxley's. In one sense, yes, he is mocking it for its lack of any sense of direction, of any intellectual ballast; in another sense he cannot help being rather impressed by its sheer brave foolhardiness, its dash and tone. Thus characters who in his earlier novels, like *Decline and Fall* or *Vile Bodies*, exist chiefly as butts of his malicious drollery can be packed into uniform and die bravely for their country (as, indeed, their originals did, too) in a wartime novel like *Put Out More Flags*. If Mr Waugh's early novels are chiefly concerned with 'taking off' fashionable society, his retrospective view of it, in his later work, grows more indulgent, and perhaps almost sentimental. In his wholly serious novel, *Brideshead Revisited*, the aristocracy are shown as, for all their waywardness, the last custodians in England of honour and faith – and this is a tenable position in itself, but hard to square with such portraits in the earlier, purely farcical or satirical novels as that of Miles Malpractice.

This difference in tone can no doubt be explained by a growing moral commitment. Mr Waugh's earliest novels, written before he became a Roman Catholic convert, set out to depict, from its comic or absurd aspect, a world from which all serious and permanent values have been evacuated, a world intent mainly on the getting of money, so that money may be spent on a 'good time.' The disasters in which such a world is likely to abound are presented in a flat, non-committal way, with an effect of shocking humour, of a joke in the worst of taste which is nevertheless genuinely funny, and with no effect at all of pathos except in so far as Mr Waugh's very indifference to the misfortunes of his characters may sometimes rouse a protesting feeling on their behalf in the reader's breast. The white slave traffic, sexual inversion, drug taking, a horrid murder in a prison cell, the lingering death of a schoolboy who has been accidentally shot in the heel by the starter of a race, the death of a gay young woman in hospital while her friends hold a cocktail party in her private ward, the sinister coincidence by which the dish presented to a young Englishman by African tribesmen turns out to be the girl he is engaged to – all these events, in the earlier novels, at least, are 'good for a laugh' or, in the case of the last one, good at least for a wry ironic shudder. It is not at all surprising that older critics like G. K. Chesterton protested that they could find nothing funny in such a novel as *Decline and Fall* at all, but on the contrary found it extremely shocking and distressing. It is a kind of humour, of course, on the verge of hysteria, but I think nobody of my generation, at least, can deny that it is irresistibly funny. Violence, I suppose, is in the air, and we are all to some extent obsessed by violence. Mr Waugh's way of turning this obsession of ours into absurd farce – for, of course, he needs our co-operation, and cannot be accused of teaching us a perverse taste all of his own – is at least more cathartic, I think, than the glum plugging away at episodes of violence, with a direct appeal to sinister impulses in the reader, by 'novelists of action' like Hemingway, Malraux, or Koestler.* Mr Waugh does not ask us to connive at anything but, in his best satirical vein, presents us rather with the picture of a society so disintegrated that death has become almost as meaningless as life. To preserve that attitude of satirical detachment, even for his first few novels, must have involved an enormous moral strain. Not only are no valid beliefs or principles represented as operative among the characters, but neither is it suggested – as in Mr Huxley's novels, for instance, it is always suggested – that at least the author and his readers know better. All foundations are deftly whipped away and we have the dizzying exhilarating sensation of walking briskly with nothing, but absolutely nothing, beneath the floor.

It could not last. Mr Waugh, like the rest of us, needed something beneath the floor, and he discovered his foundations in an acceptance of Roman Catholic dogma and in the gradual adoptance of a more and more protective and proprietary air towards that society of 'bright young people' which had formerly provided him with his most amusing and pungent illustrations of the meaninglessness of life. Thus, in his later novels, up to *Brideshead Revisited*, there is an odd mixture of tones. The bright young people may behave in a caddish or absurd way but there is often a tone of affection, or almost of admiration, in the way he writes about them and his really sharp satire is now directed more against 'outsiders.'

Finally, in *Brideshead Revisited*, the characters cease altogether to be puppets and begin to exist for Mr Waugh as people in the round. The disintegration which had aroused such hysterical laughter in the earlier novels is seen in sad perspective as part of the disintegration of belief, of standards, in our time, and Mr Waugh sees that as partly reflecting the break-down of an aristocratic society. It is only in his remarks on the sample 'common man,' in this novel, Lieutenant Hooper, that his old cruel and unscrupulous satirical humour gets full swing; though he was later to give that sinister but creative impulse a short outing in *The Loved One* in which the hero ends by cremating the heroine in a dog's cemetery. But *The Loved One* is not really innocently funny in

---

* I don't mean that these aren't important writers, but merely that there is an element of unconscious 'viciousness' in all of them.

the same way as *Decline and Fall* is. And *Brideshead Revisited* is, perhaps, as a serious novel, sometimes a little too innocent.

There is a characteristic in Mr Waugh which one can only call snobbishness; and it is not a snobbishness on quite the same subtle and excusable level, say, as that of Proust or Henry James, for it is the attitude not so much of one who wants to understand as one who wants to belong. The son of a respectable but outmoded literary critic, and the younger brother of a prolific popular novelist, Mr Waugh belongs by achievement rather than by birth to that aristocratic world of country houses, and that smart London world of Mayfair flats, towards which his attitude of wistfulness and reverence, as he grows older, seems gradually to intensify. And in his admiration for the expensiveness, smartness, and dash of that world there is an excessive innocence, just as in his very sour attitude towards the lower classes (Hooper, and the evacuees in *Put Out More Flags*) he does reveal, too clearly and probably quite unconsciously, a middle-class rather than an aristocratic habit of mind; for *noblesse*, one is always told, *oblige* and doesn't need to be always reassuring itself about its status by jeering at the awful vulgarity and inadequacy of the lower orders. It is only the well-born and the rich and gay and handsome who really engage Mr Waugh's sympathies, and this is a weakness, even from the point of view of his own religious beliefs; for we are not told that it is easier for a camel to pass through a needle's eye than for a poor man to enter the kingdom of heaven.

It can be seen, I think, from the earlier paragraphs of this section that Mr Waugh's 'world' is not a wholly representative world, and that his strictures on the decay of English society are not wholly justified. People outside his group, like Isherwood and Warner, had in the 1930s a strong and serious, if inevitably slightly confused, sense of moral purpose. So far was it from being true that the alleged decay of the aristocracy was bringing with it a general decay of English morale, for lack of leadership, that Mr Waugh himself might be considered (I do not know whether he would find this flattering) as an instance of the continuing energy and vitality of the English middle classes. It must be said that the impression Mr Waugh's own personality, as apart from his objective art, leaves on his readers is often (and perhaps notably and particularly in his later works) a distinctly unpleasant one. His attitude towards most of his fellow countrymen is one of sulky superiority, a superiority, moreover, based not on pride of intellect or the consciousness of possessing great gifts but rather on the accidents, adoptive rather than inherited, of his social position. Nevertheless, Mr Waugh is a sufficiently objective writer to keep the intrusions of his own personality into his novels down to a minimum; it is rather in his travel books, like those on Mexico and Ethiopia, that he lets his prejudices rip – particularly prejudice in favour of keeping the underdog, Ethiopian tribesman or Mexican peon, wherever he finds him, down. And these books tend to leave a nasty taste in the mouth, however much justice there may be in Mr Waugh's criticisms of the discomfort of life, for a person of his tastes, in backward countries and of the confusion of social arrangements in Mexico and Ethiopia.

His moral fault, here as in his novels, is a failure to respond to people outside his own class, colour, cultural background, as persons: a tendency to nag at them for not being Englishmen of the upper middle class, which, after all, they have had no opportunity of being: in a word, a lack of imagination, outside the narrow circle he is at home in, and a lack of charity. I think that possibly Mr Waugh has more of the real gifts of the novelist, more of the potentialities of a major novelist, than any other of the writers I have mentioned in this section, except possibly Mr Isherwood. But all these others have something that he lacks, a coherent attitude towards, if not a coherent philosophy of, life. He is not in any sense, himself, coherent. He is rather the bellicose and irate person who thinks it enough in life to stand by his friends and stick up for his beliefs, while keeping up a stiff and suspicious attitude towards all outsiders. This is quite adequate, no doubt, as a practical personal attitude, but it is inadequate as the attitude of a novelist; for a novelist ought to have a quite general sympathy with, and a quite general understanding of, human nature. Probably, however, Mr Waugh writes novels as well as they can be written on a basis of fierce, unreasoned admiration and equally fierce, unreasoned dislike.

A writer who had a great deal in common with Mr Waugh, in a drier and more bilious vein, was Mr Anthony Powell. At his most satirical, Mr Waugh has always some characters with whom we are invited more or less to identify ourselves; and others, like Captain Grimes, who may be both ludicrous and deplorable, but with whom we feel a sneaking sympathy. In his earlier work at least Mr Waugh cannot help conveying the feeling that life, in spite of everything, is great fun. Mr Powell covers a similar scene and castigates similar follies; but his characters tend to be uniformly unpleasant. In a novel like *Agents and Patients*, he harks back to the Jonsonian comedy of humours, the agents are rogues and the patients fools, and he makes us abhor both of them alike. At the most, he will sometimes make one of his characters pitiable, like the poor old gentleman in *From A View to a Death* who has the perverse but innocent eccentricity of dressing himself, in his wife's absence, in her clothes; its discovery leads to what, in another context, would be called tragedy. The skilled economy of style, the sour accuracy of observation, and the ingenious farcical inventiveness displayed in these early novels makes them good reading; but they do express a peculiarly negative attitude. Since the end of the war, Mr Powell has published two instalments of a longer novel in a rather different vein, a broader study of English social life. The first of these, *A Question of Upbringing*, is notable for the skill with which it handles two subjects that lend themselves easily to lush romanticism or to easy farce, public school and university life. The broader theme, however, is that of social demarcation. The three schoolboys, in whose study the story begins, represent three broad divisions of the English middle classes. The narrator represents, in a sense, the norm, the type of the English professional classes. A wealthier but flashier young friend, who does not go to a university, represents the commercial classes. And another friend, superficially charming but growingly ruthless, who goes to a university but does not find it necessary to take a degree, represents power and wealth. The three boys, who in the beginning seemed very like each other, by the end have each found their own quite separate places. And a comic school misfit is struggling to find his. I have heard Mr Powell's technique, in this new work, described as that of a 'dehydrated Proust.' The phrase pays proper tribute to his skill in working out large general implications from small incidents; and also to a dryness of sympathy and a power of compression which are not typically Proustian at all. His gift remains primarily that of a satirist, and his comic vision still depends chiefly on intelligent dislike. But there is perhaps implied, at least, in this later novel a more firm criticism of hardness of heart than was obvious in the earlier ones. The portraits of misfits, of the awkward or the self-assertive, are as finely balanced as ever, but if the scales were to tip it would perhaps now be on the side of pity rather than on that of contempt.

Section 6: The Last Ten Years

So far, taking the history of the English novel in periods of roughly ten years from the beginning of the century, we have been able to trace out a fairly clear and consistent pattern of development. It is not so easy to do this for the last ten years. Everything is too near us, it is hard to get the decade into perspective, and to see what names really stand out. These ten years also have been years of hurry and confusion for the writer as for other people. There were five years of war in which Great Britain was fighting, not only for the liberties of Europe and the traditional decencies of civilised life, but, at the beginning at least, for her very existence. The writer, like everybody else, was caught up in the struggle. Young writers were fighting in the ranks: older ones often had official jobs of one sort or another that prevented them from concentrating on creative work even if, in a time of national crisis, they had wished to do so. The end of the war, moreover, did not really bring with it that period of relaxation and relief which the end of the First World War had brought, at least for the intellectual. The English writer, the young writer, particularly, with his way to make, faced the same drab practical problems that confronted his fellow subjects. There was a housing shortage. That 'room of one's own,' which Virginia Woolf saw as essential to the protection of the writer's creative sensibility, was something almost impossible to obtain. The young writer just out of the army either would have to share a flat with his family or with some group of wartime friends, with whom he would club together to pay the rent. The publishers to whom he looked to encourage him were friendly but themselves handicapped by shortage of paper and shortage of staff. A book might be accepted in 1945 but not published, through one technical hitch after another, till 1947 or 1948. And if there were difficulties, there were also distractions: the new and fascinating world of literary London to be explored, 'contacts' to be made that might at some remote time prove useful but more immediately proved to be seductive time-wasters. There was the sense of freedom from army discipline to be enjoyed, and the old acquaintances to renew, the drinks, the parties. Life on this wide sociable basis can become a routine. Years may pass before the young writer realises that he is not so young as he was, that chances are slipping past him: and that on the long book which he imagined writing in the war years he has done no fundamental work at all.

Perhaps a larger obstacle, however, to the new young writers getting on with their work, was the continuing state of international tension. The young writer was often emotionally and physically exhausted by his years of war service. He wanted to look forward to long years of peace, in which he could concentrate on refining his talent and deepening his insight; but the dark and ominous clouds which overhung the European sky warned him that perhaps he was being granted only an interval, only an extended furlough, of pleasure and repose. Thus it might seem to a superficial observer that many promising young talents in England, that announced themselves in the war years, have in the last few years of peace gradually dissipated themselves over too wide a social surface. But that judgment would, indeed, be superficial. As Mr Ernest Hemingway says in the preface to his collected short stories, the writer cannot be spending all his time sharpening his tools: he must take a holiday from the problems of writing sometimes to receive the impact of life. The writer ought not to expect 'experience' to be immediately and crudely usable: but it would be a mistake to think that, in the writer who, whatever the discouragements, refuses to desert his vocation, experience is ever wasted. It sums itself up, at some time or another, in a significant shape.

How then is it likely that the experience of the younger generation of English writers in the last ten years will ultimately sum itself up? During the first five years of the past decade they have to adapt themselves to the ways of service life in strange countries: during the second five years to London literary life. They have cultivated the arts of friendship, but sometimes at the expense of solitude and awareness of perspective. They have not found it easy, in the French sense, to 'commit' themselves to some single view of life that would enable them to sift and co-ordinate multifarious impressions. Most of them cannot any longer accept the simple Marxist thesis which satisfied, for a short time, their predecessors in the 1930s. They have acquired a perhaps at first reluctant but now very genuine respect for the idea of tradition: more particularly, having seen the opposites of these in the outer world during their war years, for the traditional British emphasis on the value of tolerance, of good will, of social diversity and contrast, of rooted local habit and custom. Nevertheless, at the same time these young writers feel a growing need for some universal faith which will unite a divided and agonised world. For most of them, it is impossible to turn, as some of their elders have turned, to a simple orthodox religious faith and to the type of Toryism, based on the profound speculations of Edmund Burke, which sees in existing institutions and actually operative traditions a wisdom far deeper than that of the critical, self-conscious, rational individual: the wisdom of society itself.

For, in spite of all the fascination of Burke's thought, modern great societies cannot be thought of as developing themselves through unconscious instinct, as a great tree grows and puts out, year after year, its leaves. They seem to resemble, far more, sleep-walkers lurching disastrously through the dark. At the same time, where some genuine organic tradition still persists, it is something to be cherished: but for the over-individualised life of great cities, for what Dr Alex Comfort calls the 'telephone exchange society,' it does seem that we can no longer rely on wisdom springing from popular roots and from imitation of popular heroes, and that if we want to improve this society, to put new life into it, we must to some extent at least plan this improvement on the basis of considerations of abstract reason; yet what has been planned has never the natural, the rich and leafy, life of what has grown.

Thus it is the fate of the young writer to-day to cling to what elements of style, of tradition, of formed and stable manners that he can find in the bewilderingly fragmented world around while at the same time feeling that one of his duties is to offer what advice, what leadership he can to that much larger section of society which, at a first glance at least, seems to be almost totally lacking in manners, tradition, and style. Thus the young writer may tend to be exclusive and selective in his personal life, though in his theory of what a writer should be he probably stands for an all-embracing sympathy; similarly he may live chiefly on the culture of the past, while believing chiefly in the popular education of the future. But though he clings to this 'forward-looking' attitude which is something inherited by everyone brought up in the liberal tradition, more fundamentally, if less consciously, the recurrent disasters of history in this century may have implanted in him a profound but not openly admitted scepticism about the possibility of improving, in any permanent way, the basis and the constitution of human society. He may feel that in reality all one can do is to spread what happiness one can among the immediate circles of one's friends; to avoid adopting any attitudes or policies which are likely to be publicly harmful; and to purify one's own will and discipline one's appetites and desires. Our typical young writer of the last ten years is thus being driven in many cases from a secular to a religious view of life, and yet his whole intellectual training, which has probably been entirely secular, tends to make it impossible for him to formulate these religious intuitions of his in a coherent or rational way, or to make any outward act of faith and acceptance.

Our young writer, therefore, in his typical case, is a humanitarian agnostic, who wishes to acknowledge the element of goodness and truth, or at the very least the element of vitality, in all existing religions, philosophies, and attitudes. This general sympathy with the human predicament, and its contrasting modes of expressing itself, though a noble and admirable thing in itself, makes it difficult, on the other hand, for him to formulate his own distinctive point of view. Thus we can consider the past ten years, as they have affected him, as a period of adaptation and improvisation, a period arousing in him a deep inner uneasiness, which is nevertheless in its way an expression of goodwill. In theological terms, our young writer has to walk on a tight-rope between the gulfs of presumption and despair. He finds it hard to see any clear and happy way out of the tangles and nets in which our world to-day has trapped itself: yet he must refuse merely to throw up his hands, must refuse merely to say that evil has come and worse must happen, and the worst remains behind. A stoical indifference is no answer to our problems; there must be an active willingness to help; but on the other hand it is presumptuous to suppose that our efforts to help will have any very large or tangible result, or that we may not often be mistaken in our choice of what we think a good cause to support. One of the arguments, in fact, against the fashionable French doctrine of the writer's 'commitment' is that it is presumptuous in this sense, it assumes for the writer a kind of pontifical infallibility. But it is possible for a man to be imprudent in his moral and political choices, and mistaken in his view of the ultimate nature of the universe, and yet to be a good man and act virtuously, within the limits of human nature; for we judge morality by intentions, not by results.

The very imprecision of language which marks much verse and prose by young writers in the last ten years, if one compares it with the sharp and definite and sometimes no doubt rather jejune notions of the 1930s, reflects this new comprehensiveness and charity in the young writer's approach but at the same time this diffident, veering uncertainty of attitude. Perhaps no generation of writers has had to reconcile in the inner self a greater number of contradictory stresses, of tugs in opposite directions, than our own. In the end, if the contradictory stresses have not torn him apart, the young writer probably to-day has arrived at the position of rejecting any idea of wholesale revolution, and of accepting the link with the past, accepting the validity of tradition: but the idea of tradition, accepted after these refined agonies and these deep soul-searchings, is something quite different from tradition accepted as an unquestioned and unexamined code. Thus an air of uneasiness and hesitation seems to me to hang over much of the best writing of the last ten years: and the unity of tone in that writing seems not to depend upon any clearly formulated schemes of what must be done, and what must not be done, in the world to-day, but rather on an anxious goodwill.

Thus if much of the best writing of the 1930s was based on a clear scheme of notions; and much of the best writing of the 1920s on the proud self-assertion of the individual sensibility; some of the best novels and stories of the last ten years, on the other hand, are not based on either of these things, but rather on a clinging to what seems in human life, in a shifting and dangerous world, centrally and lastingly important.

This idea is expressed with wonderful elegance, and illustrated with striking skill, in a long short story by Miss Rosamond Lehmann, which appeared in print in the early years of the war, called *The Red-Haired Miss Daintreys*. The first few paragraphs of this story are a disquisition on the novel in general, in which Miss Lehmann says that she is very distrustful of novelists who desire to illustrate a general theme and who therefore plan out the development of their novels, in too abstract a fashion, in advance. She would have more confidence in the novelist who did not quite know what he was setting out to do but merely said, 'I want to write about some people.' Our centrally and lastingly important experiences, she feels, are experiences of intimate and affectionate response to other people, and more than that, of imaginative response: it is from such experiences that truly creative writing springs. The experiences, and the feelings that have gathered round them, are what engage the writer's conscious attention: the abstract theme, on the other hand, emerges without the writer being at first consciously aware of it.

Miss Lehmann's own novels illustrate this conception. One feels that they are based not on abstract ideas but on a varied and sensitive personal experience, which has given Miss Lehmann a deep understanding of English life. One of the best novels of the last ten years is her *The Ballad and the Source*, based on the contrast between a young girl's impression, a very favourable and romantic impression, of an older woman, and the rather grim truth about this older woman's life. The child's impression is as it were the 'ballad,' like some beautiful Scottish Border ballad based on an incident that may have been cruel and sinister enough in actual fact, but which has been made beautiful by the passing of time, the dimming of memory, and the charity of the folk imagination: and the actual facts about the older woman's life are the 'source,' like the raid or the killing, hateful in itself, which in later years the balladist is going to turn into an heroic tale. What Miss Lehmann very rightly insists on is that not only the 'source' but also the 'ballad' has its own kind of validity; and that the kind of literary 'realism' which leaves out entirely the noble fantasies we weave round other people, and the unreasonably high expectations that we form about their characters, impoverishes the experience of actual life. In all Miss Lehmann's novels, she is vividly aware of the 'glamour' of life, of the personal charm and delightfulness of people who, from a strict moral point of view, may not be very soundly based. For there is a point up to which pretences, if they are carried off with enough style, are valid. The charm and the glamour have their own reality, the superficial brilliant impression that people make on us has its own reality: if not, very often, the reality of what we take to go with it. When people's manners are more engaging than their characters, we are not to dismiss the manners as mere hypocrisy; but to think of them often as representing a genuine ideal, at which people do aim, though in general they tragically fail to achieve it. Miss Lehmann presents this sort of situation, usually, through the fresh and expectant sensibility of some young woman, her heroine; and if this heroine is to be continually disappointed, because her vitality and her imagination always pitch her expectations too high, nevertheless the vitality is perennial, and when we meet her as an older and more experienced woman – as in *The Weather in the Streets*, a beautiful novel about love – she will not have dried up and gone dead but will still be riding the waves with careless zest and risking the final shock, which never comes, against the harsh rocks of the shore.

Miss Lehmann thus carries on to some extent the tradition of Virginia Woolf, in her receptiveness to the poetry of what is transitory and pungent. Though she writes very well, she has not Mrs Woolf's distinction of style; but, on the other hand, just because we do not notice the sentences and paragraphs so much, perhaps we find it easier to get lost in the story: and the story does not tend to break itself up, as it does so often in Mrs Woolf, into a series of sharp, separate impressions. Miss Lehmann in fact can tell a story, in the ordinary crude sense of 'story,' in a more gripping and exciting way than Mrs Woolf could or probably wanted to. She has something of the roominess, the readiness to gather everything in and find a place for it, of the Victorian novelists: I do not know whether one could claim that she is a major figure, but she is certainly one of the contemporary English novelists from whom I myself in recent years have derived most pleasure.

Miss Elizabeth Bowen is a novelist who has something in common with Miss Lehmann. The world that they are both at home in is a world with traditions of space and privilege – perhaps, if one is making fine distinctions, 'upper class' in Miss Bowen's case, 'upper middle class' in Miss Lehmann's – and they both have a story to tell, and tell it on the whole in what strikes the ordinary reader as a 'sound, old-fashioned way': the interest in experiment showing itself rather in the shaping of paragraphs and sentences, the freshening up of the novelist's language, than in the structure of the book as a whole. Miss Bowen's most recent novel, her first in ten years, published a year or two ago, is called *The Heat of the Day*. It is a study of London life during the war, in the days of the great German air raids, and it evokes the tense, exalted atmosphere of that period better than any other book I know. Its story is what might seem an almost melodramatic one, of a woman (a gentlewoman, a 'lady' in the old sense) who discovers that her lover is a traitor and who is blackmailed by a government secret agent, who offers to spare the lover, if, as a reward, the lady will 'yield herself' to him. But on this harsh and what might seem this rather flashy framework, Miss Bowen has erected a living structure of words which allows us to grasp, not only a particular scene at a particular time, but a general pattern running through English life. No character in the novel (and this helps Miss Bowen to avoid real melodrama) is made wholly hateful. We are shown enough of the unhappy family background of Robert, the traitor, to realise that what has led him into a terrible and fatal course of action is no real evil will but rather a disgust at what he conceives (wrongly, but given his awful family, excusably) to be the purely commercial, purely materialistic, purely sordid and empty atmosphere of English life. Even for the government secret agent, who appears both to be neglecting his duty and to be making a most caddish use of his power, we feel sorry. He is the kind of man who has efficiency without personality, usefulness without joy. Nobody will ever love him, he will never be happy in any personal relationship; even as a menace to the heroine's happiness, he is queerly without colour or impact. Robert, the unfortunate hero (in spite of his treachery he is in a sense the hero) of the book saves the situation by committing suicide. Out of a kind of pity, the heroine is still willing to let the secret agent spend the night with her; but love was what he wanted, and love, he now realises, he will never get, so he retreats back into the drab everyday danger and routine of his life. The heroine herself is one of the most attractive characters in recent English fiction, a person whose traditional kindness and decency is bewildered by the queer inner twistedness of the two men she has to deal with but who, nevertheless, has enough magnanimity and charity to reach out towards them and try to understand them. And there is one untwisted male in the book. The portrait of the heroine's son (for she is not a young flighty creature, but a mature woman in her forties, with a son in the army) is a wonderfully vivid and attractive portrait, not in the least romanticised or sentimentalised, of the best type of young Englishman; he embodies, in a rather sad and troubled story, the spirit of hope.

While we are dealing with female novelists, one, in particular, should not be overlooked. Miss I. Compton Burnett has been writing for a long time, but though her sinister and compelling imagination has always fascinated a small group of admirers it is perhaps only in the last ten years that she has drawn the wider public into her circle. It is hard, however, to think of her as typical of any specific decade. The setting of her stories is more often than not a large country house in a period that suggests, but very vaguely, the later Victorian age; and the characters are usually members of a large and painfully ingrown family. But the outer world does not really impinge; however unbearably tense the family situation may become none of Miss Compton Burnett's characters ever really considers the obvious solution of leaving home and earning a living. The younger members of the family depend upon and resent their elders. Either the father or the mother is usually a tyrant and the parent who is not a tyrant is usually something of a weakling and a fool. The motive most profoundly at work in all members of the group is a lust for power. They exist to torment, to dominate each other, or at the very least to undermine each other with witty criticisms; but this aggressive instinct, their main drive, is civilised by a convention, recalling that of French classical tragedy, which forces them always to express themselves with extreme artificial politeness. It is in this polished dialogue that the stories are mainly told. The tension usually leads to some central episode of crime: the poisoning of a mother by her son, the exposure of an invalid to the night air so that she dies, at the least the breaking of a heart and the destruction of a will. But the criminals do not suffer the direct consequences of their acts, and even the infrequent revelation of their crimes does not disturb the formal politeness of the dialogue. The son announces at table that he has poisoned his mother, the remark is civilly ignored as evidence of hysteria, and conversation goes on as usual. In other stories, the criminal even more fully gets what he or she wants. Miss Compton Burnett appeals, in fact, to two separate tastes at the same time; that for melodrama, and that for high comedy; she may also appeal, and that is why I have described her power as sinister, to something in us that enjoys seeing wickedness triumph. The simplest way of describing her stories is as Victorian thrillers, such as might have been invented by Miss Braddon, conceived and presented in terms of comic artifice, such as might have appealed to George Meredith. Her more fervent admirers are mistaken, however, I feel, when they compare her to Jane Austen. Miss Austen's world was fundamentally wholesome. Miss Compton Burnett's is not. Apart from her children, who have a spoiled precocious charm, those of her characters who are not actively evil tend to be passively selfish and indolent; nobody is positively good. All her characters are engaged in an incessant competition of petty self-assertion, none has any general interests or principles, few any useful occupation. Their motives, too, seem fundamentally disproportionate to the narrow circle in which they have to act: Miss Compton Burnett makes her people fascinating while one is reading, but in real life their equivalents would seem self-important bores. The emotional ingrowing of large families, with its resultant horrors, is no doubt a perfectly legitimate theme; but because they are not set against a wider world, Miss Compton Burnett's people seem to lack the stature for tragedy. Their intensity and violence seem overloaded; such prizes as are open to them are not worth all that dust and heat. Their minds are subtle, but the matter the minds have to play with crude. And the artificiality of the dialogue, which does become wearing in the end (it is impossible to read two of Miss Compton Burnett's novels in succession, just as one cannot eat pigeon on two successive days), suggests that not only they but their creator is fighting a losing battle with fundamental tedium. The stories grip, at reasonably intermittent readings; they do not enrich our sense of positive life; and as a commentary on what frustrates life they are archaic. They have, also, that faint smell of evil about them. They nevertheless remain distinguished minor works of art – evoking a perhaps fortunately vanished past with elegance, nostalgia, and hatred.

One can say that both Miss Lehmann and Miss Bowen mark a certain return, in English fiction, to traditionalism. For ten, or twenty, or thirty years, some of the best novelists had been consciously rejecting tradition. In a period of stress like our own, these two brilliant women, with a woman's intuition, realise that if tradition is not something to be blindly accepted, it is not to be blindly rejected either; it is something of which the best elements must be grasped at and preserved – or it is a kind of continuing life in the community, that must be kept healthy and alert. There is a great strain of sadness in the novels of both of them, but nevertheless there is a definite note of hopefulness. Both realise that human creatures, weak and veering as they are, are capable of happiness, of loyalty, of at once showing sympathy with those who have strayed from the path of honour and strictly preserving honour themselves. Thus questions of principle, which a male novelist like Aldous Huxley would argue about, blunt-fingeredly, in an abstract fashion, they feel immediately through a kind of fineness of moral sensibility.

One often does feel that something like this is a basic difference between the temperaments of male and female writers. The male writer tends to stand back from life, to abstract from experience, to consider the business of living as a series of discrete 'problems,' each to be solved, as it crops up, by intellectual means. He looks on life rather as the administrator of an office does, the various tasks he has to deal with neatly separated in different files. Woman, on the other hand, even to-day remains a more natural and organic creature. The running of a household cannot be so tidy and abstract a thing as the running of an office, it is not a matter of solving separate and unconnected 'problems,' it is a matter of embracing and enjoying the branching continuities of life; a meal has to be cooked, a room to be made tidy, a letter to be written, a telephone call to be made, a visitor has dropped in who must be talked to, there are flowers to arrange in a bowl, and while the woman is arranging them she looks out of the window and wonders where her neighbour, Mrs Smith, is going to, walking so briskly on a rainy afternoon. Thus where the life of the male in our day tends to be compartmented off, work, home, pleasure, not one of these compartments really impacting on another, for the woman work and home and pleasure are a single organic complex. She does not separate herself tidily out from herself; she reaches out to life rather at several levels, or in several directions at once. Thus writing by women in our days often tends to have a warmth and richness, a particular charm of its own, which writing by men lacks.

THE LAST TEN YEARS

The male attitude as contrasted with the female attitude in our times can be seen very well exemplified in the very popular novels of Nigel Balchin. These have sold very well, and films have been made out of some of them, but the attitude of literary critics towards them has been, I think, a trifle cagy. They have that rather charmless efficiency which is so typical, as I have been saying, of the life to-day of the administrative male. They tend to be studies of a man who is doing a job, and doing it well, but whose life lacks the richness that comes from having settled roots and satisfying habits that he can fall back upon; they are studies, one might say, in a kind of uncushioned integrity. The two best known of Mr Balchin's novels are *The Small Back Room* and *Mine Own Executioner*. *The Small Back Room* is a story about scientists during the late war, engaged in experimental war work – hence the title, for these research experts used to be slangily described as 'the back-room boys.' It is also a story of the personal rivalries, the jockeyings for positions, the pullings of wires that seem unfortunately (side by side, of course, with much hard work and much selfless devotion) to be inseparable from the patterns of war-time temporary administration, and perhaps inseparable from the patterns of administration in general. Mr Balchin himself has been a high administrator and is a distinguished scientist, so he knows the world he is talking about inside out. At the same time, it is a criticism of his work that he tends rather to romanticise that world, and finds it hard to imagine any other one. The theme of many of his novels tends to be the old one, 'himself he could not save.' His heroes are men who inspire affection and respect in others, who get necessary and sometimes dangerous jobs efficiently done, but who suffer from a gnawing sense of inner emptiness that puts personal happiness, or even self-esteem, for ever out of their reach.

The hero of *The Small Back Room* is a research expert with a crippled foot. This causes him great pain; he can soothe the pain by drinking whisky, but whisky makes him quarrelsome. He wants simply to get ahead with his job, and he is impatient of the pattern of intrigue and wire-pulling going on around him. His ideas, which are sound and good ideas, about how his particular department should be run, are continually thwarted because he has not the art of self-advertisement, of putting himself over. At the end of the story, he has an opportunity to regain his self-respect by doing a very dangerous job – taking to pieces an unexploded bomb of a new pattern which, if he makes any mistake, will blow up and kill him. He shows the greatest courage and skill in carrying out this task, but, handicapped by his crippled foot and the pain it is causing him, needs some help at the very last stage. So, though everybody praises him, he is still left with the inner feeling of failure.

Mine Own Executioner is a story about a very similar type of man, this time a psychiatrist, who is able to give real help to others, but not to solve the emotional problems of his own life – problems which lead him to nag at his devoted wife, and to indulge in silly flirtations. Partly because the psychiatrist is too much preoccupied with his own personal problems, a patient of his – an ex-R.A.F. man whose psychosis has been immediately induced by terrible war experiences but has its deeper roots in his childhood – commits a murder and then commits suicide. Again, as in *The Small Back Room*, the hero shows great bravery towards the end of the story: by clinging on a roof, alone and unarmed, to reason with the murderer, who has a pistol. At the inquest on the murderer, the coroner wants to put the blame on the psychiatrist (who is not a qualified medical man), but his friends defend him, and he is exonerated; nevertheless he does feel in his heart that with more care and devotion on his part the tragedy might have been averted. He has a deep sense of inner failure, but he still has a job to do, and he gets on with it. The moral, in a sense, of both these novels is that to-day it is very difficult for an intelligent man to be happy or settled in himself but that he can do useful, practical work in the world.

This is an admirable moral, in so far as it goes, a moral in tune with the best traditions of English puritanism: at the same time this very puritanism, this failure or unwillingness to imagine conditions of stable happiness, this lack of any feeling for the everyday poetry of life, gives Mr Balchin's novels a notable thinness of texture if one compares them to Miss Lehmann's or Miss Bowen's. He is a typical example of the male administrative mind that I have been talking about, that sees life as just one problem after another. He does not raise the question of what it is in life that makes it worth our while to go on solving these problems, or of at what moment the kind of strained, noble conscientiousness he describes would merely crack up. None of Mr Balchin's heroes actually *has* a nervous break-down, but they all seem to me (like certain admirable administrative types that one knows in real life) to be at least headed that way. Or the alternative to the breakdown might be a certain inner slackening off, a relapsing into routine – one also knows examples of that in real life. Thus there seems to me to be a slight element of sentimentality in both these stories in that they tend to treat as a possible permanent and stable poise something which one knows not to be so; it is rather as if, in a cruder kind of story, the hero were permanently 'keeping a stiff upper lip.' The sentimentality invades the style. Mr Balchin's novels tend to be written in the first person, and the heroes, as I say, are conceived as diffident and self-torturing men, unaware of their own exceptional worth: but this conception of them as exceptional, as well as the superficial diffidence, tends to invade the writing, so one feels in the note of the heroes' descriptions of their own doings an unconscious touch of self-admiration, and in the frequent patches of 'noble' self-pity something just a little mawkish. The reader tends to project himself into, and identify himself with, Mr Balchin's heroes at a level somewhere below that of critical observation.... Nevertheless, as crisp, readable narratives, as giving a detailed and accurate picture of one side, at least, of modern life, Mr Balchin's books are well worth reading.

One novelist of the 1940s deserves special attention as carrying on, more definitely than any of his contemporaries, the tradition of the novel as a comic or satirical criticism of manners. Mr Angus Wilson is an official in the Reading Room of the British Museum, a point of vantage which must present him with a fascinating view of the eccentricities of scholars; more broadly, it must offer him a useful cross-section of the more literate English public generally. Few people with intellectual interests in Great Britain have not used the reading room at one time or another, and within its more coherent limits it resembles a little one of these great London railway stations where, if you wait long enough, you will see everybody you know. Acquaintance with the melancholy of those to whom reading is an addiction, the indifference to time of enthusiasts, the burrowing persistence of cranks, has probably sharpened Mr Wilson's sense of the individual as a type. He is one of the few contemporary novelists who, without forgetting their social roots, tends to see people as 'characters' almost in the Dickensian sense. He has a firm grasp also of what at a first glance appear to be totally disparate social scenes: the smugness of a Scottish university, the dignity and decay of an English country house, the sodden bonhomie of a flashy London night-club, the stiff self-righteousness of progressive opinions in the suburbs, the wanton extravagance of a wealthy hostess in Mayfair, all seem equally familiar to him. He isolates the essence of such atmospheres, again in a rather Dickensian way, by bold flat caricature and by concentration on the self-betraying trick of speech; and with this there sometimes goes an extravagant Dickensian fantasy, and a touch of Dickensian sentiment, particularly about the decent and inarticulate young. Mr Wilson has also something of what Bagehot, too contemptuously, dismissed as Dickens's 'sentimental radicalism'; he sees cold and narrow, or arrogantly selfish, social sympathies as symptoms of some basic inadequacy in personal generosity; but he can also sketch in, with sardonic objectiveness, the dry and doctrinaire fanaticism of the Left.

Mr Wilson is perhaps at his best in his two volumes of short stories, *The Wrong Set* and *These Darling Dodos*. His one novel, *Hemlock and After*, shows both the qualities and limitations of a writer, whose gift is for the vivid isolated episode, in working out a coherent sustained narrative. Page for page, chapter for chapter, *Hemlock and After* is immensely more lively than the ordinary novel; the critical question is about its total effect. Yet it has a very important general theme. In the character of his hero, Mr Wilson tackles the problem, centrally significant for our day, of the liberal humanist (probably all that is nicest in us is a hangover from the liberalism of the last century) who is suddenly and reluctantly confronted both with the sense of the transcendent, or the absolute, and the fact of evil. The hero, a distinguished writer, who, though a married man with children now adult, has allowed play to his homosexual impulses for the sake of 'the full life' suddenly finds that far more sinister urges than he imagined, including an urge towards cruelty, underlie his mainly sentimental fondness for the company of handsome and clever young men; and while he is recovering from this shock about his own nature, he discovers also that his tolerance has abrupt limitations when it comes to the abnormality of others. He finds himself morally impelled to expose, and thus to drive to suicide, an acquaintance who has been corrupting immature girls. The hero's state can be regarded from different points of view as one of disintegration or of self-discovery. Is his new road to self-completion mainly, after all, just the old road to hell? Yet after his death – a death rather imposed on the book, for the sake of a tidy ending – there is a suggestion that his painful and sometimes apparently cruel honesty may bear good fruit in the lives of others. The 'moral' of the book may be not that he was 'wrong from the start' but that no attitudes are absolutely right and that his, dangerous, and difficult to sustain though they were, represented a higher though therefore more painful and unstable level of integration than most people's. If he has always been an unsettling influence is that not because, like Socrates of whom the title reminds us, he has been a dangerously honest man – refusing to accept the Platonic 'noble lie,' the middle-class English decent pretence, or the revived myths of fashionable religion and politics?

Mr Wilson's characters in this novel, other than the hero, are of a rich variety of type and treatment: the cosy, vulgar, wicked procuress who seems to have stepped out of some unwritten, because unprintable, Victorian masterpiece: the sensitive, neurotic, saintly lady who belongs to the world of Virginia Woolf: the good adolescent boy who might have stepped out of a franker Talbot Baines Read story about the dangers of London life, and the bad one who belongs to the most mocking and scabrous tradition of picaresque romance, almost to the tradition of Petronius. The shifts of view are a danger. We jump about. The story as a whole exists at several levels that seem incongruous with each other, of perception in depth and cartoon in profile, of subtle comedy and pain explored gently juxtaposed with violent melodrama and bawdy farce. These successive projections are never quite brought into common focus. Partly, of course, this disparity of moral levels *is* an objective feature of our society. Mr Wilson knows that every household is, makes, and projects its own world, and that worlds which seem utterly separate can have odd and sinister meeting-places; *what* we are is partly *where* we are. Yet one feels that about certain fundamentals Mr Wilson has not made up his mind. His attitude to life has something in common with that of the early Aldous Huxley though the hero of *Hemlock and After* more resembles, if such a thing were possible, an English Gide. It will be interesting to see whether Mr Wilson's future development is, like Gide's, towards a scrupulous and sensitive avoidance of at least dogmatic transcendental commitments, towards what might be called a rejection of faith for religious reasons; or, like that of Mr Huxley, towards a rationalised mysticism.

Another very masculine writer, and one very much concerned (but more profoundly concerned) with the public side of life, who has produced notable books since the war is the late George Orwell. Orwell had already made a reputation before the war for novels based on personal experience, like *Burmese Days* and *Down and Out in Paris and London* and for books on social problems, like *The Road to Wigan Pier*. He belongs to a wider history than that of the novel. His fierce satirical passion allies him to Jonathan Swift: his blunt, harsh honesty and passionate defence of the underdog, to William Cobbett. Orwell is a writer in a well-known tradition in England, that of the gentleman-radical. Educated at Eton, he was not a man of the people by birth: he had knocked about the world in various jobs, as a police officer in Burma among other things, and had known much of the grimness of the life of the poor and also of the humour and sturdiness of it. Unlike so many radical critics of social arrangements in the years between the wars, he had remained a passionate lover of England, of the English people even in their earthiness and limitations, of everything that struck him as true and vital in the English tradition. The poet Roy Campbell, who fought for General Franco in the Spanish Civil War, where Orwell fought on the other side, nevertheless cherished a warm admiration for him and has described him in a recent article as a 'valiant, generous heart.' Orwell died in 1949 when only in his early forties: the general hardship of his life, and the injuries he had suffered in Spain, had worn down a sturdy constitution. He died of tuberculosis; and he wrote his last novel, the terrifying *1984*, on a remote island to the west of Scotland, when, if he had obeyed his doctors, he should have been taking life easy in a Swiss sanatorium. He never spared himself, took life hard, was always a fighter; and if he had not an immediate social or political cause to fight for, he would fight his own bodily weakness.

Orwell's passionate love for the English common people is shown, outside his novels, in books like *The Road to Wigan Pier*, published before the last war, and *The Lion and the Unicorn*, published during it. What is remarkable about these books is their lack both of sentimentality and snobbery. He writes about the actual culture of the working classes – the culture that reflects itself in boys' twopenny magazines and in vulgar comic postcards, in fish and chip shops, in eel bars and whelk stalls, in miners' choirs, in street corner oratory – without trying to make it out more grand and important than it is, but without any patronising tone. If the English masses are philistine, so, to some extent, is Orwell philistine himself. He thinks there are more important things in the world than taste and refinement; loyalty, courage, humour, generosity being among these. He knows how drab and constricting working-class life in large industrial cities often is, and he does not grudge the working classes the garish or pathetic pleasures that sweeten it, though he wants them, too, to take a more responsible attitude towards life. His radicalism was based on a firm belief that, if they are let alone, and not deliberately misled, you can trust the instincts of the people. Though he was a firm supporter of the Labour Party, as the popular party, himself, he hated the type of long-haired, short-sighted 'progressive' who wears odd clothes, eats a vegetarian diet, combines his Socialism with all sorts of eccentric notions about art, religion, or sex, and expresses himself in a kind of bleating and superior verbiage. He distrusted doctrinaires of whatever kind: distrusted all evasion of plain fact and straight feeling, all abstract and wordy and pretentious thinking about politics. He was even something of a jingo, distrusting foreign influences, from the Left and not only from the Right, on British life. Thus he perhaps comes near to making articulate the instinctive prejudices and unformulated principles, of the ordinary English man in the street, or man in the pub, than any other contemporary writer.

His temperament was much more like that of a radical of similar temperament, on the opposite side, Roy Campbell, than like that of the Leftist poets and novelists of Auden's generation; Auden himself Orwell once described incisively and contemptuously as a 'gutless Kipling' – a coiner of slogans for which he would not be willing, when it came to the push, to make a personal stand. Thus the angry, impatient tone of Orwell's writing, though so radical in its intention, was one that might sometimes be approved by old-fashioned Tories and disliked by the more squeamish or the more sensitive of his own 'progressive' friends. He was swinging a great flail round his head, and it was as likely to knock out the supporters cheering behind him as the opponents cowering in front. This fearlessness of Orwell's, his contempt for official party-lines, made him a formidable figure: and in a wider sense it is this uncomfortable, passionate, tactless honesty of his that, as a writer, makes him significant.

The two works of fiction produced by Orwell in the years since the war were social allegories. *Animal Farm* is not only an allegory but a fable. In this story, some farm animals get tired of their servitude to men, and start a revolution to run the farm in their own way, but are betrayed by the more cunning and self-seeking of their leaders into a worse servitude. Orwell had in mind the Russian revolution of 1917 which seemed to him, after having started off with high ideals and noble hopes, to have degenerated into a hypocritical tyranny. Though *Animal Farm* is a pungent, it is a slight book, and perhaps the symbolism of the fable is unfortunate; it might be taken to mean, what was not really Orwell's intention, that just as it would be foolish for animals to rebel against human control, so, such is the innate difference between them, is it impossible for oppressed masses to rebel against ruling classes.

One cannot accept quite seriously (as one can accept, say, the big men and the little men in *Gulliver's Travels*) the idea of the rebellious animals. They are obviously, like many animals in fables, men in disguise; but on the other hand, the illusion is spoilt when real men, and not only animals, figure in the fable. In other words, *Animal Farm* does not quite hold together as an allegory: *Gulliver's Travels* can be read merely as a story, but in *Animal Farm* we have to be constantly thinking of the *meaning* of the story, in contemporary terms, to avoid noting the inconsistencies of the story as a shape in itself.

Orwell's last novel, *1984*, is on a much vaster scale, a terrible study of what the totalitarian state may, in our century, develop into, if it is given its head. Orwell describes a society in which the driving motives are hatred, fear, the lust for cruelty, and in which the ordinary citizen lives in a continual state of degradation, of terror, or of both. The society he describes has deliberately rejected all genuine and objective standards of behaviour: in particular the standards of charity, joy, truth. It is perhaps a criticism of Orwell's general conception that it is hard to see how the kind of society he describes, a society rejecting the very notion of objectivity, could persist for long. It would collapse fairly soon, deceived by its own lies, rendered stupid by its own propaganda, and robbed of nerve by its own terrorism, into some kind of barbaric decay: yet the barbaric decay, which might have the seeds of new life in it, would at least be better than the kind of perversion of civilisation that Orwell describes. Nevertheless, we have evidence enough at present to show that societies such as Orwell describes can at least establish themselves; can hold power for a considerable period; are infinitely more aggressive, during that period, than traditional civilised societies, and therefore in a position to do almost incalculable damage to traditional decencies of behaviour.

Orwell's terrible picture of the deliberate evil of which man is capable owes, perhaps, something to the famous, sinister, and very important writer of the French Revolutionary period, the Marquis de Sade. Sade had imagined the possibility of a society based, not, as most human societies so far have been based, on an imperfect good will, but on a positive lust for power for its own sake, and a positive lust for cruelty. Sade was, however, though a man of brilliant intellectual gifts, a madman: he took pleasure in imagining a society of this kind. Orwell, who is one of the bravest defenders of human decency in our age, feels, as he imagines this society, the profoundest horror. But his vision is definitely, like Sade's, a vision of evil, and in *1984* (written,

we must remember, by a dying man) that vision seems almost unredeemed by hope: Orwell sees in *1984* almost too clearly, almost
unbearably clearly, how the noblest ideas and the highest purposes
can be perverted, by the active, intelligent wickedness of a few, and
the passive stupidity of the many, to the most perverse and horrible
purposes.

When we read this terrible book we should not, however, yield
ourselves completely to despair. That would never be Orwell's intention, to crush our last hopes. We should realise rather what a very evil
thing we have to fight in our time (to fight in our own hearts, as well
as in the outer world) and we should strengthen our wills for a long
and implacable struggle. Orwell did not intend *1984*, as some critics
have thought, as an attack or a satire upon the very idea of Socialism.
He was all his life a staunch supporter of the British Labour Party; but
he differed from most political writers to-day, whether of the Left or
Right, in that he tested his political principles by his traditional feelings
for honour and decency, and not his traditional feelings for honour
and decency by his political principles. He wrote not out of any
abstract doctrine swallowed whole, and lying like lead upon his
stomach, but out of a wide, and deep, and thoroughly if painfully
digested experience of life. He loved the British common people
because he had shared their hardships in the lean years between the
wars, and knew them, with all their qualities and all their limitations
and shortcomings and positive faults. He loved personal liberty because
all his life he had fought to preserve his own intellectual and moral
independence, at whatever cost in estrangement from admirers and
friends. He loved that honest and direct comradeship of man to man
which can transcend, in the happy few who are capable of it, barriers
of nationality, colour, opinion, class. He loved courage and he loved
ordinary happiness (though he rather hated the cold and selfish pursuit
of pleasure), and he hated anything that tended to intimidate people
or make them unnecessarily miserable. So in the end he became a
fighter not for any party, or any slogan, or any theory, but for justice
and truth themselves, so constantly threatened, so persistently sapped
at, in our world. Perhaps no writer of his own generation (of the men
born, that is, in the first decade of this century) has been such a morally
impressive figure as Orwell; built on so gaunt, so haggard, and so
heroic a scale.

Younger British novelists of to-day, set against the background
of Orwell's achievement, often seem to be evading total problems:

treating selected aspects of life, rather than life as a whole. Thus the books of William Sansom or of Denton Welch, to mention only two of the younger novelists who have been very highly praised, do seem taken up with expressions of the personal view, the special sensibility, life not so much as it is, or might be, in itself, but as it looks from a particular personal perspective, seen through one pair of eyes. Denton Welch began to make his name in his 'teens with a brilliant travel book about China and went on publishing occasional stories and novels, obviously in most cases grounded in personal experience, after an accident had made him a chronic invalid. He died a year or two ago, after enduring much pain, and many periods in hospital, still a very young man. The adolescent and the invalid are in everything he writes, the adolescent's innocent and passionate simplicity of vision, the invalid's acute, painful sensibility and his hunger for distraction. Mr William Sansom, a more robust person, happily still with us, has imitated the allegorical manner of Kafka and has also written vivid sketches, impressions, 'stories' in a certain sense (but one thinks how the 'story' to-day can fade into the meditative essay or the descriptive article) based on his experience in the war in the National Fire Service and later travelling about Europe. I still remember very vividly a story of his about the National Fire Service called *The Wall*: describing how the wall of a bombed and burning house collapses while a fireman is climbing up it. It was a memorable and disturbing recreation of what, fortunately, is not a common experience. But it was a notation of that experience: not a 'story' in the sense of having a plot, or involving a clash of characters, or a development of character. Similarly, on his travels, Mr Sansom has a sharp eye for the oddly picturesque person-ality and an exceedingly vivid, if sometimes rather arbitrarily selective, perceptiveness about the visual surface of life. But one is often more aware of scenes and characters than of an 'action,' even of the anecdotal sort. Both Welch and Mr Sansom write beautiful sentences and para-graphs: both create little scenes and episodes that come painfully and vividly alive. But it is rather like flipping through somebody's snap-shot album: one feels the lack of a strong, continuing moral theme (or a theme accessible to the reader, at least, for, as with the snapshot album, a theme may be latent for the writer) that would bind the bright and beautiful fragments into some coherent whole.

One feels also in Welch and Sansom (and in certain others, less known and gifted, who may be considered as of their 'type' or their 'school') something like a fundamental lack of curiosity about the inner workings of other people. People are described as trees or flowers or other details in a landscape might be described, with a scrupulous care about their value as isolated strange objects, that are also elements in a pattern: but without a fundamental informing sympathy. What one feels lacking, in fact, in this kind of writing, as an evocation of life, is some strong habitual context of ideas or feelings; characters are seen, like fish in an aquarium, lucidly but estrangingly, through glass; the writer has no deep *rapport* with his characters; his point of view is too much that of the spectator, too little that of the participant.

This air of rather excessive 'objective detachment' (not truly objective, since the writer should be in, and aware of, the same kind of general predicaments as his characters) and this 'fragmentariness' that goes with it are, perhaps, too common in contemporary English fiction by younger writers. The unsettling circumstances of the time (let me revert here to my themes at the beginning of this section) have left many young writers not only without a 'faith' in the ambitious sense of the word, but without any very fixed and stable set of 'working principles': without even the feeling of having inherited a conventional code of behaviour which, whether or not it is 'right' by the highest standards, is at least 'moral.' It is not very good for the novelist or for any imaginative writer to have to think out too many of his basic ideas for himself (the artist and the philosopher are two opposite types of human creature) and perhaps one of the reasons for the many failures to develop of promising young writers in our age is that they cannot merely concentrate on their proper creative tasks: they have to think out and justify their own philosophies of life, their own codes of behaviour. Writers like Welch and Sansom in preserving a deliberate blankness of aspect about general values, and fundamental problems, are at least attempting to concentrate strictly on the creative writer's proper task: but then, if he is not a philosopher, he at least needs to be nourished by some philosophy, or by some complex of stable social values. The writer who because of his strict artistic conscience deliberately ignores, or for the time being sets aside, these larger problems of belief and conduct which beset us all to-day is rather like the man who, in ordinary conversation, talks in a very witty and vivid fashion but who contributes nothing to the topic which everybody else, until he came in, had been passionately discussing. This is not to say that writers should be ideologues: but it is to say that it is disturbing when one feels that they are, as it were, bouncing energetically up and down in a kind of moral vacuum.

What applies to young writers of some fame like Welch and Sansom is even more true of the more obscure and struggling young writers of my own immediate generation, writers who went through the war, who have been endeavouring in the last five years to settle down in London, carry on with their work, and at the same time earn some sort of reasonable living, and who are faced to-day with the unsettlement of a new threat of war. These grew up in childhood in a time of tension with war looming over them, spent their young manhood in far countries, have been adjusting themselves ever since to new situations and to a continuously overhanging cloudily ominous sky. This kind of tension, if prolonged over too long a period, ceases to be fruitful for creative writing. One retains one's good-will and one's persistent hope that what is wise and tender in human nature will in the long run conquer what is stupid and angry, but the nervous anxiety of our time does certainly inhibit concentration on the creation of any considerable literary work, any work on the grand scale, and it makes it hard to arrive at that working habit of life which every good writer needs.

A writer should be conscious about his writing, he should have the most intense and supple consciousness about that, but much of the rest of his life should pass as in a kind of pleasant trance or dream. He should drift about from scene to scene, from friend to friend, from conversation to conversation, simply taking things in in a quiet and calm way. All this, if he is lucky, if he is alert, if he is really a writer, will build itself up in his mind as sentences, paragraphs, pages, chapters of convincing prose. But the too rapid and too mechanically conscious and sometimes too jarringly painful changes and adjustments of our own world tend to blur and confuse all such impressions. The poet perhaps is in a different case from the novelist, and in a luckier one, he can condense and refine his impression of a place, a group, a situation into perhaps a dozen lines, but the novelist is more closely tied down to documented plausibility. He must describe how institutions work, how people look, how they talk, and if he is shifted too rapidly from scene to scene (and from hope to hope, and from assumption to assumption), his impressions are likely to lose their sharp accurate edge, and, more profoundly, it becomes difficult for him to 'connect' – to relate the moral atmosphere of one scene to the moral atmosphere of another, perhaps apparently completely discrepant. This is a great age for journalists, who can visit a country for a few weeks and skim off the cream of it in vivid and garish prose, but not such a good age for the novelist who must sink, very deep indeed, into the mind and habit of a community. Possibly, for that very reason, the novel as an art-form may be coming to an end, and what we need, perhaps, in our odd, violent, unintegrated age, is rather the exact and sensitive record of personal experience: the diary, the autobiography, the travel book, some flying joy of perception caught on the wing. It is possible to make a clear shape of the merely personal life and to reach out to other persons of similar temperament. But it looks less and less true, to-day, that the more we let our social experience mature, the clearer the shape it will take: our angles may merely become more obtuse, our perspectives muddled.

Perhaps some of the best writing of the last ten years is the hastiest writing, impressions scribbled by soldiers in army camps, on coarse paper, with blunt pencils, by the light of a candle in their tents. It is very hard to make a solid and lasting pattern of the strange confusion of our time. Nevertheless, there are in London, I think, perhaps two, or three, or four young men, among those one knows, of course (there may be very many unknowns), who have it in them some time to write the novel which will catch, without false abstraction or tendentiousness, the strange rhythm of our time, with its continual over-hanging tension, its storms, and its calm, fatalistic drift. The question is this, however: when and how will they get the odd six months of almost complete isolation and security, of frigid and exact perspective, that will enable them to write it? There is too much hurry: what Matthew Arnold called the 'strange disease of modern life' has now become the customary disease, everybody's disease, the disease regarded as a normal state of health. But if we have less to show in work from the younger men in the last ten years than in previous decades of English literary history in this century, I myself do not believe that this is due to some failure of talent, or dying away of genius, in our generation. I rather think that the pressures are too hard, and yet I have a deep faith that the passion of the writer (one of the very deepest and most persistent of all human passions) will resist somehow and surmount the pressures.

CHAPTER THREE

THE DRAMA

Section 1: The Weakness of the Victorian Age in Dramatic Literature

The nineteenth century, a century so strong and so rich in other kinds of literature, was peculiarly weak in the drama. It might be almost true to say that between Sheridan's *The School for Scandal*, written towards the end of the eighteenth century, and the early comedies of Oscar Wilde and George Bernard Shaw, there was no English working playwright who could produce acting plays that had any literary interest; and, on the other hand, there was no Englishman of letters, whether novelist or poet, who could produce plays that would have held the attention of an audience on a stage. Even as reading matter, indeed, the verse dramas of the great Romantic and Victorian poets tend to be quite the weakest part of their performance. Byron's poetic dramas, for instance, show all the worst sides of his poetic character – the hasty, careless writing, the taste for garish melodrama, the tendency to strike poses. They have nothing of the wit, the flippancy, the gay mastery of light verse which makes *Don Juan* still the only English poem of its length which can be read right through merely for entertainment and pleasure. The plays of Keats are deplorably weak imitations of the surface mannerisms of Elizabethan drama, with none of the Elizabethan drama's bite or grip. There are some plays of the Romantic period which have more intrinsic interest than those I have mentioned, for instance, Wordsworth's *The Borderers*, and Shelley's *The Cenci*. But the interest of these two plays is rather as curious, not quite edifying revelation of the poet's psychology, than as living constructions presenting real plots and life-like characters. Wordsworth's play, in fact, was a stiff study in the kind of morbid state of mind which he imagined might really result from the complete acceptance of the rationalistic and egoistic philosophy of Godwin. He wanted to show that if we do not trust our feelings, our habits and our instinctive reactions as a moral guide, we might be led by sophistical reasoning into acts of desperate wickedness.

Shelley's *The Cenci*, a finer play, was taken from an actual historical episode, too horrible and too powerful *in itself* to be artificially transmuted into anything but *superfluous* poetry. Shelley's intentions are high, but the fascination of the story of *The Cenci* is for him obviously a rather sinister and unhealthy one; and the language of his play lacks originality, it is made up of scraps of imitation from Elizabethan drama, and in imitating he has weakened and vitiated his originals. Shelley's *Prometheus Unbound*, on the other hand, is in its way a real masterpiece of original lyrical inspiration, but one cannot imagine it really being acted; it lacks the body of a real drama.

In the later poets of the nineteenth century, the poets of the Victorian Age, Browning, Tennyson, Swinburne, Matthew Arnold, even the original psychological impulse which gives some life to *The Borderers* and *The Cenci* has vanished away. The plays of all these writers are excessively, in a bad sense, 'literary.' There are imitations of Greek classical drama, like Swinburne's *Atalanta in Calydon* or Matthew Arnold's *Merope*. There are imitations of Elizabethan drama, like Swinburne's plays on Mary Stuart, or Tennyson's on Archbishop Becket, or like Browning's plays on an even wider variety of historical themes. Of all these plays it may be said that here and there they contain pages of fine writing and even of genuinely poetic imagination, but that one cannot imagine them being acted, and that their writers show, and perhaps would wish to show, no real and intimate feeling for the stage. This is even truer of the one Victorian poet, Thomas Lovell Beddoes, who in a strange and fantastic fashion did manage to create, in the Victorian age, some genuine echo of the word-magic of Elizabethan times. If you were to read an isolated page from Beddoes' plays, you would probably say this is a dramatist with the same sort of genius as Webster or Ford, or Cyril Tourneur; but when you attempt to read the whole play you find a complete lack of consistency and purpose in working out a plot, and an interest in death, in ghosts, and the romantic supernatural, which robs Beddoes of any power of imagining living characters in a possible situation.

One might say that the whole immense, deplorable Victorian 'literary' drama springs from the romantic heresy expressed in the famous essay of Charles Lamb's, that it is much better to read the plays of Shakespeare than to see them acted on the stage. The imagination of the sensitive reader – this is what lies behind Lamb's theory – can embody *Hamlet*, for instance, in a more satisfactory fashion than any actor, on any stage. But unless a dramatist writes for the stage he loses touch with the limitations of reality. It is only the awareness of an audience that keeps him, for instance, from writing speeches which are far too long, from substituting the rhetoric of ornament for that of action, and from diversifying his work with whimsies and humours which may amuse himself in his study, but which would make any audience, in any theatre, yawn its head off. Shakespeare, in fact, was misunderstood by critics like Lamb; there are many passages in his plays of what look like bad or hasty writing that do justify themselves in performance; he was an excellent and, in fact, often an unscrupulous craftsman of the theatre. His plays are not shaped on the classical model, but they have nevertheless a living shape of their own, and the danger of the romantic approach to him was that poets tended to think that dramas could be constructed out of fragmentary poetic conceits, noble isolated speeches, Elizabethan mannerisms, without having been felt in advance as wholes.

What is true of the failure of great poets in the drama is also true of the failure of such a great novelist as Henry James. James, who had been a dramatic critic, had a 'sense of theatre' and an uneasy awareness that the literary playwright would have to come to terms with the demands and the standards of the commercial theatre. But the successful commercial plays of James's own time, with which he was best acquainted, were the so-called 'well-made' melodramas of the contemporary French theatre in which actresses like Sarah Bernhardt starred. The psychology of such plays was as crude as could be; the dialogue has no literary quality; the themes had no moral validity; all one could say about them was that these plays were skilfully constructed, and gave great actors and actresses an opportunity to thrill an audience.

James's own refined and delicate talent was at the opposite extreme from this sort of crude and cynical commercialism and he observed bitterly, after the rejection of one of his own plays by a manager, that 'you cannot make a sow's ear out of a silk purse.' Perhaps if he had not attempted to flatten, to simplify and to vulgarise his own astonishing talents to suit the demands of the theatre, he might have made more of a success on the stage. So at least the critic William Archer thought. But James had never the courage to write his plays with the same contempt for the more obtuse part of his audience as he displayed in his stories and novels. A writer like Dickens, again, had a genuine dramatic imagination, but in his amateur acting, and his public readings this imagination revealed itself as that crude sense of melo-drama which provides us with so many of the weakest, and coarsest, or least edifying passages in his novels.

Thus, just as the Victorian poets failed to produce a great tragic dramatist, so the Victorian novelists failed to produce the kind of high comedy which, in Congreve or in Sheridan, gives us a genuine criticism of society. To sum up we might say that, so far as prose comedy goes, a certain conventionality, prudishness, or smugness made it impossible for Victorian writers to produce comedy which would be a really vital criticism of current manners and ideas. One centrally important subject to the comic dramatist, the relations of the sexes, was more or less taboo in the Victorian age. In the novels of the time, the young women tend to be extremely innocent and marriage for most of them is regarded as the end of their emotional lives. Anything outside marriage is regarded as 'vice,' an occasion for regretful moralis-ings, or as 'scandal' which may bring about the ruin of family life and these subjects are treated by Victorian novelists melodramatically. More serious contemporary subjects, like the vexed question of women's independence, are not treated at all.

This explains the extraordinary and hysterical rage with which the dramas of the great Scandinavian, Henrik Ibsen, were received when they were first presented on the London stage. No dramatist could be more profoundly moral than Ibsen is, but it shocked the London critics very much that, for instance, in *A Doll's House* Nora, the heroine, leaves her husband, a dull domineering husband, who seeks to crush her personality and keep her permanently in a childlike, irresponsible state, and that Ibsen obviously approves of the step Nora is taking.

One might say that the drama began to revive again when drama-tists claimed the right, as Ibsen claimed the right, to discuss serious social and moral problems in a calm, sensible way. That was one important factor in its revival. The other was the rather *blasé*, cynical, *fin de siècle* atmosphere of the 1890s, which allowed men like Oscar Wilde, without perhaps seriously questioning the moral assumptions of the great Victorian Age, to treat them with a certain frivolity, make polite fun of them. The element of mockery had come back to the stage rather earlier than Wilde with the comic operas of Gilbert and Sullivan. Rather hard-hitting satire was accepted in these comic operas because it was disguised as burlesque or fantasy, because these two men of genius appealed to the insatiable Victorian appetite for nonsense –

for the sort of comic dream-literature provided also by Lewis Carroll or by Edward Lear. Wilde's own very best comedy, *The Importance of Being Earnest*, which is, as far as its construction goes, a typical late-Victorian farce, is deliberately nonsensical in its characterisation and motivation, like *Charley's Aunt* or *The Private Secretary*. Wilde uses this farcical form, which has no literary value in itself, to express his flippant, detached, and dandified attitude towards life. The sparkle of his wit keeps the absurd thing alive, and it is still revived very frequently and with great success, on the London West End stage.

As always, when the dramatist is in a weak position, the *actor* tended to dominate the Victorian stage. It would be wrong to say that though the drama was in decay in the Victorian Age, the theatre was necessarily in decay. Out of plays with no literary value, an actor like Sir Henry Irving could construct spectacles which genuinely enthralled and terrified his audiences. The English stage under Irving had something in common in fact with the kabuki stage in Japan, in which the fine settings, the wonderful acting, and the audience's interest in, and knowledge of the stories, make up for a lack of separable literary value in the acted texts. The text was almost nothing to Irving when he acted Shakespeare; it would be drastically cut, except for his own part. It *had* to be drastically cut, for Sir Henry's manner for instance of delivering one of Hamlet's soliloquies might make it last for minutes with many pauses instead of the short time in which an Elizabethan actor, in the 'two hour traffic of his stage,' would reel it off. Sir Henry's manner of delivery quite destroyed the effect of Shakespeare's words as verse, while his manner of production distorted and truncated the plays, but his own strange, original, personal genius left the audience with an undeniable memorable experience. But he was no more memorable in Shakespeare than in trashy current plays like Bulwer Lytton's *The Lady of Lyons*, or in a worthless melodrama translated from the German, *The Bells*, in which according to all contemporary accounts he gave his most impressive performance.

Another great Victorian actor, Sir Herbert Beerbohm Tree lacked Irving's powerful stage personality, but attracted attention by the lavish scenery of his productions of Shakespeare. The time which such scenery took to mount again led to a drastic cutting of the text, but people were pleased by the feeling that no expense had been spared in honour of 'the Bard.' Thus when in the 1890s an actor like Forbes Robertson started restoring some of the scenes in *Hamlet* which had always been cut – for instance, the last scene in which Fortinbras says,

'Go bid the soldiers shoot,' and a salute is fired over the dead Hamlet's body – this seemed to critics of the time, like Bernard Shaw, and in fact was, a startling innovation. Unfortunately, perhaps, in their reaction from the reign of the actor-manager, new dramatists like Shaw went too far in the other direction, became too anxious that the dialogue by itself should make all the theatrical effect, and ignored the poetic and dramatic value of spectacle.

Thus the 1890s saw the rebirth of English prose comedy, and this was to have a prosperous fifty years in front of it. Shakespeare also began to be produced with some regard for the value of his own text, for the conditions of the Elizabethan theatre for which, after all, he had written his plays, and for the conclusions of modern Shakespearean scholarship. But the reaction against the shoddy and showy side of the Victorian theatre – a theatre which nevertheless had, as I have been trying to show, its own element of bizarre poetry – postponed the revival of a living and contemporary poetic drama in England almost till our own day.

Section 2: The Revival of the Drama in the 1890s

It is an interesting fact that the two men who brought back vitality to the English drama in the 1890s were both Irishmen. Since the eighteenth century Ireland has contributed a very high proportion of great writers, great orators, great dramatists and great poets to the English tradition. The Irish are remarkable among the peoples of the British Isles for their fluency of speech, their ready wit, and their taste for rhetoric. Shaw and Wilde, besides being famous dramatists, were famous talkers, famous social figures. They were, however, men of very different character.

Both came from that Protestant Irish Ascendancy which has on the whole contributed more men of genius to English life and literature than the Roman Catholic tradition of the Irish peasantry and working classes. Shaw however represented the Puritan side of the Anglo-Irish tradition, where Wilde was more built on the model of the swaggering and amusing Irish adventurer of old novels and plays. Wilde was a man of the world, a man of pleasure, who needed a life of ostentation and luxury and whose vanity and appetites finally landed him in disaster. He was not a deep or thorough or passionate thinker as Shaw was; his attitude to ideas was essentially a playful one. He is full of witty paradoxes, but if one attempts to arrive at his fundamental philosophy of life it seems to consist of selective borrowings from more creative thinkers, from Walter Pater, from Ruskin, from William Morris and from the famous painter Whistler. Whistler, who was as great a wit in ordinary conversation as Wilde was, accused him of 'peddling in the provinces' the ideas which he had stolen from his betters. He thought of Wilde as a kind of populariser, vulgariser, or middle-man of ideas. There is the famous story of Wilde remarking on some witticism of Whistler's, 'I wish I had said that, Jimmy,' and of Whistler replying, 'You will, Oscar, you will.'

Wilde's originality then was not so much in his thinking as in his personality, in a certain grace and impudence which enabled him to deploy his second-hand material with the most striking social effect; Yeats, another contemporary of his, and another Irishman of the same social class and religious background, said of him that he should not have been a writer, but a man of action, and certainly he aimed, not as the writer does, at the greatest depth and finish, but rather as the man of action does at the most striking immediate effect. His success both as a writer and a man was the success of the social entertainer, and it is as 'entertainment' that his plays have survived. Three of his plays, *Lady Windermere's Fan*, *An Ideal Husband*, and *A Woman of No Importance*, are built on the model of the conventional social melodramas of the time. They are given sparkle and literary interest by the flashing, if sometimes flashy, wit of the dialogue. *The Importance of Being Earnest*, on the other hand, is built on the model of the popular farce of the time. Wilde in fact took up the ordinary commercial type of play of his day, dressed it up with a new smartness and elegance so that clever people could enjoy its trite situations or its mechanical absurdities and not lose their self-respect. He is not necessarily to be blamed or reproved for this, for much great drama of the past, the early plays of Shakespeare, for example, or the plays of Congreve or Sheridan, can be considered as a rehandling and a raising to a higher level by a man of genius of the average product of the time. Except, however, in *The Importance of Being Earnest*, we are too conscious in Wilde's plays of the contrast between their 'serious' element, which is merely melodramatic or merely sentimental, and the passages of epigrammatic wit which are not really adapted to the plot of the play or to the characters of those who pronounce the epigrams. What Wilde did unscrupulously and remarkably well has been done with sometimes more scrupulosity, but hardly ever with such sparkling wit, by the long series of British dramatists who have taken over his role of the social entertainer in the last fifty years.

From Wilde descend more or less directly the Somerset Maugham of such plays as *Our Betters* and the Noel Coward of such plays as *Hay Fever*, while at a lower literary level the comedies of such a writer as Frederick Lonsdale and to-day the lighter work of somebody like Terence Rattigan are very much in his tradition. In fact it might be said that Wilde is the father of the comedy of pure entertainment in our time just as Shaw is the father of the comedy of ideas. This kind of comedy of polished wit and gaiety, which skims the deeper issue of life, has in our own day become temporarily exhausted. It was remarkable how even the plays of a really brilliant craftsman of the theatre like Noel Coward have 'dated' so that a play like Coward's *Fallen Angels*, which struck the audience of the 1920s when it was first produced as rather daring and shocking, could be revived recently in London by two famous comediennes, Hermione Gingold and Hermione Baddeley, in terms of pure burlesque.

Social manners change so rapidly in our own time, that the comedy of manners dates more rapidly than any other type of drama. Such comedies are not so much true to life itself, as to the current falsifications of life; and with the lapse of even ten years we become jarringly aware of this. The modes of speech, the attitudes to life which ten years ago seemed smart and emancipated and up-to-date, to-day seem as odd and tasteless as the fashions of dress in old snapshots. If Wilde's plays of almost sixty years ago seem still more lively and contemporary than Coward's plays of only twenty or thirty years ago, it is because Wilde's wit acts as a preservative element. Coward has not so much 'wit' in the real sense, as smartness and flippancy, and smartness and flippancy do not stay fresh. Somerset Maugham's comedies show certainly a more solid construction than Wilde's and the plotting of a play like Maugham's *The Circle* is certainly wonderfully ingenious. But Maugham's wit is too obviously rather mechanically modelled on Wilde's, and while his grasp of human nature, or of some aspect of human nature, is remarkably shrewd, he lacks that affection for his characters which helps to give theatrical inventions permanent life.

So we can say that the artificial comedy of the last fifty years in England does not really compare with the artificial comedy of the Restoration, of the period that begins with Wycherley and ends belatedly with Sheridan. Artificial comedy *should* of course be conventional, but the conventions invented by Wilde and developed and exploited by his successors were not sufficiently penetrating and elegant. They did not permit a sufficiently deep and subtle criticism of social life. They were too much bound up with two different kinds of coarseness, that of melodrama and that of farce. One can see this very clearly if one looks at one of Somerset Maugham's most successful plays, *Our Betters*, which I have mentioned already, and compares it with the novels and short stories of Henry James. On a similar theme, the effect of English social life on rich American women who marry into the European aristocracy, Maugham's assumptions, if one compares them with those of James, are altogether too crude and simple. His Americans are either of an impossible nobility and innocence, or too completely bowled over by the alleged corrupt glamour of European high life. His English aristocrats are altogether too parasitical and too eager to acquire money. There are none of the fine shades and hesitating delicacy on both sides that make James's stories so fascinating. The play is an effective moralistic melodrama, diversified with some good broad comedy verging on farce. It is like a piece of network strongly and capably constructed but with the meshes so large that most of what matters in life escapes through it.

In Noel Coward's plays, on the other hand, the more slangy and careless dialogue, and the more informal manners presented, do occasionally give us much more of the illusion of actual life, but when Coward's characters are faced with a serious or subtle situation they, too, have no way out but the way of sentimentality or of angry hysteria.

One might say that the failure of artificial comedy in our own century is partly the failure of society itself to establish and to recognise a code. High comedy gets its point from the recognition and the exposure of current infractions of some high and genuine code of behaviour which most people find it too hard to live up to. When there is an ultimate confusion and scepticism about what such a code might be, comedy loses its perspective and the comic writer loses his most important instrument. Not one of the plays that I have mentioned as representative of artificial comedy in this century can compare, for instance, in subtlety and depth with such a novel as George Meredith's *The Egoist*. Meredith had a clear idea of what human behaviour should be and a clear perception of how people fall short of what it should be, and of how they deceive themselves about their falling short. He wrote in a style too strained and pretentious to make it possible for him to succeed in the theatre, or to think of succeeding there. But he had a more exact and adequate conception of the nature of artificial comedy than any of the writers whom I have mentioned.

With social comedy, or the comedy of ideas, it might on the other hand appear that we have a more cheerful story to tell, but in its essence it is the same story. George Bernard Shaw, the father of the comedy of ideas in our time, was a man of intellectual genius, not merely of personal genius, on a much more impressive scale than Oscar Wilde. If Wilde represented the ebullience and the frivolity of the Irish character, Shaw represented its stern Puritan seriousness. That came out in his life, a life so very different from that of Wilde, the vegetarian meals instead of banquets at Claridge's, the cups of black coffee instead of magnums of champagne, and the life of poverty, of industry, and of comparative failure, which was his until well after his fortieth year. He had failed as a novelist, though he had made a certain reputation for himself, both as a dramatic critic and as a critic of music, long before he had his first theatrical successes. As a dramatic critic, in fact, he helped to create the taste by which he himself later was to be appreciated. His book, *The Quintessence of Ibsenism*, put across his own interpretation of the great Norwegian dramatist – an interpretation which perhaps did not do full justice to the element of deep and painful poetry in Ibsen, to that slight degree of confusion and hesitation in Ibsen's own moral judgments on his characters which gives his plays even to-day their peculiar, uncomfortable tang of reality, or to the extent to which this great 'dramatist of ideas' was full of inner doubts about all ideas, including his own.

Shaw was very much more a conscious partisan of his favourite ideas than Ibsen was and he was less deeply interested than Ibsen was in individual human character. The difference in the depth of genius in the two men can be stated simply: Shaw has never written a play which, under the surface of prosaic realism, has all the elements of poetic tragedy, like Ibsen's *The Wild Duck*. He has not Ibsen's profound sense of the 'pity of things.' What he does have is a greater mastery of dramatic dialogue than any other English dramatist since Congreve, combined with a gift for lucid and graceful exposition of new ideas which might remind one of another great Irishman, the eighteenth-century philosopher, George Berkeley, the Bishop of Cloyne. His plays are not only a series of lively and entrancing performances, but a kind of running commentary on the burning topics and leading ideas of the age. Because his approach to these ideas is a dialectical one, not like that of his rival and contemporary, H. G. Wells, a sentimental one, we can read his passages of abstract discussion with the liveliest pleasure even when the topics are no longer burning and the leading ideas no longer give anyone a lead.

His plays on the whole are of two main kinds. There are those like *Mrs Warren's Profession* or *Widowers' Houses* or *The Philanderer* which tackle some urgent contemporary problem, and depict a contemporary social scene rather in Ibsen's manner. There are those like *Man and Superman* or *Back to Methuselah* which allow themselves much more fantasy and freedom in their development and are mainly concerned with the exposition of Shaw's own philosophy of life. Thus in *Man and Superman* the most exciting passage, purely from the reader's point of view, the dialogue between Don Juan and the Devil in Hell, contributes nothing to the action of the play and is generally omitted in performance. *Back to Methuselah*, again, has, properly speaking, hardly any dramatic development at all, but is rather a panoramic series of scenes to illustrate Shaw's view of the significance of human history and its probable future development. There are other plays like *Getting Married* in which Shaw seems to fall between the two stools of the particular situation grasped and the general exposition of the idea, and presents rather a large but inconclusive discussion within the framework of a somewhat untidy plot. He sometimes, in fact, uses the drama, as Wells used the novel, as a kind of 'hold-all' for all the ideas that are at the moment engaging his mind, whether these ideas have any intrinsic relation to each other, or to the fable which he has invented to illustrate them, or not; he is sure that his unending spontaneity in creating amusing diversions in his dialogue will carry him through. How very well and solidly he can construct, however, is shown in such a play as *John Bull's Other Island* or in *Saint Joan*. *Saint Joan* might appear an exception to my statement that, for all his great gifts, he is incapable of creating a tragedy. Nevertheless, to me at least, this play does appear to have the values of an inspiring and ennobling pageant rather than those of tragedy in the proper sense.

There is a lack that one feels in Shaw, something brittle and heartless about his optimism, and his assumption that some immanent spirit – what he calls 'the life-force' – is somehow or other, through all the disasters of history, always working towards greater good. This belief in an immanent spirit working through history, a belief which has something in common with the philosophy of Thomas Carlyle, makes him strangely indifferent to the values of the liberal tradition, the values of tolerance and respect for hard facts, and too ready to welcome all the 'men of power,' from Lenin to Hitler, who have appeared in such uncomfortable profusion on the European stage in our century. He is far too ready to excuse the excesses and inhumanities of these institutions in human history, from the Inquisition to the Ogpu, which have at various times attempted to impose an orthodox point of view upon the mass of men not by argument but by terror. His belief in the 'life-force' makes him suppose that wherever there is might there must be some mystical right, even though from an ordinary point of view of human decency there is nothing but bloodthirsty despotism. Yeats, who had a far deeper and more tragic sense of the age of calamity which we are now living through, once described a dream he had about Shaw in which he saw the great dramatist as a sewing machine, clicking out words mechanically, but all the time grinning, grinning, grinning. . . .

What this great man does lack is a sense of poetry. That can be seen when, in one of his most charming comedies, *Candida*, he brings an alleged poet on the stage and makes him talk in the bastardised watered-down lingo of a fifth-rate advertising hack. It can also be seen in his attempts at blank verse and in his irreverent criticisms of Shakespeare, the grand coherence of whose mind Shaw is quite unable to grasp; and thus there are few modern writers whose greatness one more readily recognises, and yet about whose fundamental attitudes of life one has more reserves, than George Bernard Shaw.

If the history of artificial comedy after Wilde is on the whole a history of degeneration, so is the history of the comedy of ideas after Shaw. None is a complete success in this genre; neither Galsworthy nor James Bridie nor J. B. Priestley has Shaw's stature or Shaw's wonderful gift of creating subtle, muscular, and living dialogue. Galsworthy's plays are carefully constructed and very well-meaning, but one is too much aware all the time, when reading them or watching them, of the author's intention to present an example and state a case. As in the mediaeval morality play the fact that the characters must represent certain points of view means that they are not able to develop and that there can be in the working out of the plot no real reversal of situation, no real poignancy or surprise. Galsworthy's dialogue, again, though sober and careful and fairly sensitive, lacks Shaw's pungency and wit. It has the same subdued realism, vitiated by a certain sentimentality, as has the dialogue of Galsworthy's novels.

Mr Bridie on the other hand had something of Shaw's wit, fertility of invention and gift of giving the reader or the audience a sharp jog when a jog is needed, but he never really learned how to construct a play. His three-act plays generally resemble three different very brilliant first-acts of some ideal play which he has never had the patience to construct along a single line of development and argument.

Mr Priestley, again, is certainly not at his best in such plays, as *An Inspector Calls*, which, in their allegorical exposition of some simple thesis, very much recall Galsworthy's, though perhaps Mr Priestley's general philosophy of life is more like Shaw's. He is at his best in such pieces as his amusing farce of local colour, *When We Were Married*, or in such sensitive studies of the atmosphere of middle-class life as *Eden End*, or in such a play as *The Linden Tree*, in which he mirrors very exactly some of the confusions and the disillusionments of contemporary post-war life in Great Britain. His quality as a playwright in fact is a certain solid sensitivity to the atmosphere of ordinary living, and though one must praise his tireless readiness to experiment with new forms, as in *Johnson Over Jordan*, or with new technical devices, as in his various plays on themes connected with the problem of time, it is as a recorder, perhaps, rather than as an intellectual interpreter, of the contemporary atmosphere that Mr Priestley has dramatic importance. One may feel that he would have achieved more in an age in which it was sufficient for the dramatist to record and that his intellectual preoccupations have to some extent inhibited the development of his very real sensibility to background and character. He might have achieved very much in that tradition of the realistic presentation of the problems of provincial life which in Manchester in the 1910s did seem to be producing a new, a strong, and a local tradition.

It is a pity that the centring of the English theatrical world in London and the demand for plays of intellectual topicality has tended to prevent playwrights on the whole from exploring the more solid and settled, and therefore richer and more rewarding, atmospheres of English provincial life. It is a lack in the broadest sense of 'atmosphere,' a lack of the quality of 'felt life' that one must complain about in the more serious English drama of the last fifty years. For all Shaw's undeniable greatness, there is equally undeniably sometimes a certain airy thinness about his texture, and it is notable that the one play of his, *John Bull's Other Island*, in which he goes back to the world of his ancestry and his childhood to Ireland, has more of this brooding and atmospheric quality, more of this quality of 'felt life' than any other of his performances. A certain rootlessness in fact in the personal lives of English dramatists in the last fifty years has reflected itself in this lack of richness and body and poetic depths in their work. They have worked too much with the surface of the mind, with the conscious mind, and their deeper and more obscure feelings about life have never found a wholly adequate expression. It is a sense of this inadequacy in the prose drama of this century, striking and admirable as it is in many ways, that has led in recent years to the attempt by writers like Mr T. S. Eliot, Mr Stephen Spender, Mr W. H. Auden, Mr Christopher Isherwood, Mr Christopher Fry, and Mr Ronald Duncan to revive the poetic drama. It is too early to say whether this attempt will be wholly successful but it is certainly a step in the right direction.

Section 3: Suburban Domestic Drama

Neither the drama of ideas fathered by Shaw, nor the comedy of pure entertainment fathered by Wilde, made a direct appeal to the typical English suburban audience. About Shaw, the remark might be, 'Very clever, no doubt, but a bit above my head, and I do get sick of all that talking for talking's sake'; about Noel Coward in his riskier moods, 'Very amusing, no doubt, if you're broadminded, but frankly I'm old-fashioned about that sort of thing, and it's not the sort of show I'd like the children to see.' One can imagine this sort of conversation taking place over bridge and tea in one of these dormitory suburbs about an hour by train from London, which offend the architectural purist by the frantic individualism of their houses, but nevertheless are very charming in their way with their trees, their pure air, the riot of flowers in the gardens, and the odd contrasts of the various building styles.

The suburb is neither the country nor the town. The Industrial Revolution pushed more and more people into the towns in Great Britain but the desire to get away from the 'shop,' the crowdedness and inconvenience of London flats if one is bringing up children, the expense of a house with a garden in London, the wish of busy office workers to get into touch with nature, if only at week-ends, all these pushed the new middle classes out to the edges of London again; and the same kind of process was taking place in all the larger industrial and commercial towns. There was thus brought into being a way of life which, if it lacked urban sophistication, lacked also the deep, slow, natural rhythms of genuine country life. The social centre of the English village is still the parish church. In the suburb, that centre is often rather the local tennis club or golf club. Parasitical, in a sense, both on the country and the town, with no function other than a residential one – or, more deeply, a function of escape – the suburbs are strangely insulated from the pressures of the life about them. Suburbanites belong to the middle classes. They would not claim to be 'upper' middle class, but would be properly offended if you suggested they were 'lower.' If they come in little direct contact with the lower orders, except as shop-keepers or servants, they are also incurious about the upper classes (and particularly about what one might call the intellectual upper classes, about literary and artistic circles). They would not claim to be 'fashionable' or 'advanced,' but they would insist, and rightly, that they are not 'common.'

They are neither poor nor rich. The fathers, who go up to the city every day by train, have probably sound, subordinate jobs in some old-established commercial firm. They will save up to send their sons to a good minor public school, but in very few cases think of putting them through a university. At eighteen, the boys may become bank clerks, or may become articled to a solicitor, or a modest opening may be found for them in the firm in which their father works. It is hoped that the girls will marry, but perhaps they are given a course at a business college, or train in domestic science, or become nurses. Because of its isolation in its suburban fastnesses, and that insulation, of which I have spoken, from disturbing currents of feeling and thought, this section of the middle classes (and one might describe it as the dead centre of middle-class life in Great Britain) represents one of the most stable factors in our national life. Its young men, in any great war like the last two, provide a high proportion of the new officers. It is a very intelligent, staunch, and capable class but not in the least an intellectual class. It has probably few books in its pleasant, sunny houses and these accumulated rather at random over the years. When it wants something new to read, it goes to the circulating library at the local chemist's. Father chooses a detective story, mother a slightly sentimental novel of family life. To read much, and to read books other than novels, is thought slightly odd. It is odd, too, to discuss general topics too intensely. Bridges can be crossed when we come to them. For the outsider, the atmosphere of suburban life is likely to seem a little complacent and smug, but the other side of the smugness is the staunchness which this section of English society always shows in times of crisis. England, after all, owes a great deal to her philistines. A too lively imagination, a too vivid and ominous pre- monition of change, too widely diffused among the people, is not always a source of national strength. And the sort of suburban English men and women whose traits I am trying to sketch in, in this summary fashion, would not be in the least offended, I am sure, at one's assertion that imagination is not one of their notable characteristics.

Out of this kind of negative virtue, however, with its wariness of involving itself in intellectual complications or getting out of its emotional depths, no very profound drama or literature can be expected to emerge. In the 1920s and 1930s, people of this class, when they ran up to London or the nearest large town to see a play, looked for a kind of drama which would reflect the comfort and the safe boundaries of their own lives. And since a demand, on a free market, always creates a supply, they were given the kind of drama they wanted.

One can almost give a generic description of it. In retrospect, one play of this sort does not sort itself sharply out in one's mind from another. The setting is the living room of a suburban villa, with French windows opening out on to the garden, and through these French windows young people in white flannels wander in and out with tennis rackets under their arms. The play perhaps begins with a comic servant dusting the furniture and describing to a curious visitor the various endearing characteristics of the family. The young people are probably minor characters. The heroine is as likely as not a sweet, fluttering, managing mother (in her forties, but still very attractive) in whom every suburban matron in the audience can see herself. The young people's complications are put in to show her powers of management, but the main plot is perhaps the wistful revival and the gracious laying to rest of some romance in her own past life – perhaps the return of some old admirer, bronzed and still handsome, from the Far East. Nothing will come of his return except that it arouses her husband, who is such a nice man, but who perhaps has been taking her too much for granted, to a new attentiveness. Or perhaps the admirer can be shunted off on a daughter. The dialogue of the play does not aim at wit or incisiveness, but at an effect of pleasant natural chatter.

The author? At various times in the past twenty or thirty years it might have been (though it is invidious to mention names where so many playwrights have made a success in this genre) A. A. Milne, or Dodie Smith, or Esther McCracken, or John Van Druten, or Merton Hodge, or Daphne du Maurier. But however often one sees it, and whoever the author is, and however the local colour may be altered or the emphasis shifted from time to time, it is always 'a very nice play.' The plot is sometimes a little thin, perhaps; but the very cushioning of the action by the conventions of middle-class decorum allows one to sit back in one's stall with a reassuring sense of safety.

In dealing with the work of writers who would not claim to be more than honest entertainers, and who have given so many people so much harmless pleasure, one should avoid, I know, being heavy-handed. Yet if we look back, I think, at the play which seems to me to be the original ancestor of all suburban domestic dramas, Gold-smith's *She Stoops to Conquer*, it is impossible, I think, to avoid the conclusion that they represent a certain decadence. Like the plays I have been talking about, *She Stoops to Conquer* is notable for the amiable, almost too amiable, golden mellowness of its mood – one thinks of Yeats's phrase about Goldsmith 'sipping from the honeypot of his mind.' Yet we do see, nevertheless, that the rural society which Gold-smith describes is at once more fully integrated and more vital than the suburban society of the plays of A. A. Milne and Dodie Smith. Tony Lumpkin is alive in a way in which the young man with the tennis racket under his arm is not; Mrs Hardcastle, compared to the attractive mother in her forties of the latest West End success, is, for Goldsmith, almost an *unkind* portrait: and yet she is permanently alive in a way in which that mother, and her successors, and her predecessors, all weaving together in a ghostly unity in one's mind, are not. Lastly, the dialogue of *She Stoops to Conquer* is, for the eighteenth century, almost naturalistic; it has none of the polished artificial point and antithesis of Congreve or Sheridan. Yet it is alive on the page as well as on the boards; the play is a contribution to literature; the modern suburban comedies I have been describing are not.

The suburban domestic drama is a special instance of a phenomenon of the inter-war years which is worth touching on – the phenomenon of what Virginia Woolf called 'middlebrow literature.' By this she meant the abundance of books and plays which are reasonably well con-structed, which have had some pains taken with them, but which are not intended to make any real disturbance, any sharp impact, to un-settle in any way anybody's feelings or convictions. The popularity of middlebrow literature had something to do with the limitations of suburban existence as a training-ground for discrimination in the arts. Great drama or literature is generally aristocratic in its regard for finish and form, but has its roots, on the other hand, deep in a popular culture. I have described already the insulation of suburban life both from any kind of aristocracy, whether of birth, intellect, or manners, and from the life of the people at large. That insulation leads in many cases to a feeling of emptiness, which is not, of course, reflected in the suburban domestic dramas I have been talking about. Or at least not consciously reflected; for the more critical spectator of such plays is conscious of a certain airlessness, he misses room for his mind to move in, he wonders what life can be like in such circumstances when no great issues are ever mentioned, where all moral problems are taken as solved, where all the talk is an endless going over and over of family gossip.* It is what everybody takes as charming, soothing, and re-assuring and a few days of it would drive the more critical spectator mad. . . . But there is a sense at least, I think, in which suburban women particularly (for the men after all have their work to take up their time and to diversify their lives) turned to this kind of play, as they turned to a similar kind of novel, to dissipate a sense of inner emptiness and fatigue. It gave them a flattering picture of what their lives were not but what they might have day-dreams of them as being. And we may observe, rather severely, that it is *never* the business of the writer to encourage day-dreams; *never* his business to flatter.

Thus our reasons for rejecting the achievements of the middlebrow in drama and fiction are not reasons of intellectual self-conceit. They have to do rather with deep and sincere doubts about the wholesome-ness of the product, even for those most addicted to it, for those whose great consolation it has become. One can, out of an effort of good will, attempt to surrender oneself to the impact of the sort of play and story I have been talking of, but, if one has cultivated one's sense of dis-crimination at all, one will be overcome in the end by an oppressive feeling of listlessness. There is often quite a high finish on products of this sort, but there is never any real inner 'go.' In the genuinely vulgar, the genuinely lowbrow product, on the other hand, there is this 'go.' When Marie Lloyd, the great vulgar music-hall singer died, Mr T.S. Eliot pointed out that she and her like represented something which the lower orders in England had and which the middle classes appeared to be losing – a deep and genuine recognition, and enjoyment, of the pattern of their own lives. Marie Lloyd's song, 'I'm One of the Ruins that Cromwell Knocked Abaht a Bit' caught up, echoed, diversified and fantasticated, and flung back to a delighted audience a part of their own lives – with no holds barred, with no genteel reserves of decorum – in a way in which no West End drawing-room comedy does. Marie Lloyd's song, one may say, had life in it, but the West End comedy has machinery that keeps it in motion.

* The most recent equivalent of the suburban domestic drama, for even wider consump-tion, is probably the very popular – and unending – radio series, *Mrs Dale's Diary*.

One can think of similar contrasts outside the strict realm of litera-ture. One thinks of the London pub, vulgar and ornate, with its frosted glass, its gilding, its barley sugar wooden pillars, its signed photographs of Georges Carpentier and Vesta Tilley; and then one thinks of the genteel, jazz-modernistic lounge of some road house twenty or thirty miles from London, built a few years before the war to cater for passing motorists. The pub has been there three parts of a century, gay, elaborate, ugly, all the time accreting more life and character. The roadhouse was perhaps built fifteen or twenty years ago. Already, in that time, its thin, rootless smartness has acquired an almost ghostly air. A lack of density, of thickness, of the pressure of 'lived life,' is what we have to complain about in all suburban pleasures and especially in suburban art and literature. The insulation of one class from another, of one way of life from another, however peaceful and tolerant an insulation, in the years between the wars in England, was not wholly a wholesome thing.

Perhaps things are changing now. The suburban middle classes are having a harder time since the end of the war. They cannot get servants as they used to; they have probably, because of the petrol rationing which has only recently come to an end, laid up their cars; even if only because they are so surprised and shocked not to find a Conservative government in power,* they are tending to take a new interest in social and political questions; their young people have been unsettled, from one point of view, or had their horizons broadened, from another, by the war. The suburbanites retain, of course, all their old moderation and cheerfulness and staunchness. Are they likely also to acquire a new imaginative grasp of the significance of their own kind of life, and its relation to the life of the rest of the nation? All I can say is that some of the most promising younger poets I know in London come from this suburban background and have begun to write about it in an imaginative way.† For the rest, we shall see.

Section 4: The Irish Dramatic Revival

Some of the criticisms that I have been making of the new realistic drama in England are made with great vigour by the Irish dramatist, John Millington Synge.

* Written before the last General Election.
† See Iain Fletcher's *Orisons, Picaresque and Metaphysical* (Editions Poetry London), par-ticularly the long, queer, and moving poem called *The Agony of Dying Houses*. The setting is Bromley, Kent.

In his preface to his most famous play – which has elements in it at once of farce and tragedy – *The Playboy of the Western World*, Synge pointed out what an advantage the Irish dramatist had over the contemporary English dramatist in being able to draw upon a rich and racy peasant speech.

'When I was writing *The Shadow of the Glen* some years ago,' he wrote, 'I got more than any learning could have given me from a chink in the floor of the old Wicklow house where I was staying, which let me hear what was being said by the servant girls in the kitchen. . . . In countries where the imagination of the people, and the language they use, is rich and living, it is possible for a writer to be rich and copious in his words, and at the same time to give the reality, which is the root of all poetry, in a comprehensive and natural form. In the modern literature of towns, however, richness is found only in sonnets, or prose poems, or in one or two elaborate books which are far away from the profound and common interests of life. One has on the one side Mallarmé and Huysmans producing this literature, and on the other Ibsen and Zola dealing with the realities of life in joyless and pallid words. On the stage one must have reality, and one must have joy; and that is why the intellectual modern drama has failed, and people have grown sick of the false joy of musical comedy, that has been given them in place of the rich joy found only in what is superb and wild in reality. In a good play every speech should be as fully flavoured as a nut or apple and such speeches cannot be written by anyone who works among people who have shut their lips on poetry. In Ireland for a few years more, we have a popular imagination that is fiery, and magnificent, and tender; so that those of us who wish to write, start with a chance that is not given to writers in places where the springtime of the local life has been forgotten, and the harvest is a memory only, and the straws have been turned into bricks.'

Synge died when still a comparatively young man, having written only a few plays, but for their combination of what he called reality and joy, of profound human insight and richness of language, these plays are rare among the dramas of this century. It might be questioned, however, whether they genuinely belong to the English tradition, or even whether the beautiful language they are written in with its many Celtic tricks of syntax and word order, and its abundant local idioms, is really 'English' in a strict sense. Certainly, they do not provide a model for a young man setting out to write plays in Birmingham or Manchester, and it is clear that Synge's tricks of language might

in a lesser dramatist become mere mannerisms, as they do to some
extent in his last unfinished tragedy, *Deirdre*. Synge is on the whole
saved from mannerism by his heartiness and earthiness but in the
dialect comedies of Lady Gregory, for instance, one feels that the local
colour is being laid thickly on a substratum of ideas that has almost
something in common with the world of suburban cosiness that we
were considering in our last section.

Again, admitting that *The Playboy of the Western World* is a dramatic
masterpiece, we might still ask whether it is a masterpiece of 'contemporary' drama or rather more essentially a piece, in the wide sense,
of 'pastoral' writing: of writing, that is, which evades the current
issues of life in a complex society by inventing, or at least depicting
with a certain added glow of poetic tenderness, a world of simpler
characters and simpler problems than those of the actual world.*
James Joyce, at least, who was as great a master of language as Synge,
did not dismiss the intellectual drama of Ibsen as a failure and did not
see the solution of the Irish writer's problem as involving a retreat
from urban complexities and an exploitation of the richness of peasant
culture. One of Joyce's earliest writings was a tribute to Ibsen and his
one play, *Exiles* deals, in Ibsen's manner, with contemporary problems.
Its characters are subtle and evolved, its statement of its issues an
intellectual one, its background urban.

One may say, perhaps, that, great man though Synge was, his
'programme' involved an undue degree of artificial simplification and
that it is the task of the dramatist to-day, not merely to look for the
raw poetry of rustic speech and life where it still survives, but to make
a poetic and dramatic shape out of the outwardly intractable and even
outwardly anti-poetic material of the life that he and his friends lead.
The weakness of Synge's programme can be seen not only in the
rather too couthy 'kitchen comedies' of Lady Gregory, but in the
plays of W. B. Yeats, where the most absolute mastery of language, and
a deep and real feeling for the folk roots of Irish tradition, somehow
fail, on the whole, to compensate for a lack of dramatic 'body,' a lack
of that gritty complexity and harsh solidity, which we ask from the
plot and the characters of a 'real play.' In some of Yeats's very last
plays, like *Purgatory*, he seemed to be developing towards a harsher
and more effective sense of dramatic reality, but on the whole the
impression that most of his plays leave upon us is a pleasant, but faint,

---

* For this notion of 'the pastoral mode,' see William Empson's brilliant book, *Some
Versions of Pastoral* (Chatto and Windus).

one, like that of a tapestry scene, rippling and moving through water. They are very beautiful but very remote and far less genuinely dramatic in force of language or concentration of character than Yeats's purely lyrical and meditative poems of his personal life.

The most promising Irish dramatist, after Synge, was Sean O'Casey, who does seem to have realised, at least in his earlier plays, the dramatic inadequacy of the pastoral attitude – the dramatic inadequacy, that is, of setting one's characters in a setting that is not one's own, assuming the existence in them of a simplicity and directness which is not in oneself, and thus shelving, for the time being, the proper statement of one's own problems. O'Casey grew up in the Dublin slums, and he writes about them; and if his attitude towards them is a warm and generous one, it is not in the least sentimental. His earliest and best plays, *Juno and the Paycock, The Shadow of a Gunman* (which is somewhat slighter than the first) and the splendid *The Plough and the Stars* (this was the flag of the Irish Republic for which the Irish patriots rose at Easter in 1916) are harshly realistic tragedies. They are shot through, nevertheless, with a broad and deep and effective humour – the vital humour of the Irish poor. The Irish 'troubles' give O'Casey a background which enables him to introduce plausibly the acts of violence which he needs to resolve, in a tragic sense, what might otherwise be the merely static pathos or humour of his scene; thus the atmosphere of these wonderful plays is sometimes like that of a music-hall crosstalk act (but of a kind that could only be invented by a genius) interrupted by a murder. No writer of our time has caught the whole atmosphere of working-class life more beautifully than O'Casey, or has been able to raise that atmosphere, as he has, to the pitch of tragic dignity. His plays are poetic in their total effect, but in detail they are sharply realistic. O'Casey listened to the language of the Dublin poor as Synge had listened to that of the Irish peasantry, but with a different purpose. He was not looking for cadences out of which he could artfully construct his own poetry but, like a reporter, looking for the effect of language which – whether or not it would be poetic or beautiful – would be unmistakably true to life. One does not ask, reading these early plays of O'Casey's, what his style is like; one simply believes that all his characters say exactly what he makes them say. This complete illusion of reality is a very rare thing in the theatre, indeed.

Thus, we might say that, though O'Casey is not a 'lord of language' in the sense of Synge or Yeats, he is more properly a dramatist of our own age than either of them; in that he does know exactly what a given range of characters, over a given range of situations, will say. Unfortunately, he knows this only in reference to a sharply defined milieu – the Dublin tenements of his boyhood and youth. His gift is one of specific sensitivity. When he enlarges his theme, he loses his touch. In his later plays, *The Silver Tassie, The Star Turns Red, Within the Gates, Red Roses for Me*, and *Oak Leaves and Lavender,* he deserts the poetic realism of his wonderful early Irish plays for a kind of symbolic expressionism, whose failure lies, precisely, in a lack of genuine poetry. His characters no longer talk in their own style, but in a style that O'Casey has invented for them; in a florid and rhetorical language which is always aiming at, and for ever falling short of, poetic eloquence. Moreover, they are no longer, except in snatches, real people – they are symbols of various social attitudes that O'Casey disapproves of or admires, like the characters in a mediaeval morality play. The melodrama is now obvious, the pathos overweighted, and the humour, when there is any humour, has lost its old music-hall earthiness and gaiety. We can no longer believe – as in the earlier plays we completely and unquestioningly believe – in the detail of what is happening at the 'realistic' level. And O'Casey has not the verbal art which could make us believe in it at any other level. In a country of poets, he was, in his beginnings, a great prose dramatist (though with the underlying poetic vision which the greatest prose dramatists, Ibsen, Tchehov, always have). It is his personal tragedy that he has attempted to transform himself, by a sheer effort of will, into the overtly poetic dramatist which he was not fitted to be.

He is trying to-day to give his characters and actions a symbolic reality. But the characters of Mr O'Casey's earliest plays, Juno and Jack Boyle, 'Joxer,' Nora, and Fluther, have not the reality of symbols, they have something more important and harder to achieve, the reality of flesh and blood; perhaps a more tangible and poignant reality than that of the characters of any other dramatist, in the English language, of this century. Possibly Mr O'Casey was right in feeling that he had exhausted that early vein of gold, and possibly he was right in leaving Ireland, in the fear that if he remained there his dramas might become provincial, but the fact remains that he is a dramatist of undeniable genius who seems, since he cut apart from his roots, to have lost his way.

Another Irish dramatist who, for reasons that it is harder to divine, has never quite fulfilled a splendid early promise is Mr Denis Johnston.

He is a younger man than Mr O'Casey and his second play, to which he mainly owes his reputation, *The Moon in the Yellow River*, had its first production, at the Abbey Theatre in Dublin, in 1931. In some of his interests and attitudes, as in some of his stage techniques, Mr Johnston has, in fact, perhaps less in common with the general tradition of the Irish theatrical revival than with such typical writers of the 1930s as Mr Auden and Mr Isherwood; a very fascinating non-realistic play of his, *A Bride for the Unicorn*, a poetic fantasy in prose with much incidental social satire and some verse choruses, very much resembles in flavour their *The Dog Beneath the Skin*. The hero, again, of Mr Johnston's *Storm Song*, a play about the making of a film in the Aran Islands, is very much a typical hero of the Auden generation. He sees his art as one of social documentation, he resents the commercial interests that strangle it, and at the end of the play he deserts the heroine (who is an emancipated representative of the old landed aristocracy) to go on studying the art of the film in Russia. 'Like many of his type,' Mr Johnston tells us, 'he would probably call himself an anarchist, while meaning that he was a communist, though in fact he is neither, being an artist – which is the last thing he would admit.' Mr Johnston's background is obviously a different one from Mr O'Casey's. He touches in lower-class humours and patches of Irish local colour, with a masterly hand, but he has not O'Casey's intimate feeling for the tragedies of Irish working-class life, and his best characters, like the disillusioned Catholic, Dobelle, the romantic rebel, Darrell Blake, and the German engineer, Tausch, in *The Moon in the Yellow River*, are extremely articulate people – almost as articulate sometimes as characters in Shaw – who belong to the 'ruling few.'

In this play, Tausch, the German engineer, is in charge of a power-house in a remote part of Ireland. The period is that of the early days of Irish independence, when the government in Dublin has still to deal with sporadic partisan activity by extreme Republicans who disapprove of the compromise treaty signed with England. Tausch has to confront a charming captain of partisans, Darrell Blake, who wants to blow his power-house up, but only superficially for political reasons. Fundamentally, Blake is defending a traditional way of life, the Ireland of the peasant and the craftsman, against the deadening order of managerial industrial society. Tausch, for his part, is defending not only his power-house, but his ideal of the rational ordering of the world through science. Both are completely honest men. Dobelle, in whose house most of the action takes place, is a more complex character. Both Tausch and Blake seem to him to be fighting for illusions. His attitude to life is ironically defeatist. Years before, in accordance with Catholic practice, he has let his wife die in childbirth, rather than save her by sacrificing the child. Unconsciously, he has revenged himself on his daughter by refusing to love her; more consciously he has revenged himself on the Church by 'returning God his ticket.' He has not lost his faith, but he has lost his hope and his charity. The eternal torments of the damned and the sufferings of the living are, for him, much too high a price to pay for the eternal bliss of the redeemed. Dobelle is too humane and fastidious to give himself deliberately over to evil, but all positive human enthusiasms now seem to him mistaken and futile; perhaps life itself seems to him a misfortune, and the creation of the world, from a rational human standpoint, God's great mistake. Dobelle is the most profoundly conceived character in the play, and though he takes no active part in the debate between Tausch and Blake, his more inclusive, even though temporarily negative, attitude suggests their limitations. In mere verbal combat, Tausch's heavy-handed German seriousness loses ground all along to Blake's poetic wit. But Tausch unconsciously breaks the sporting rules of this sort of situation by calling in a local police official, Commandant Lanigan, an old comrade of Blake's in the days of the troubles. For Lanigan, heavy, inarticulate, and sullen, there is one practical solution to the problem, and he takes it. The power-house may be saved now, but it will certainly be blown up some time if Blake survives. So he shoots Blake dead. Tausch is morally overwhelmed; he has called in the law to help him, and it has behaved illegally. And as a final irony his power-house (farcically incompetent attempts to destroy it have been going on all through the play) is in the end blown up after all. All that emerges positively from the action is that, as a result of this violence, Dobelle is shaken out of his negative attitude, realises that his daughter needs his love, and regains his hope and his charity. The play can be read as an extremely brilliant farcical melodrama, just skirting the verge of tragedy, but its fundamental significance, perhaps, is as a modern morality. Tausch, Blake, and Dobelle represent not so much three Shavian 'points of view' as three stages in the progress of the soul: the practical, the poetic, the religious. Dobelle represents the latency, the negative pole, of an attitude that could reconcile Tausch's blind science and Blake's irresponsible poetry; but to do so it needs to be awakened to life by a kind of 'shock treatment.'

Storm Song, an extremely interesting, but less successful play, deals perhaps with too many conflicts on too many levels, and resolves some of them rather perfunctorily. There are two main groups of characters, a set of young English people making a film in a group of islands off the west coast of Ireland, under a famous continental director, and a set of Irish aristocrats, robbed of their old power, and turning to culture, whisky, or bitter grumbling about the younger generation, as a diversion. The film director, Szilard, who dies at sea in a storm making the last shots of his great film, is less a character than a symbol; he represents for the play the heroic attitude rather as airmen, mountaineers, and explorers do for the poetry of the Auden group. Gordon King, the hero, who attracts the heroine, Jal Joyce, away from the defeated aristocrat, Martin Burke, hero-worships Szilard and his feelings for Jal can never be equally important to him; when he leaves her at the end of the play to go to Russia he is still following symbolically in the dead Szilard's footsteps. For him, as for many young heroes of the Auden generation, social activities have in the long run more glamour than the personal life, and he is more at ease in practical comradeship with men than in any emotional relationship with women. In his hopefulness, his courage, his impatience, and also in a certain unconscious callowness and callousness, he is very much a type of his decade. Thus in spite of its loose ends, *Storm Song* has a peculiar interest as a documentary record of typical attitudes of the 1930s. A very young reader would find it good background reading for the study of Auden's poems and Isherwood's novels.

A Bride for the Unicorn, a poetic play in prose, has prophetic rather than documentary importance. It anticipates the central part played by myth in the work of writers like Robert Graves, Edwin Muir, and Kathleen Raine in recent years, and its central theme is that dealt with by Mr Graves in *The White Goddess*. A young man, who has just left school, meets a beautiful masked woman who goes with him to a room in a hotel. In the hotel, he meets a number of old school friends, who chaff him, and when he goes back to the room the masked woman has vanished. All through the rest of the play, she haunts him, but he does not find her. He marries somebody else and settles down and, with various old school friends, who typify conventional attitudes, has adventures in the fields of commerce, war, and politics. His adventures are at once a satire on the general contemporary situation (particularly, perhaps, on the recent history of Ireland) and a gay but poetic parody of the exploits of various classical heroes. Without the presence of the masked woman, they can never attain to tragic seriousness; not only with the hero, but with all the other characters, lightly sketched in as they are, one has the feeling that the real life of the adult can never be *as* real as memories of schoolboy comradeship and of a first experience of romantic love or initiation into sexual maturity. (The old school, the original assembling of comrades, looms as large in the plot, though it is not given the same poetic underlining, as the elusive goddess.) In the end, the hero, John Foss, finds the masked woman again, but with her finds death. He embraces her cloaked figure and 'it collapses in his grasp into empty air, and he falls dead upon the ground, holding to his heart the folds of the garment.' (This is an aspect of the White Goddess on which Mr Graves has hardly touched, that perhaps her existence must be imaginary, perhaps no real woman can satisfactorily embody her.) John's companions mourn for him, as for Adonis. This is one of Mr Johnston's most original and fascinating plays, but I imagine Mr Graves, for instance, might find something sinister both in the fact that her status, as I have said, seems to be almost that of a subjective illusion, and in the other fact that Apollo, her male supplanter (the god, for Mr Graves, rather of rhetoric than of true poetry), plays such a prominent part in the choruses:

> Sing of your brother, Phoebus, of the golden hair
> Who rules Parnassus and the Delphic stream
> Flowing from the fair Castalian hill.

In the long run, in fact, the moral of the play might be that the main social use of the goddess has been as a spur of impossible hope to keep the hero going through a round of useful practical activities. Ambivalent as its theme is, and rather sketchy as its execution sometimes is (with a flavour of brilliant conversation, of charade), *A Bride for the Unicorn* has nevertheless gaiety, pathos, and charm. Mr Johnston has written no plays in recent years, but he is still a comparatively young man, and it is to be hoped that he has still something to offer us. Among dramatists of the 1930s, he stands almost alone for his flexible stagecraft, his grasp both of general social situations and particular types of character, and his mastery of witty yet natural dialogue.

Since the time of Mr O'Casey's early plays, Ireland has not produced any other dramatist of the first rank, and it may be that the peculiar social tensions, the atmospheres of exultation and crisis, which fostered the geniuses of Synge and Yeats and O'Casey, have now vanished from what is, at the present time, merely a rather sheltered and remote and, in intellectual matters, rather cautious and puritanical farmers' republic. It may be also that when Synge said that the peculiar raciness and vivacity of Irish speech and life had only a few more years to run, he was right, and that now that the study of the Irish language and of Celtic mythology have become, not the passion of rebellious enthusiasts, but a burdensome task for schoolboys, the sense of Irish destiny may have lost something of its old magic. At all events, there was a time when it did seem that Dublin rather than London was going to be the centre of everything new and interesting in the English-speaking theatre; but, in spite of splendid isolated achievements, that hope has not been fulfilled.

Section 5: The Revival of the Poetic Drama

We have seen that by the 1930s all the various types of prose drama which we have been considering might be said to have reached a dead end. In Shaw's later plays, for instance, such as *The Millionairess* or *The Simpleton of the Unexpected Isles*, we feel that fantasy is being substituted for plot, caricature for character, the reiteration of old, settled notions for fresh thinking. And the prefaces to these later plays, though written (as the plays themselves, to give them their due, often are) with as much sparkle as ever, show a certain loss of emotional touch with the moral issues of the age. A brisk and cheerful consideration of the uses of extermination as a political method, for instance, might have seemed an amusing paradox in the 1890s: in the 1930s, when Hitler was forming his plans for the general extirpation of the Jews in Europe, it was too topical to be funny. But for Shaw the violence and cruelty of Hitler, of Mussolini, of the Tcheka in the early days of the Russian revolution, were all simply means, though no doubt imperfect means, by which the 'life-force' in our time was achieving its purpose; a view possible to take only if, like Shaw himself, you are fortunate enough to live in a civilised country, a country sheltered from all these horrors, in which nobody would dream of lifting a hand to harm you however much pernicious nonsense you write. But for that humane and liberal society which had done so much to foster and protect his genius, Shaw had never a word of courtesy, even in these years when it was so soon to fight, against the new barbarisms, at once raw and decadent, for its life. His great countryman, Yeats, who was no more of a liberal, but had a high chivalry and in spite of his arrogance an innate gentleness of temperament, knew better. Thinking as Shaw thought that the rule of law, the society which respects liberty and protects the individual, were things gone in our time for good, he nevertheless saluted their memory:

> We too had many pretty toys when young;
> A law indifferent to blame or praise,
> To bribe or threat; habits that made old wrong
> Melt down, as it were wax in the sun's rays;
> Public opinion ripening for so long
> We thought it would outlive all future days.
> O what fine thought we had because we thought
> That the worst rogues and rascals had died out!

Yeats saw with a poet's eagle eye at once what should be obvious now, some thirty years after he wrote, that the attack of violent, passionate, ignorant men on the majestic, crumbling fabric of the nineteenth-century liberal idea was not 'progress':

> Now days are dragon-ridden, the nightmare
> Rides upon sleep: a drunken soldiery
> Can leave the mother, murdered at her door,
> To crawl in her own blood, and go scot-free;
> The night can sweat with terror as before
> We pieced our thoughts into philosophy,
> And planned to bring the world under a rule ...

Yeats, in fact, recognised what is obviously the case that, as far as the high traditions of civilisation go, our time is a time of loss. Shaw, for all his dialectical gifts – 'the philosopher turned demagogue,' Robert Graves has called him – was reluctant to admit this. He had always relied on argument, lacking the poet's more profound and more immediate grasp of reality, the simple 'feel' of the age. He was dogmatic as well as dialectical; and one of the dogmas he had always accepted (trimming it up in the garments of his 'life-force' religion or philosophy) was the old Victorian Liberal one of automatic progress. Rejecting so much that was so much more true and important in Liberalism, he retained that. Progress is automatic, the result of an immanent spirit driving onwards through history; therefore the 'strong men' at any given moment, the Hitlers, Mussolinis, and so on, must be the instruments of progress. ... But one must not suppose that Shaw had (as Carlyle had, for instance) a sneaking appetite for brutality in history, for exhibitions of the smashing mailed fist. His humanitarianism, however thin and abstract, however fundamentally unconcerned with individual suffering, was perfectly genuine. But he lacked imagination; he could not know – as the most ordinary man in the street would have tended to suspect – that the 'strong men' he praised would cling desperately to power even if it involved the total ruin of their countries and that if they killed and tortured many people, it was often less for any high-minded or even practical reason, than because they enjoyed doing so.

If the drama of ideas, in the hands of its greatest living master, was failing to grasp the realities of the age, the drama of entertainment and suburban domestic comedy were both in the 1930s (and the process has continued into our own decade) growing more pallid and insignificant. It was notable that Noel Coward in the 1930s tended to turn away from the comedy of entertainment, which may also be a comedy of social criticism, to plays of sheer patriotic and sentimental spectacle like *Cavalcade* (effective on the stage but unbearably dull to read) or romantic musical comedies like *Bitter Sweet*: these latter rather recalling the style of a successful confectioner of romantic spectacles, who does not, however, quite belong to a history of literature, the author-actor-producer, Ivor Novello. Younger playwrights, more or less in Coward's tradition, like Terence Rattigan, had even less genuine wit in their pieces than Coward had and aimed, on the whole, at some fetching combination of lively farce and sound sentiment. There were still in the 1930s, of course, as there are to-day, certain sober and honest craftsmen of the theatre such as Mr J.B. Priestley, with his solid feeling for the backgrounds and atmospheres of the more thoughtful and serious kind of English middle-class life, but even Mr Priestley's constant experimentation, either with technical devices involving some new conception of time or with various kinds of modern allegory or morality play, showed that he, like most people, felt that the tradition of realistic prose drama was needing, in the 1930s and the 1940s, an injection of fresh blood.

It was in these circumstances that various writers who had made their reputation and had their training not as dramatists but as poets were to make the attempt to revive that tradition of the poetic drama which had been dead, if not since Jacobean times, at least since the Restoration. Most people would agree that the Restoration dramatist Thomas Otway's tragedy *Venice Preserved* is the last English play in verse till our own times which can claim at once to be a work of literature and a piece of 'good theatre.' The revival of the poetic drama in the 1930s and the 1940s took various forms, and it was in a sense significant that the new attempts at poetic drama had a much closer connection with the deeper religious beliefs or social attitudes of their authors than had most of the prose drama of the time.

Thus Mr T. S. Eliot (who is certainly the most important name in this context) commenced his career as a practical dramatist by writing a pageant-play to encourage the collection of funds for the building of new London churches. The pageant-play was called *The Rock*. The outline of this play, and many of the details of it, were suggested to Mr Eliot by other persons, and it is scarcely either a 'play' in the proper sense or typical anywhere of Mr Eliot at his best, though it has some fine rhetorical choruses; but it undoubtedly gave Mr Eliot useful practice in stagecraft. Mr Eliot's second play, *Murder in the Cathedral*, written to be performed in Canterbury Cathedral at the yearly Canterbury Festival, commemorated the death of St Thomas à Becket, Canterbury's famous martyr, who had been murdered in the very Cathedral where Mr Eliot's play was first performed. So the impulse behind this play too was a religious rather than a properly theatrical one.

Nevertheless, *Murder in the Cathedral* is closer to being a drama in the real sense than *The Rock* is. It makes, again, a particularly effective use of the chorus; and perhaps the women of Canterbury, who make up the chorus, have a more impressive dramatic reality even than the dignified and impressive but rather thin, flat, sharply outlined character of the protagonist himself. If St Thomas strikes us, in the end, as failing to have reality in depth – as being rather a symbol than a person – the other characters in the play have even less independent significance, are personifications of various simple abstract attitudes, meaningful only in relation to St Thomas himself. The real 'action' of the play, in fact, lies not really in the violent killing of St Thomas at the end but rather in his confrontation with, and his triumphing over, various temptations, of which the most serious and dangerous is the temptation to accept his martyrdom, not out of Christian humility and obedience and the wish to bear witness to God's truth, but out of spiritual pride. The drama, in so far as there is a drama, is thus strictly 'interior,' and the outward value of the play is rather that of a spectacle and a commemorative ritual. Thus, in spite of marking an advance on *The Rock*, *Murder in the Cathedral* still belongs to the special religious occasion rather than the wider world of the theatre; and to get the most out of it, one must approach it in a religious frame of mind.

In Mr Eliot's third play, however, *The Family Reunion*, he is at last beginning to acquire a proper sense of the stage. This is no longer a religious work, with edification or commemoration as its primary aim. The setting is one of English aristocratic country-house life and the plot is concerned with the return of a young nobleman, Harry, Lord Monchensey, to his ancestral home, of which his widowed mother wishes him now to become the head, settling down happily to his traditional status of local grandee. It is soon obvious that Harry is tormented by anxieties and fears of his own and is both indifferent to, and in fact hardly consciously aware of, his mother's schemes for him. These anxieties and fears are personified, not only for Harry but for his chauffeur, and of course for the audience, as the Eumenides or Furies, who pursue Harry (who has murdered, or thinks he has murdered, his wife) as they pursued Orestes after he murdered his mother, Clytemnestra: and these archaic and frightening beings, with their glittering eyes, do in fact occasionally stare through the French windows of the manorial living-room. Mr Eliot was looking, as he has explained, for a symbol of remorse and guilt which would be more widely acceptable in a largely sceptical, agnostic, or pagan age like our own than any overtly Christian one. Gradually in conversation with a sympathetic aunt and cousin, Agatha and Mary, the story about Harry's wife (he asserts that he pushed her overboard off a passenger steamer on a dark night and has been 'on the run' from the Furies ever since) comes out. It is not made quite explicit but we do feel either that this belief of Harry's that he has killed his wife is a hallucination or else that what is haunting him is something more complex and more deeply rooted than a single violent act. In an attempt to help Harry to recover his spiritual balance and to get at the roots of his sense of trouble, his aunt Agatha reveals to him the tragic circumstances connected with his own birth. Harry's father, the late Lord, had not loved his wife Amy but had passionately loved her sister Agatha and had wished to murder his wife. Agatha, though she returned his love, had persuaded him not to commit this crime, partly because Amy at that time was about to have a child. The child of course, turned out to be Harry. Harry can thus feel that his own obsession that he has killed his wife is simply a kind of inherited, unconscious memory of his father's desire to kill his mother. Whatever Harry himself may be guilty of, it is something far deeper and wider than any guilt of his that he is expiating. Agatha also lets Harry know that she feels that she, rather than Amy, is spiritually his mother, for she had genuinely loved Harry's father, as Amy, who cared only about her place and her possessions, never had. Harry now realises that the Furies are not instruments of blind vindictiveness but rather of purification; and he is like Orestes too, in that when he has been driven finally to the place of his purification, the internal divisions that have rent his family and are now, as it were, personified in him, will at last be reconciled. But the place of his peace will certainly not be his ancestral home; so Harry sets out again on his travels, in his expensive car, accompanied by his chauffeur, and this shock, and the disappointment to all her hopes, kills his mother.

There are a few technical remarks to be made about *The Family Reunion*. The verse has perhaps fewer easily memorable or obviously eloquent passages than that of *Murder in the Cathedral*, but the reason is that Mr Eliot is now aiming at catching the tones, idioms, and rhythms of contemporary speech; so the 'poetry,' in the obvious sense, is muffled and subdued. Similarly, the 'formal' element is muffled and subdued; instead of the elaborate choruses of *The Rock* and *Murder in the Cathedral*, there are a number of minor characters – less important uncles and aunts of Harry's – who occasionally express their thoughts in unison, thus giving an ironical effect of a background of well-mannered, well-intentioned dimness and incomprehension, to which Harry's inner sufferings are disturbing from their very lack of everyday palpableness: if only it were something that an aspirin, a hot-water bottle, a day in bed, a drink after a tiring journey, an understanding talk with a fellow man of the world, or, at the very outside edge, a consultation with a nerve specialist could put right! Yet for all their pathetic kindness and inadequacy these faded gentlefolk have their own kind of sensitivity too, and feel uneasily that there is something in Harry's predicament beyond their intellectual and moral grasp. Here, in fact, we have an adaptation of the tragic Greek chorus to the purposes of a modern 'serious' play and also, occasionally, to those of ironic or comic relief. Contemporary reviewers of this play who complained that Mr Eliot had flattened out his poetry in it missed the point. The first requisite of any play is that, within its own convention, it should convey the illusion of reality; a richer use, however, of language would have destroyed the play's grey, tense, edgy contemporaneity of atmosphere. One might almost say, if the statement does not sound too paradoxical, that Mr Eliot was looking for the verse equivalent of what Synge called Ibsen's way of 'dealing with the realities of life in joyless and pallid words.' He needed a kind of dramatic verse which, whatever other virtues it had, would at least have those of prose; especially the prose virtue of convincingness.

Some critics had, indeed, even felt this grey quality in his non-dramatic poems. 'Eliot,' says Yeats, in every way temperamentally his opposite, 'has produced his great effect upon his generation because he has described men and women that get out of bed or into it from mere habit; in describing this life that has lost heart his own art seems grey, cold, dry. He is an Alexander Pope, working without apparent imagination, producing his effect by a rejection of all rhythms and metaphor used by the more popular romantics rather than by the discovery of his own, this rejection giving his work an unexaggerated plainness that has the effect of novelty.' One does not expect one great poet to be fair about another, and this seems to me very unfair; there is a grain of truth in it, however, and especially in his two plays of modern life, *The Family Reunion* and *The Cocktail Party*, it is the case, I think, that Eliot, seeking above all things to convince his audience of the reality of what they are listening to, has aimed especially at this 'unexaggerated plainness.' There are moments of high eloquence and there is a submerged rhythm making the speech more exciting than prose – but it is submerged, an underswell, it does not often break in foam on the surface.

Apart from the fact that the poetry is submerged in *The Family Reunion*, it might be said that the drama, in so far as one thinks of drama involving a violent or crucial *action* of some sort, is submerged too. Miss Helen Gardiner, in her very perceptive study, *The Art of T. S. Eliot*, makes the observation that what is novel in this play, and what leads perhaps to its lack of complete effectiveness on the stage, is that it sets out to dramatise not guilt but sin. Guilt springs from some specific thing we have done; the sense of sin from our general human condition; it is therefore hard to illustrate it in a dramatic way since there is no particular state of affairs to which it can be related rather than to any other – it is involved more or less in everything we think and do. On the other hand, some people are blind to it, as nobody is blind to a specific instance of guilt; and to those who are blind Harry is likely to appear a mere neurotic, badly in need of treatment, but of more expert treatment than Agatha can give him; and the Eumenides are likely to appear a tactless piece of archaic poeticising, which rather destroys the illusion. Certainly, though *The Family Reunion* is a far more ambitious and interesting play than *Murder in the Cathedral*, its effect on the stage is an oddly (and unsatisfactorily, because not I think consciously or intentionally) ambiguous one. The main characters, or at least the characters with whom Mr Eliot seems to be most in sympathy, Harry, Agatha, and Mary, are in a sense too transparent, too spiritual and introspective – there is something very 'materialistic' about the stage and we like a character to become an opaque and solid manifestation; something not so much that grasps itself, as that *we* grasp. But Harry, Agatha, and Mary are so nearly pure minds, so much presented in terms of consciousness and so little in terms of unconscious habits of speech, feeling, behaviour, that they elude us. We cannot imagine them *outside* the particular context of the action. We do not know what Harry was like before he turned up and he seems almost to vanish away from us completely when he finally steps outside the door. But Hamlet and Falstaff go on existing for us both when they are off stage and also after the play is over: and in *The Family Reunion* the character of Amy, the mother, with whom Mr Eliot is not so anxiously in sympathy, whose 'inner states' do not interest him much, by her very opacity acquires a solid theatrical power, which does not belong to the more 'spiritual' characters in the piece. Amy's death is perhaps the most moving thing in the play, at least when one sees it performed; much more moving than Harry's final departure. It is very wrong, of course, to think of Harry as a mere neurotic and weakling: but one might say that the heroic element in his character is not made manifest with sufficient crudity. The distinction between his being on the run at the beginning, with the Furies after him, and his departure at the end, not as a fugitive now but rather as the modern equivalent of a pilgrim or seeker, is a distinction which it is hard to make dramatically palpable. And the sympathy which Amy arouses, without, probably, Mr Eliot's intending to arouse it for her to that degree, makes Harry's general attitude of indifference or absent-mindedness towards her estranging: as if Mr Eliot were saying, 'We are all sinners, of course, but what happens to the more earthy and practical-minded sinner is, really, of little interest.' All this tends to dislocate the moral pattern of the play. Yet if on the whole we must judge it to be a failure, it is a failure more distinguished and more intrinsically interesting than the normal commercial, or even than the normal literary and dramatic, success. It has the touch of genius in it.

Mr Eliot's latest play, *The Cocktail Party*, is, on the other hand, a success at all levels, including that of accessibility and acceptability in the ordinary commercial theatre. It does seem to surmount that gap which lies between the poet's privacies of sensibility and that obvious, direct, and crude appeal which is necessary in a successful play; to surmount that more confidently than any of his previous dramas. It is a comedy, and in the light and gay texture of its witty conversations it beats, on his own ground, such a dramatist as Mr Noel Coward at his best. At the same time, *The Cocktail Party* has a profoundly serious underlying theme, that of the various kinds of self-deception in which even cultivated and pleasant and well-meaning people tend to indulge, as one might indulge in a drug, in our uneasy society; and of the way in which self-deception prevents people from living the life and doing the work they were meant to do, from following their true vocation.

The play begins with a cocktail party at which the host is exceedingly embarrassed because he does not know all the guests. They have been invited, and the party arranged by his wife – and shortly before the curtain goes up, he has discovered that his wife has left him, without notifying him where she has gone. He keeps up appearances as well as he can, pretends that his wife has had to pay a sudden visit to an aunt in the country, but an eccentric guest whose name he does not know stays behind after the others have left and shows both an uncanny penetration into the host's state of mind and an apparent knowledge of his secret. In the next act, it turns out that this guest is neither a brilliant madman nor a supernatural visitant, both of which he at a first glance might seem to be, but rather a famous Harley Street psychiatrist. And in a scene in which he confronts the distraught husband and the wife who has temporarily deserted him, it becomes clear what are the roots of the failure of the marriage. The husband is a capable and clever man, but a man dogged with a sense of his own inescapable mediocrity of spirit, and in particular possessed by a guilty feeling that he can never love anybody adequately. This has been made clear, in fact, already in the first act, where the husband, in an interview with a young woman, with whom he has been having a love affair, has refused to welcome the fact that, now his wife has left him, he is 'free.' It is not that his wife's leaving him has suddenly made him feel that it is, after all, his wife he loves. It is rather that he hates having his habits of life broken into, and that he thinks more of the social ridicule and awkwardness which may follow his wife's desertion of him than of his personal feelings, confused and dull feelings in any case, for either his wife or his mistress: and his coldness and timidity and irritable self-centredness have the effect of completely disillusioning the latter young woman, not only about the husband, but about human relations in general, so that she too comes to consult the psychiatrist. The wife, on the other hand, who has been having her own love affair – with a young man, a man much younger than herself, verse comedies of Christopher Fry. I shall quote a speech from one of them, in which it can be seen that there is an abundant richness of fanciful detail, not to be found in that speech I have quoted from *The Cocktail Party*: but neither on the other hand is there the massive and compressed moral strength of that speech:

> For me
> The world is all with Charon, all, all
> Even the metal and plume of the rose garden,
> And the forest where the sea fumes overhead
> In vegetable tides, and particularly
> The entrance to the warm baths in Arcite Street
> Where we first met; – all ! – the sun itself
> Trails an evening hand in the sultry river
> Far away down by Acheron. I am lonely,
> Virilius. Where is the punctual eye
> And where is the cautious voice which made
> Balance-sheets sound like Homer and Homer sound
> Like balance-sheets? The precision of limbs, the amiable
> Laugh, the exact festivity? Gone from the world . . .

There our essential feeling is one of playfulness; the lines very gently mock the woman who is mourning just a little more eloquently than her feelings justify for her dead husband, while at the same time allowing a lyrical quality to her grief: as in such lines as

> Trails an evening hand in the sultry river.

There is a great facility of phrases and images, and, in fact, if I were to quote the whole of this long speech from Mr Fry's comedy, *A Phoenix too Frequent*, I do not think the reader would have a sense so much of the development of idea and character as of a surprising fertility in the various ornamentation of a static theme. What is remarkable about Mr Fry's verse comedies, *A Phoenix too Frequent*, *The Lady's Not for Burning*, and *Venus Observed* is this playful and fantastic wealth of language, which at moments might almost recall the young Shakespeare, the Shakespeare drunk with words, of a play full of conceits and quibbles and speeches written not as dramatic speeches but as lovely youthful lyrics, such as *Love's Labour's Lost*. But Mr Fry's weakness is possibly that of those brilliant but meretricious dramatists of phrase and situation, not of theme, action, or character, Beaumont and Fletcher; he lacks a coherent conception of his play as a whole. His plays have often the air of wonderfully clever improvisations and though I left the only one which I have seen performed, *The Lady's*

Not for Burning, having enjoyed every moment of it, I would find it hard to compress the series of vivid and pleasant impressions with which the play left me into any very coherent account of the plot or the theme. Watching the play, too, I had the sense, about episodes as well as speeches, that Mr Fry, like somebody telling a story to children, was 'making it up as he went along.' This fecundity of episodic invention, like this 'fowth of language,' are both, of course, very exceptional qualities in our grey, inhibited, rationed time. One does not expect the age to foster the copious and florid talent, any more than one expects to have the fountains flowing with wine on state occasions or whole oxen roasted, in a hard winter, upon the frozen Thames. The agreeable anachronistic shock of Fry's careless abundance of episode and epithet may have indeed been one contributing factor to his remarkable popular success.

It is too early, I think, to pass any very definite literary judgment on Mr Fry's work but one may say that it fills a need in our time and may be the precursor of a more gay and gallant attitude to life, than our own is, in coming generations: but at the same time, it has something of the quality of a *soufflé* very light and very delicious, but liable to collapse into a flat pancaky mess if it is left too long to grow cold after it is taken out of the oven. One does not know how it will taste or how it will look in five or ten years. (Was there not a Mr Ashley Dukes, twenty years or so ago, who was going to restore to the prose rhythms of drama something of the sprightly elegance of Congreve? And where are his works now? One can never be sure how long a borrowed glow will last.)

One might mention in this connection the great success of the verse plays of Stephen Phillips in the 1890s and in the early part of our own century. These had an immediately captivating quality upon the stage, but after a certain lapse of time their spangles ceased to glitter and their rapid rhetorical speeches lost that look of vital convincingness. I would not say that this is likely to happen to Mr Fry, but I would say that if he is to develop his great quality as a dramatist, he needs to acquire a harder and perhaps a sadder sense of structure both in language and event. At present one cannot honestly say whether the language of his plays is really poetry or a skilful imitation, almost more stunning at a first glance, like artificial pearls of a large size and a beautiful rotundity, than the real thing.

These are the two names of poetic dramatists that one can mention as having stormed and held the West End stage. When one thinks, on problems which are perhaps permanently insoluble at the merely human level – nor the values of comedy – that is, of the statement of human problems which are permanently soluble, but which the run of men, through their average shortcomings, as often as not quite fail to solve. The tone of these plays has a kind of bright, evangelical eagerness, an air of superior knowingness, and a hint of 'the good time around the corner': it was perhaps only through adopting some thin and abstract final optimism of this kind that young men, in the 1930s, could face with cheerfulness the actual distresses, dangers, and horrors of the time. These plays typically reflect, in fact, the confusions of a critical, transitional decade: and that gives them an historical interest, which may well keep curiosity alive about them in times to come, in spite of their lack of permanent satire and permanent pathos. But they were certainly bad models for the young poet in a more sober decade, a decade perhaps with a longer and sadder perspective, like our own.

The other names that one has to mention in this section are more or less, at least so far, minor names; and must be dealt with more rapidly. On the whole, if the tone of mind and the mode of expression among young poets in the 1930s was predominantly political, to-day it is predominantly religious: and it is, of course, those young poets whose religious attitude has, like Mr Eliot's, a traditional and orthodox bias, who find it easiest to dramatise this attitude. It is difficult to dramatise the more common attitudes of partial acceptance, of hesitation, and of doubt. Mr Norman Nicholson, Miss Anne Ridler, Mr Ronald Duncan, are three young dramatists whose plays cannot be said yet to have quite moved out of the shadow of the church porch; they are at the stage of *Murder in the Cathedral* or even of *The Rock*, rather than at the stage of *The Family Reunion* or *The Cocktail Party*. A too obvious wish to edify, to preach at the audience, weakens their plays as drama still, though not necessarily as poetry. Mr Duncan is probably the one of the three who has so far the largest grasp of the possibilities of the stage; and he reinforces his piety by a vein, lacking in the others, of often crude, surly, and schoolboyish, but often also rather effective satire: as well as by a vein of rich and sensuous lyricism, which reflects, as it were, a pagan substratum underlying his top layer of Christian belief. Many of Duncan's qualities are to be explained by the fact that he earns his living as a farmer: that therefore he has something of the countryman's natural distrust of the 'city slicker,' and, what is rare in English literature, the peasant's strong and passionate sense of concrete ownership and his distrust of government interference. On his remote

West of England farm, Duncan grows his own tobacco, bottles his own wine, thus making himself as independent as possible of a government which taxes such luxuries; curses the government forms which farmers have to fill in to-day; and vents his anger at government interference, and his sturdy feelings about the farmer's independence and the importance of local traditions, in a regular feature in the *Evening Standard*, called 'Jan's Journal.' Before the war, he expressed the same intransigent attitudes in a vivid and acrid little magazine called *The Townsman*. He is thus a personification of what the conventionally 'progressive' person would call 'reaction': and without identifying myself with that person, I do nevertheless feel that Duncan's attitude to life, though no doubt in its way a gallant one, does not take cognisance of a wide enough range of facts. Thus in the satirical antimasque to his religious masque, *This Way to the Tomb*, he reproaches ostensibly from a Christian point of view the democratic creed for being international, not based on blood and soil and the natural rhythms of life. But so is Christianity international and so does it transcend, and sometimes break down and transform, local traditions and customs. It is not such an 'earthy' religion as Mr Duncan would instinctively like it to be: and it is religion that inculcates a spirit of charity, not always to be found in his own writings. The world which, in the more satirical parts of his plays, Mr Duncan attacks with such rough anger is after all the world, with all its faults, which we have to live in: and the world which, from the Christian point of view, we have to help to redeem. It is a weakness in a dramatist if certain kinds of background, attitude, personality arouse in him not the desire to understand but simply a wild unreasoning anger; and I feel that this weakness is Mr Duncan's. His own anger arouses a responsive anger in that townee intellectual audience (I dare say I myself am representative of it) which dislikes having its face slapped and its head buffeted by a vociferous country cousin who often does not seem to know, in any deep and intimate sense, the sense which might make his malice fertile, the world that he is attacking. For all that, the ability to rouse anger is a sign of vitality; and Mr Duncan's is a vital talent. And he has other gifts too, gifts which when developed with a less hasty energy, may make him an important dramatist.

Mr Nicholson and Mrs Ridler have, on the other hand, more to learn about the craft of the theatre than Mr Duncan: and they have, unlike him, a gentleness and sensitiveness of temperament, a spirit of wide charity, in their plays, that is likely to make their work more